T0247780

Spencer Keasey

A Nice Guy Like Me

A MEMOIR

ISBN: 979-8-35097-772-1 (print)

Memory Press, LLC

Cover photos by Ric Ide

To all those I've touched and all those who've touched me

*"...but one thing is for sure:
they'll never look at a gay porn star the same way again."*

—Peter Crawley
The Irish Times
Review of *Two Boys on a Cold Winter's Night*
Dublin Gay Theatre Festival, 2009

Winter, 2007

⌄

I t took three credit cards and three hours to get to rehab. Three days for the drug fog to clear and three weeks before the guilt, shame and despair started to fade. It took the full three months to realize I would use again.

Ten weeks in, we decided to have a talent show. Addicts can be a creative lot; those genes that drive us to create also give many of us a propensity toward self-destruction. It was unusual, however, to have so many creative types shipwrecked at the facility at the same time, the counselors said. Our core group, everyone at least ten years my junior, spent much of our free time using the meager collection of art supplies or singing around an upright piano left by the nuns. Shortly after my arrival, once I'd called my mother and came clean that I was in rehab, I had her send several of her piano song books. It wouldn't be my last request for sheet music while I was in a rehabilitation facility.

Our band of misfits was energized by the rehab's youngest client, Lora, an 18-year-old drinker and cutter. We were infected and energized by her new addiction-free energy. Yes, we'd have a talent show. All would be welcome. It didn't take much to get me enthused, ham that I am. After ten weeks clean in rehab and with two more to go, I felt like a kid again. I was healthy and clean. Healed, even. Fixed. Cured! That had been my hope and goal when I put $24,000 on three different credit cards the previous New Year's Eve. I'd hit bottom and needed to get clean. Several days before, with the intention of killing myself, I'd tried to shoot an eight-ball of meth into my arm. It was a veterinary needle, thick in girth, meant for subcutaneous injections for our cat.

But I went to rehab not only because I was desperate, but because I wanted to be taken care of while I processed and figured out what had happened to my life. That's what I tried to convince myself during the drive to the former convent 40 minutes north of Montreal—that it would be a retreat as much as it would be rehab. Henry, my ex—after 17 years together, calling him "ex" instead of "partner" was still hard—had driven me from what I still considered "our" home just south of the Canadian border in the Northeast Kingdom of Vermont to the Montreal airport, where he left me on the curb to be picked up by the Clear Haven van for the last leg of the journey. The further the van took me out of the city and into the rural towns of Quebec, the more confused and spellbound I became. When we reached our destination, a red brick school-like building done in the institutional architecture of the fifties, the facility was barely visible through the walls of snow. It was a snow-capped volcanic island upon which I was to be a castaway. I couldn't decide whether I was entering hell—the obvious choice given what I'd just done to myself—or heaven, because of the gleaming white snow. While I don't believe in a heaven, per se, what's after death for me is a place covered in snow. Henry was completely right when he'd suggested that I take Thomas Mann's *The Magic Mountain* with me. I spent my first days pretending I was in Mann's sanitarium high in the Alps, snowed in and safe from the world's myriad colors, which I no longer knew how to see.

After the initial shock of having most rights stripped from me and being assigned to a room with a roommate who looked as close to a biker gang-member as I could imagine and who didn't move for three days, I fell easily into a routine of classes, meals, and activities. Clear Haven was based on cognitive behavioral therapy, the reason why I chose it as opposed to a more traditional and common 12-Step program. I needed to quit, yes, but there was a lot of baggage I needed to work through with professionals—not just with other addicts. I'd learned from my vast experience with the 12 Steps—by which I mean one meeting a decade prior at the start of my first stint of sobriety—that sort of rehab wouldn't work for me. I needed science. And I needed a 90-day commitment—30 wouldn't cut it. I lost a lot in the shipwreck of my using but knew there was still a lot left to salvage, repair and put back to good use.

Now, months into my stay and with my young rehab-mate Lara egging me on, I knew what to do for the talent show: everyone had already heard snippets of my song. With every new client entering the facility, the "upperclassmen '' would introduce me as "Spencer the gay pornstar who's on Broadway." Most of the rehab patients weren't the sort to know the difference between Broadway and off-Broadway, and I stopped trying to explain it to them. I'd been, at least up until my drug meltdown that Christmas, the "Perky Little Porn Star," my moniker (and the name of my solo number) in the musical *Naked Boys Singing*. The nickname was appropriate only in terms of my being a pornstar—being "perky" wasn't how anyone would describe me during my career in the adult industry. Now the residents wanted to hear it, the whole song, not just the snippets I had shared, and with the choreography. It had been three months since my last performance in *Naked Boys Singing* at the New World Stages in New York City and 11 weeks since calling the producer—while in a psychotic break from the drugs that were meant to blow out my heart—to tell him I couldn't return to the stage where I was due back in two days.

Some clients were fascinated by my minor fame. Few could say they knew a porn star. Sadly, few knew anyone gay and certainly no one knew anyone who was HIV-positive. I had let it all out over the previous weeks in classes, sharing with as complete an honesty as I was able to offer at the time. It brought me closer to many fellow patients and further away from a few others. Those watching the talent show, both patients and staff, those who cheered and laughed during my song, all helped me in some way during my stay. They shared, I shared. They supported and they comforted me, as I did them. Rehab was comfortable—almost too comfortable in that it had become a retreat from real life. It had become my magic mountain. I was also really good at it, if one can be good at rehab.

The morning after the talent show, I and some other folks gathered around the ancient computer with dial-up to find out what happened the night before at the GayVN Awards, the Oscars of gay porn. Over the previous two years, having made only nine movies, I'd racked up six nominations including Best Newcomer. I won one for Best Threesome for having sex while hanging from a trapeze, something I jokingly warned people not to try at home. Apparently they loved me overseas as well, because I won the Best-Non European Actor at the David Awards, the European version of GayVN. Readers of MEN magazine ranked me fourth on the list of the current top pornstars.

This supporting-actor nomination was different, though. Even after landing in rehab, I had no regrets about being in porn. Drugs and alcohol were never a part of my film career. I was always clean and sober on the set. I was proud of my work because of the opportunity to act in many of these movies. The sex wasn't acting. That desire, need and energy were real. It was the combination of story and sex, of dialogue, character, and cumshots that launched me into a different echelon of performers. The acting nomination meant something to me; it offered a validation beyond my ability to fuck on camera and to fuck well, and I craved that validation. I needed proof that I was good, that I was successful, hot, manly, talented, and that what I did mattered—that *I* mattered. While I'd attained a certain level of introspection after ten weeks in rehab, I would need many more years and additional facilities and therapists to truly understand the root causes of my need for validation.

That morning, I learned I'd won the GayVN Award for Best Supporting Actor for my performance in Michael Lucas' *La Dolce Vita*. In class later that day, I announced that I was retiring from porn. Clear Haven was the perfect place to make this decision. These people knew my journey—they could relate. I knew that staying in the business after leaving the safety of this place, surrounded only by white snow, would be reckless. There were already too many risks to my sobriety and recovery in the colors of the real world that I was about to reenter. Retiring from porn became part of my written relapse prevention plan. Retiring from porn would also, along with landing in rehab, make a perfect ending to the book I dreamed of writing when I started my porn quest. In fact, I told myself *My Porn Quest* would be a good title.

The day after I was released from rehab, 91 days after I'd arrived, I carefully examined the salt-covered floor mats of my Volvo in the hopes of finding a tiny shard of crystal meth I might have dropped while driving to Vermont before Christmas. Had I found one, I would have used it. A week later, I had a martini. Two days after that, I was immersed in meth, Manhunt and madness. While my porn quest may have come to an end, my fall, as well as my epic journey home to a place of healing and recovery, would continue for years.

Preface
Winter, 2024

⌄

his started out as a porn memoir. I'm not exactly sure what it's become. The what, how and why of this story are all distinct things. The what and how are static: this is how it all happened and these are the events or actions that took place on this adventure. What follows is an account of the how and the what, from the surprising to the inevitable, from the titillating to the painful, from the foggy to the graphic. (That is your warning!) It covers a fast and furious ascent in the adult film business at the end of a decades-long golden age of gay porn—before the iPhone, before Grindr, Scruff and OnlyFans, before sex on camera became as commonplace as seeing a bird out a window. It spans the two and a half years I spent as Spencer Quest, how within two weeks of initially contacting Titan Media, I was filming in Palm Springs and offered an exclusive contract, and how over the next 30 months I captured magazine covers, features, a sponsorship, international fame, multiple industry awards, and a stint headlining a show off-Broadway. It also covers my equally fast and furious fall into a purgatory of addiction, mental health issues and self-destruction. It was, just like life, both a beautiful and a traumatic journey.

The why is more elusive and remains so even after two decades. As someone who cannot help reflecting, perhaps to a fault, my understanding of the why is still evolving as I mark the twentieth anniversary of my first film. My original fear when I started writing this book was that I would overly mythologize the story, describing some epic adventure as though I were one of those heroes with a thousand faces. But the fact is that's exactly what this journey was, and what I'd intended it to be from the very start: an epic adventure, a quest, if you will. I chose my porn name for a reason. After all, aren't we all on our own epic quests in life? The story probably isn't that different from yours in its hows or whys, even if the whats may be vastly different.

Writing the first draft of this book in an eight-month daily ritual—assembling its bones—was like walking on broken glass. I love a challenge, even if it may make me bleed. As soon as I started writing, it felt like my addictions had all lined up on a balcony, throwing bottles three stories down that smashed at my feet. I stood there looking up, encouraging and taunting them, and then I started tiptoeing through the shards. Eventually I began intentionally stamping my feet on the sharp edges. Getting my story out became more important than the long journey of recovery I'd been on since retiring from the business.

But writing this was a necessary and essential part of that recovery as well, so I had a conundrum. I knew that revisiting my past would put me at risk of slipping back into it, but I also knew I couldn't move forward without writing this. I wanted closure on these chapters of my life, to gather them in a book with a hardcover that I could stick on a shelf—one that would contain the things I was tired of fighting. Then, instead of being derailed by unexpected memories, I'd be able to choose whether to take that book down and page through it again. It would be my choice.

The months I was writing the first draft weren't all painful. I managed to learn and conquer Rachmaninoff's *Prelude in C# Minor*, I started acting and painting again and hit a personal open water swim record of four miles. Some of that glass in my path was beach glass, gently smoothed by years of tumbling in the surf. Writing this was its own odyssey with all the trials and travails, all the wonders and riches, one would expect when retelling tales. Love and joy and suffering and pain can promote growth and forge identity. By the time I started working on the second and third drafts in the following three months, adding the blood and guts, the muscle and skin to the story, the soles of my feet were thickly callused and I could tread more easily, often with a smile and a skip to my step. I even managed to sweep up most of the glass behind me.

While I've tried to be as honest as I can about my own behaviors and any damage I did or may have unwittingly done, much was lost during these years. Meth days were not always clear days, and memories tend to be filtered through our subsequent life experiences. They are not always accurate but instead are interpretations of what we think happened. I have no qualms with saying that maybe my recollections are bent. Bent, but not broken. It's been proven that the same memory changes each time we recall it. Even though I still have all my personal and professional emails from 20 years ago, I've also forgotten many incidents. I've forgotten many people. I've used industry names but have changed others. And I've intentionally—and with good, necessary and compassionate reasons—excluded people, including some of the most significant people in my life at the time. During my short tenure in the business, I met the man who is now my husband. I won't be weaving him into the story because this isn't his story; just know that there was someone, many people actually, who cared deeply for me and supported me along the way through both the highs and lows.

The most important thing in this retelling is to be clear: I blame no one or anything for my own decisions. I was faced with tasks, puzzles, mazes, riddles and challenges on this quest, and I was the one who made the choices given me. I believe in serendipity but also in a universe that responds to my own intention. I do believe things happen for a reason, but to me, when I'm balanced, clean and stable, the "reason" isn't divine intervention even if the messages and the signs I see appear to be so. The things and their reasons aren't elusive lessons we can't seem to grasp in the face of great loss or pain, although how to find peace through meaning is always the lesson. The reason things happen is simply the law of cause and effect. We are created by our experiences, not defined by them. Our choices are based on a cause. The reason, the why of this story, thus includes life episodes that formed me, some episodes in which I did harm to others and others in which I was harmed. Life lessons. Even when the cause was abuse or trauma, there is a story and reason behind *that* cause, a story behind the person doing the damage. Every cause is rooted in another cause. My father's treatment of me had a cause, a logical one which, with some patience, you'll discover later.

Yet, every experience, even the traumatic ones, has been a gift because I'm still here and every person I touched or who touched me is a hero on their own journey. And for those I wronged, I ask for forgiveness. While I wrote this for me, I truly hope it might help someone else, even just one person.

It was my intention when I sent those photos to Titan that I would write a book, that I would embark on an adventure and have a story to share. I got exactly what I asked for, something to write about. I had no idea it would take 20 years to tell.

"My story isn't pleasant, it's not sweet and harmonious like the invented stories; it tastes of folly and bewilderment, of madness and dream, like the life of all people who no longer want to lie to themselves."

—Herman Hesse
Demian

Chapter One

⌄

This isn't a story of my childhood although this story, like all of our stories, is rooted in those formative years and so some details may be helpful before I dive into the what and how of my becoming an adult film star. This introduction is an initial whirlwind telling of these years, and while you may find yourself saying, "Whoa, hold up, tell me more," please know that I will. We're starting with an outline of my first two decades, an overview which includes self-harm and sexual abuse. My dropping bombs, casually throwing something traumatic at you and then breezing forward, isn't meant to frustrate. These are the past events that began to come to the surface during my years in the industry, so I will go back to them and give them their due once my porn quest begins.

Up until I was about three years old, it was my father who "raised" me during the day while my mother worked to support us. My sister, two and a half years older, had the benefit of a stay-at-home mother during her first years of life while my father spent those years doing this job or that, including being a debt collector who, even in Lititz, PA, our small town in Amish country, carried a gun while he knocked on doors. My father ended up going back to school at night at Elizabethtown

College in 1968 to become an accountant, however, which meant before I turned one-year-old, my mother left for work each morning leaving me screaming and in a tantrum at her daily departure.

When I was old enough to stand at the door looking out at her as she got in the car, I would be inconsolable. This image is still one my mother reflects back on as one of her most traumatic for a 22-year-old mother. It wasn't just that I was upset, it was that she was leaving me with him, my father who, while he may have had a basic understanding that he should give me security and comfort, was incapable of giving it. He didn't know how to give it and didn't understand how a lack of nurturing at this age would forever affect his son, even though he was familiar with the feelings of abandonment—his own childhood having been marked by it in a different form. He also demanded quiet throughout the day, so I spent a lot of time learning to tiptoe around him in between biting and scratching my sister who seemed to get from him what I didn't. My acting out, my intentionally seeking out attention no matter how it came to me, whether it was a scolding or punishment, started early.

My sister was clearly the one my father loved. She was his princess while I was the troublemaker, the crier, the bedwetting, night-terror-screaming child who probably would have tested any father's patience. Even as a toddler I could recognize that he was capable of affection because he gave it to my sister. I didn't understand why he withheld it from me. I got used to feeling like an annoyance to my father early on and would eventually write a story in my head years later that I was the unplanned child, not my sister who actually was unplanned, that I was the extra mouth to feed, and that my father resented me because I existed.

But with every difficulty in my life, there has always been some beauty. We lived next door to my mother's parents, sharing a wall with them, and while my grandmother didn't have time to provide all the maternal love I missed during the days when my mother wasn't there, she gave me all she could. Including ice cream. My grandparents owned and operated an ice cream factory, Rosey's Ice Cream, that sat just yards behind the house. My grandfather would churn out flavors to deliver to the schools while my grandmother would serve soft-serve swirls and scoop comfort to town foot traffic, including local Mennonites who came into the cone shop. My mother was a Rosenberg, a family that had a long history of providing food and panaceas to others, whether it was Rosey Burgers from the lunch wagon in the Lititz town square (a continuing century-old tradition) or tonics at town fairs all along the East Coast. My great-great grandfather was a well known traveling medicine man whose own handmade tonics, including Rosenberg's Great Century Oil, claimed to fix just about any ailment.

This juxtaposition of feelings of fear and abandonment I felt on one side of the house with my father and the feelings of love and comfort from the Rosey side of the house became a familiar pattern during my childhood into my teen years. I'd spend decades trying to reconcile the opposites but would learn early from my father that I "had nothing to complain about '' in life and that, even as a toddler, I'd better stop acting like a baby during what he considered my overly emotional moments. His disdain for crying meant he'd send me to the happy side of the house where my tears would dry—a relief for me, but a disappointment as well. When I was an adult, my grandmother told me that I'd come over to their side in tears and ask why my father wouldn't play with or throw the ball to me.

We moved to Audubon, outside Philadelphia, when I was around three years old, after my father had finished his degree and started working for Price Waterhouse in the city. My world changed drastically. Suddenly my mother was present during the day and my father was not. I began to get love and attention from my mother and from the other mothers in the apartment complex. But by this point I had already turned into a sullen, sad, lonely, overly sensitive and somewhat angry child. I didn't know how to interact with other kids and didn't know how to be a "normal" kid, one that wouldn't bother my father and that would know how to play with other kids.

While my mother, now that she was home during the day, was the most beautiful, wonderful, kind and caring person I could have hoped for as a child, I was still scared for when my father would come home. During those hours my father was at work, I tried desperately to forge an identity that gave me the attention I craved from him. I still wanted his love. I would do anything to make him smile because if he did, maybe he'd not scold me the next time I did something "childish," as though a three-year-old should know that once you hit the age of three, acting like a baby was no longer appropriate. My need to please him started early, so while I had the tendency to steer clear of him when he came home miserable from work, a nearly daily occurrence, if I sensed he'd had a good day, I'd try desperately to get a smile and a touch.

There was another side of my father which, when it appeared, confused me. While there were occasional moments when I had a fleeting sense of security and comfort when he was near, there were also rare moments when I was shocked by the collapse of his hard exterior. One such moment I've carried with me to this day, cherishing its significance because it still proves to me that there was always something more to my father.

In 1971, an ABC movie of the week, *Brian's Song*, showed me a side of my father I would only ever see again a few times in my life. It was a true story of two Chicago Bears players, played by James Caan and Billy Dee Williams, who were close friends at a time when racial divides were clear even in football. When James Caan died from cancer at the end of the movie, my father cried—hard. I didn't know what was happening and didn't know why; I just knew it was a movie about football and that it was sad. The one thing my father did love was football. He had been a star football player in a blue-collar high school in York, Pennsylvania. He could have been on the football team at Penn State had he not decided on playing cards freshman year and getting my mother pregnant instead. I didn't understand any of that, of course. I just knew he liked football, wouldn't play with me and teach me how to throw a ball—and now apparently it was okay for him to cry, but not me. Boys didn't cry; that had been made clear, and even though I wasn't quite four years old, I was so confused. I didn't know at the time how significant that moment and that movie would be for me throughout my adolescence, teen years and into adulthood.

Resulting from the long period of feeling abandoned and lacking attention while living in Lititz, my main coping mechanism at this time, an early form of the dissociation I'd use in my life moving forward, was to become the goofiest kid imaginable. Disney mania had resurfaced across the country with the opening of Disney World in Florida in 1971, so it was these cartoon characters with whom I found companionship and my first experiences with escapism. Their faces were on my shirts, pajamas and sheets. My mother had a Disney piano songbook and spent hours playing songs from classic shows with me sitting next to her singing along. Our bedtime stories were from Disney Golden Books. When I say I was goofy, I mean I was, well, Goofy. I'd take on the slapstick mannerisms of the character before changing to another Disney character. I'd become Pluto when I barked at the dinner table with a chicken leg bone in my mouth. I made people laugh. I was a jokester. I got attention and a feeling inside that felt good.

It was at this time that a neighbor, my mother's best friend in the apartment complex, taught me how to talk like Donald Duck. Not only did I catch on quickly, I was good at it and I suddenly realized I could have a new identity when I used the voice. Oddly enough, by speaking like Donald Duck, I had found my own voice. Most kids in the complex didn't appreciate it; speaking like Donald only made me weirder and less desirable as a playmate. But most adults thought it was adorable, and because I spent so much time alone and with my mother, it was usually her friends I would entertain. I talked like Donald Duck a lot. Donald took over my normal speech, and while my father initially half-smiled when I first used it with him, his face soon betrayed that it had quickly become an annoyance. But being able to distinguish between positive attention and negative attention from my father wasn't something I knew how to do yet. So I kept using the voice in the hopes of getting something, anything, from my father that didn't cross the line after which he'd demand my silence.

What happened next, between the years of 1972 and 1974, was a series of adventures. They added to my confusion as to how to manage my conflicting feelings, fear warring with my newly discovered feelings of excitement and awe. My parents called these moves "adventures" probably in the hope of appeasing an easily terrified child. In 1973, when my parents were 27 years old and already with a five-year-old and a seven-year-old, we moved into a dilapidated 18th century colonial home in Collegeville, Pennsylvania. It was such a mess that the entire basement was literally filled with over a century's worth of trash and debris that reached the ceiling and came up the steps to the first floor. There were bats in the attic I'd hear above my head at night. Our black lab dog would stand at the foot of the stairs looking up to the second floor and growling all night, his hair on ends, even after all the bats had been forced from the house. When my grandmother visited, she swore she heard other sounds at night.

There was also an enormous hole in my bedroom wall that had to remain there because it was the access to the pipes that needed to be dealt with when my parents eventually tackled renovating the bathroom on the other side of the wall. While they tried to hide it with a Disney themed stretch of fabric, I knew the hole was still there—and it terrified me nightly. The sounds, smells, spiders, rodents, holes in the walls and in the floors that seemed to have no end all worked their way into my imagination. It's no wonder I developed an obsession with horror later on, especially after reading the Amityville Horror when it first came out. That house seemed like home; it was familiar. Any fear I felt and expressed to my parents in tears was dismissed and reclassified by my parents, who told me, "it's an adventure." For me, this started a lifelong habit of making myself walk, even dive, into fear in order to have an adventure. I learned that it wasn't an adventure unless it was scary.

It continued to be a lonely time for me. My parents were distracted with renovating the house that happened to be in a neighborhood with no children my age. My sister found friends easily. I had no choice but to entertain myself and gauge the extent to which I'd purposely get into trouble so that I could get some attention but not fall victim to the full force of my father's ire. Being threatened with the belt he used on our dog was too far to the bad side of the attention spectrum. Having witnessed and heard the pain my father inflicted on our dog, whom I loved dearly but my father never seemed to have wanted in the first place, made me fully believe he'd do the same to me if I couldn't do anything right. When I dropped lit matches down an uncapped but disconnected gas pipe in the corner of my bedroom, he made me sit for hours at the dinner table until I ate the very last canned pea on my plate, something I couldn't do without retching on each one. That was relatively easy punishment compared to the threat of a belt.

He was drinking a lot at this point while he worked on the house, something I would also do in my twenties. I never knew what would happen when he was in that state. But then he then decided to move us to Cape Town, South Africa, through an opportunity given him by Price

Waterhouse. It was another move for the family, more extreme of course, again labeled as an adventure. But once we got there, my father drank more, because that's what everyone did. My loneliness grew, as did my attempts at attention by talking like Donald Duck to entertain my parents' new friends.

It was in South Africa that things started going really wrong, and while it's hard to describe the emotional distress my father inflicted, I feel that my childhood ended our first year there, when I was seven. The energy dynamic in our family shifted; my mother, who once could protect me, suddenly seemed to lose her power. My father threatened me at the kitchen table in a new way, with what felt like hatred and disgust in his eye. He'd mock me in front of other adults and if I'd cry he'd rub his clenched fists over both eyes and pretend to cry, saying "Wha.. wha.. wha…I'm such a baby." He scolded me for the smallest thing.

Then one night, he forbade me to ever speak in a Donald Duck voice ever again—or else. There's nothing like an "or else" from a father that's previously threatened you with a belt to give a threat weight. And in that threat, he stole the one sense of identity I'd managed to find comfort in the prior four years. I'd loved the world of Disney—my place within that world, within the characters, the stories, the music. Imitating those characters had become my tool to make people laugh.

This may seem insignificant to some, and in reality I had already switched to becoming a Hardy Boy and not a Disney character, but the threat wielded the power to completely change how I would walk through the world. The cute coping mechanism, a child dissociating from himself by slipping into a character, was gone and would need to be filled by another form of dissociation. I ended up simply not talking at all when I was near my father, not wanting to say anything wrong. But my deepest desire was still to make him happy, even though I apparently didn't know how.

This threat came at the same time my parents were also caught up partying, doing what most young adults in their twenties in the early 1970s would do if they found themselves in a bohemian life of beach, sun, and booze, as they did in Cape Town. They became somewhat negligent and subsequently thought nothing of my hanging out and playing with an older teenage boy next door. He molested me at the age of seven years-old, and in doing so, he built the foundation of my adult identity– one that would be built on power, sex and the ability to please.

I still struggled with being a loner once we returned to Pennsylvania after Cape Town and then a year in Buffalo (where our house literally looked like the Amityville Horror house and I'd have to escape to the terrifying basement to get away from my father.) I was now nine and faced a sense of abandonment as my parents now engaged in a different type of behavior, one involving a neighborhood couple. As a direct and intentional reaction to my father now outright asking me at the dinner table, "why don't you have any friends," "why don't you DO something," or simply telling me, "you're getting fat," as well as a reaction to feeling like my parents forgot I existed when I wasn't at the same table, I tried to kill myself by emptying all of the medicine in the bathroom into my stomach. I only succeeded in starting a 15-year addiction to cold medicine, which had a similar effect as taking acid. This is when I first experienced "splitting." With enough cold medicine I would essentially become another person; this was dissociation on a new, more powerful level. I'd answer to and go about my day as the Spencer people knew, but I secretly knew I wasn't Spencer anymore. I was someone else completely. Someone with powers, someone who could read minds and someone off of whom the comments from bullies at school and the bully at home would bounce without hurting me. On bad days, I'd take a double dose of cold medicine, chug from a bottle in the liquor cabinet and go to school.

Then, in seventh grade, I found the time-honored lifeline of many a tortured, lonely gay kid—the drama club. For the next five years, with some help from puberty, I turned into a leading man, starting with *The Music Man* in eighth grade and then working my way through *Brigadoon, Bye, Bye Birdie* and *The Sound of Music* by senior year of high school. My mother still shares the story of how dumbfounded she and my father were when they saw me on stage the first time in 7th grade. They didn't know I had it in me to stand in front of an audience and become someone else. It was like they started seeing me for the first time. They had no idea that I'd been pretending to be someone else for a very long time.

As I grew, I got handsome and more confident until I managed to find a place within multiple communities in high school. By senior year, even the jocks and cool kids accepted me and gave me some level of respect in part because I was out, proud, and carried myself in such a way that said, "I don't give a shit what you think." I graduated eleventh in my class of 250; I was smart when I put my mind to it, but I'd also learned how to fudge, lie and cheat. I wrote myself out of gym my entire senior year by stealing a pad from the doctor's office when I broke my foot in the fall. A good friend a year older than me had given me all of her writing assignments from her senior year, which I turned in as my own in my senior Honors English class. The teacher gave me A's and praise, not realizing she'd read the same papers the year before.

I was actually a well-adjusted kid during my teen years. I was kind and respectful toward my elders, if not always toward my parents. I'd worked as a busboy in restaurants since I was fifteen. I'd also sneak into those restaurants and steal cases of beer after my shift, successfully building up a small distributorship in my closet. I was the one to go to for booze and I had some crazy parties in high school.

After I graduated high school, my father told me that he wouldn't pay for anything other than an in-state college. So I chose the University of Pittsburgh, hoping to get a dose of what it was like to live in a city. Shortly after moving there, I met Henry, the man with whom I would spend the next 17 years—and the man who would end up taking the photographs I submitted to Titan in 2004.

Laying out these early decades of my life at such a pace and in so few words may seem lazy, but again, this is my porn quest, not my autobiography. Still, the patterns of behaviors that paved my path forward through those decades are important to know at least on a basic level. I understand that what I went through in childhood that played a role in my starting a porn career at 36 years-old pales in comparison to what so many children have gone through in childhood. But my therapist, a trauma specialist, has made it clear: what I went through was in fact traumatic no matter how much I dismissed it throughout my life. I was sexually abused at an extremely early age regardless of how many decades I suppressed the memory. It happened. It was traumatic. It changed me.

It's sad that, even now, I feel like I have to justify my experiences as being severe enough to do the damage into which I'm about to delve. My father's treatment of me may not have been physical or consistently cruel, and in fact may not seem like much of anything to those who haven't spent a lifetime dealing with the repercussions of emotional abuse. But the scars exist. I ended up making a lot of erratic, impulsive and just plain bad decisions based on scars I didn't know I had at the time. Even the ones I could see at the time, I brushed off. "That little thing? Oh, that's nothing."

But the fact remains that I was scared of my father for much of my childhood. That fear left a hole where I might have had his healthy and necessary affection. Instead, I'd spend a lifetime trying to fill that emptiness with the affection and attention of other men. It would be a constant craving and I would learn to use everything in my power to get it.

Chapter Two

⌄

In 2001, fourteen years into our relationship and three years prior to him taking the photos I initially sent to Titan, Henry and I left Pittsburgh where we'd spent half our lives to search for a place to start our next chapter. You and I need to go back yet again, to those young adult years now, because just like my early childhood, these years with Henry were formative. We know the young male brain doesn't stop growing until his mid-to-late 20's, and one of the last areas to mature is the prefrontal cortex which controls decision making. It's a very interesting fact that, along with genetic and learned behaviors, can hardwire a person. So in other words, my behaviors in the first 10 years with Henry fired synapses, released neurotransmitters, and made me who I was carrying forward into the decision making of my 30's and beyond.

From the moment I saw Henry on the University of Pittsburgh campus my freshman year of college, I wanted to save him. He reminded me of my father. I could sense his broodiness from across the quad, and because of that broodiness I felt not just drawn to him, I felt like he needed saving. It surely had something to do with my relationship with my father, but I was still a child and unaware of the reasons behind my needs and drives at the time. I was drawn to and wanted to shower this boy with attention and affection. It took decades of time and multiple trained professionals to explain the logic in the illogical need to give affection to someone who reminded me of my father. I connected "attention and affection" with the concept of being saved, a connection I eventually learned was derived from my childhood desire to be saved from my own pain with attention and affection from others, especially male figures.

Henry was wearing a sweatshirt that read "The Hill School," which was a fancy prep school in eastern Pennsylvania, so I assumed he'd gone there and fit into my prep-school fantasies from reading books like *A Separate Peace, Brideshead Revisited, A Boy's Own Story* and *Demian*, or from watching the film *Another Country* with a young Rupert Everett. (The movie poster hung on the ceiling above my bed senior year in high school, along with a poster of Rob Lowe in the movie *The Hotel New Hampshire*.) Henry looked like James Dean—deep brown eyes, hair flopping over his forehead and partially covering one eye. I fell deeply in love as only a 19-year-old sensitive gay boy can.

It turned out that he didn't attend The Hill School but instead lived on the other side of the fence from it, in the blue collar neighborhood of Pottstown, one of the many former steel towns in Pennsylvania. He just owned the sweatshirt and wore it like anyone else who might purchase an Ivy League sweatshirt to wear even though they went to a state school. It turned out that his moodiness, which I chalked up to a Jack Kerouac disdain for the common, was more an outsider's envy of a life above his upbringing. Regardless, it was a moodiness I felt compelled to conquer. I knew it well, that dark energy—it was my father's. People talk about straight men marrying their mothers, or girls marrying their fathers, but I don't hear a lot about gay men marrying their fathers.

Besides being brooding, Henry also fulfilled my romantic need to find a creative type. For weeks, I walked past him after last call at the Upstage, a dive bar, on Tuesday nights, which was New Wave night. He'd be sitting there in the window of Mr. Donuts, surrounded by homeless people who flocked there to use the restroom, reading massive works of literature, or writing and sometimes drawing. He appeared to be a gifted artist from what I saw through the window.

One night after the bar closed when I was very drunk, I walked in to Mr. Donut and plopped myself on the seat in his booth. He let me sit, but with good reason was dismissive. I was a stranger after all, and he went back to reading *Middlemarch*. He was likely hoping I'd get the message and leave, but I stayed, forced him into conversation, and soon knew that I wanted to take care of him. With the same intensity of need I had felt all my life of wanting someone to pay attention and take care of me, I also needed someone else to take care of. I assumed his energy, the aloofness, the sly smirk and the unwillingness to reveal himself, were because somehow he had been damaged like I had been.

My father had been hurt as a child, too; that's what I had told myself. My father must have been hurt so badly, that's why he hurt me. I wanted to give Henry what my father could never give me, what my father must not have gotten and in the process, I would save him. I would save us all not realizing this thinking was the first sign of my developing savior complex, a complex which was likely initially instigated by reading Richard Bach's *Illusions: The Adventures of a Reluctant Messiah* years before. My need to feel special in high school led me to start believing it was possible that I, too, could be a messiah (not *the* Messiah) and subsequently could help and heal those around me.

I'd had previous sexual experiences before meeting Henry when I was 19—what limited experience I could find in Lancaster County in the eighties. I'd been out since my sophomore year of high school and was immediately confessing my undying love to the queerest-acting boy in glee club, as well as slipping notes and literary quotes in the lockers of others on whom I had deep crushes. I'd wait around the corner and watch as the unsuspecting beautiful boys found and read the notes, glancing left and right to see if the girl they assumed had left them the note was making herself known. No one was out in the early eighties in my high school; the idea that the note-writer could be a boy was unimaginable.

At the age of 16, a voice from heaven provided the opportunity to potentially get those experiences I was craving. The voice, actually the loudspeaker in my homeroom, announced that The Loft restaurant in the city was looking for busboys and to see Mrs. Duffy, everyone's favorite and fabulous English teacher who always dressed to the nines. I knew that The Loft was above The Tally Ho, the only gay bar in Lancaster County. That afternoon, I drove the seven miles downtown and was immediately hired. I quickly became the new mascot for the restaurant—not just because I was fresh, young, tall, and blonde, but also because my father had drilled into me a work ethic rare in someone my age. I busted my ass and made a lot of money; the waitstaff appreciated someone who could anticipate their needs and ensure they never had to ask me for the breadbasket or remind me to refill the water glasses. I was always one step ahead of them—something that would easily translate to having sex on camera.

Because the two businesses, the restaurant above and the gay bar below, were owned by the same people, after the end of a shift in the restaurant late at night, I'd head down to the bar and hang out with the adult staff. The first time I stepped into the cavern of lurking men, I sat on the bar against a wall with a sconce shining down on me, in a spotlight, for all the guys to see. I liked being seen. I loved having all those hungry eyes on me. I suppose that's where it all started, when I realized there was a world out there where I'd be able to find the attention and male affection I was desperately searching for since I was a child. And I did. I "dated" multiple men in their twenties. Because my parents were often absent during my teen years, on sailing trips or such, I woke up in strange apartments, hungover and having to drive the winding miles through Amish farmland to get to school on time. Or it would be the middle of the night and I was completely high, barely able to stop my convulsive shivering, a side effect of the pot, as I struggled to control the clutch of my '72 Volvo. It didn't happen a lot, but it happened enough that I soon realized I could hold power over men. This was when I learned how to seduce. It was when I realized I was brazen and confident, that I had no fear and could get what I wanted when it came to men.

But while I was obviously often at the mercy of my raging teenage hormones, what I wanted wasn't just sex. What I really wanted was affection and desire and the sense of being needed.

There were these few encounters and a couple of boyfriends in high school before I graduated. When Henry and I met in early 1987, my freshman year and his junior year at Pitt, the AIDS epidemic was still getting its footing. For those of us coming of age at that moment, the outlook was bleak. We knew we would never be able to explore our sexuality as openly and freely as the gay men who'd come of age the decade before. Even before we had a real chance to find and live in a gay community, we were told to tread carefully into sex. But we were also told that even if we did tread carefully, we could still die trying. Even so, by college, I'd had many more gay experiences than Henry—all within the safe confines of Amish country, far from the epicenters of the epidemic.

I was Henry's first. We started dating with all the angst and intensity of young lovers. Henry and I essentially sheltered ourselves from the sexual dangers of living in the gay world. It's possible that our parents had been correct that we were too young to be so enmeshed, but we also knew it was safer than the alternative. It's because of that I'm alive. Had I followed my passion, theater, and gone to New York City for school after high school, I'm sure I would've gotten HIV and ended up dying of AIDS before there was good treatment. With my need for affection, my need to attract and lure, to feel others' desire and to give pleasure— along with my propensity to self-destruct—I would have been just another casualty in the crisis.

We did have the opportunity to experience, albeit briefly, one of those big cities, an epicenter, during the summer of 1987, just months after we met. Henry and I found ourselves in Victoria Station in London, using our remaining money to eat at McDonald's. An older man walked up to us while we were standing by a trash can with our luggage and asked if he could be of assistance. Clearly he had an eye for lost young men. We told him our story of having traipsed off to Crete with one way tickets for promised but nonexistent jobs, how we didn't want to go home yet, and how we managed to make our way through Europe, get robbed in the Milan train station and land in London with five quid. He zipped us off in his Jaguar to a penthouse on Kensington High Street. We spent the summer as shiny accessories to a wealthy group of gay men; in essence, we were boytoys, squeezing money and places to stay while trying to have as little sex as possible with our "daddies." We did have sex—it was a part of the transaction, of course—but Henry and I made a pact to only have sex with these guys if it was absolutely necessary, and always with a condom. We were able to manipulate several months' worth of support this way, including a place to stay and pocket money, before we made our way home with our tails between our legs.

In the fall of 1987, after being justly punished by my parents for flunking out of freshman year and for stealing the deposit for what was supposed to be my sophomore year at Pitt to buy the tickets to Greece, Henry and I returned to Pittsburgh and moved in together. That first year living together was awash with blackout drunk episodes, the final one landing me in the hospital with 20 stitches after I threw a TV and shoved my head through a closed window. Ironically, given my later philandering, it was actually Henry who cheated on *me* first, which turned out to be a gift. Unlike my future secrecy and lies, he immediately came home with a confession and a kitten in hand. I forgave him quickly and easily. We were just two kids trying to find our way into individual identities, not understanding who we were to ourselves, let alone understanding who the other was.

Chapter Three

⌄

We spent the next fourteen years trying to figure out who we were both as individuals and as a couple. We finished school, got jobs, bought a house and built a remarkable life together. By 2001, after nearly a decade and a half together, being a couple was the easy part. We were Spencer and Henry; we were a 'we' to the extent I could barely say "I" anymore. Among our friends, we were the couple, gay or straight, with the most years together. Now, having spent nearly half our young lives together, we decided it was time to move and leave Pittsburgh, the only home we'd ever known.

This was a significant decision, the one that changed the trajectory of our lives and relationship. It was the beginning of my quest, albeit not yet specifically my porn quest. Tired of the city, we wanted to dedicate ourselves to living an artistic life. We were already living creative lives to a certain extent, I suppose, but we were becoming distracted by city living and the other work necessary to support those creative endeavors. So we moved in with my parents in eastern Pennsylvania and proceeded to drive 16,000 miles throughout New England looking for that new beginning, that place we envisioned in our own romantic fantasy. There was always an image of a dock in my mind, with a beckoning green light across the water straight out of *The Great Gatsby.*

We had a little money. When I was twenty-four, eight years earlier, we'd bought a run-down, three-story gingerbread Victorian in Shadyside, the trendy and upscale neighborhood of Pittsburgh. The run-down house was on the edge of the neighborhood, one street from the bus lanes that cut a swath through the city and separated Shadyside from the harder, forgotten neighborhood of East Liberty, which is how we got it for $55,000. But, like my parents when they'd bought their ruinous old 1700s farmhouse when I was three years old, I saw that both the house and the address had potential. I felt it in my bones, like the house was calling me, like buying it and fixing it was a chapter I had to work my way through in order to get to the next part of my journey. It had been converted to three apartments in the 1970s, a butcher job that had destroyed most of its original beauty. I decided I would renovate it myself. Never having used a hammer in my life (I remember my grandfather attempting to teach me how to hold one at the very end of the handle when I was younger, but my wrists had been too weak), I proceeded to gut the first two floors. I tore down walls, pulled out toilets, tubs and sinks, removed lathe and plaster ceilings and the knob and tube wiring, ripped out floors and paneling—all in an attempt to remove the traces of the 20-year-old conversion and to begin a restoration that would honor the original design

The demolition and destruction of the house's interior didn't take much coordination, skill, or knowledge—but the rebuilding of what I'd torn down did. As I'd done so many times in my life, I sought out books (it was pre-internet days) and taught myself how to do everything from framing to drywalling to wiring and plumbing to cabinet-making and roofing. I designed and decorated, cast concrete fireplace mantel pieces, routered and made my own trim molding, and painted faux parquet floors. The confidence, drive, determination and energy—all of it was because of the voice in my head telling me I could do it. It told me I was competent and that I was man enough, that I could do the work despite the other voice in my head, my father's, saying I was neither a man nor competent.

Like most people, I was plagued by voices from my past. But the voice telling me I could do these things was different; it didn't belong to a real person but instead to something I'd created and given birth to a long time before. It was a familiar voice, a driving force throughout my life constantly keeping me on my toes, on high alert and running from failure, as much as it encouraged me to believe in myself. Fear of failure, fear of not trying and fear of regret weren't an option with that voice in my head. It was a backseat driver, steering me toward perfectionism and, in precarious times, towards a cliff of grandiosity. It was the same voice, though, that provided a sense of comfort and a sense of self as a child during times when both had been deprived or stripped from me by external forces. It was a voice that took over in moments of vulnerability and a voice that became dangerous in moments of mental instability.

And yet, after eight years of slowly transforming the house, floor by floor, room by room, Henry and I decided to move on. It wasn't an easy decision. I loved Pittsburgh. It was a perfect city to me. Since I'd arrived there for my freshman year at the University of Pittsburgh in 1986, I'd felt entirely at home. And I loved the house. My investment in the renovation was the greatest endeavor of my life—and continues to be, alongside my recovery. It occupied nearly every waking moment of my existence for all of those years. The house lived in my dreams, too—dreams that often provided answers to challenges I was facing during the day, such as how to run the new wiring up from the basement to the third floor through 150-year-old timber joists. To this day, I still dream of demolition and renovation. The house was my child, my love, and eventually my savior as I tried to fight my addictions and stay sober through my late twenties.

But having been raised on adventure, on drastic change and risk, the call towards starting a new chapter in a new home, in a new state and with a creative purpose was strong enough to alleviate some of the pain of losing such a significant piece of me. Also significant was a continually developing sense that avoiding making choices, and hence being stuck and not living a full life, would crush my soul. Fortunately, we hit the jackpot. All the work on the house paid off, and my intuition had been correct; over the previous eight years, this edge of Shadyside became the trendy, up-and-coming side with new restaurants and large-scale renovations of prime properties. Realtors clamored to get our listing. Within a day of our house hitting the market, someone offered cash—well over asking, quadrupling our initial investment, and with no inspection. That was a good thing, because I hadn't gotten a single building permit for any of the work I'd done.

Our next chapter was partly based on location, on finding that perfect place to land. The problem with chasing our dream of a creative life was not understanding the cost of real estate in New England. But where else would we go to live a creative life other than New England? Henry and I had both been English literature majors. He was a poet and I was an English teacher, so our literary foundations were naturally built, at least partially, on the words of New England writers.

After selling off our furnishings and belongings and moving what was left—mostly books and my piano—into a storage unit in Lancaster, we moved in with my mother and stepfather with our 14-year-old apology cat we'd had since the fall of 1987, when Henry and I first moved in together in Pittsburgh. We then scoured all six New England states, naturally drawn to the cost-prohibitive coastlines with their docks I loved so much, and eventually landed in Vermont with its Green Mountains. It was the last of the states on our map and our last hope. Real estate agents in more expensive Southern Vermont all but scoffed at our age and our naïveté—but mostly at our finances and the paltry size of what we could provide as a down payment.

The further north we went, however, the possibilities of ownership became more real and our down payment offering became viable. But we had to go all the way to the top of the state, two and a half hours up I-91 to the 45th parallel, in order to find something we could afford. That turned out to be a Christmas-card log cabin on ten acres of woods, five miles south of the Canadian border. We moved in on Henry's birthday in late August, 2001, just weeks before 9/11 brought the world to a halt. While our mailing address was Newport, the town at the foot of Lake Memphremagog, the 31-mile glacial lake that reaches far into Quebec, Coventry was our actual address. But it was too small a town to even warrant using its name. No one said they lived in Coventry, population 1,000. There were no taxes in Coventry because the revenue from one of the largest landfills in New England brought in enough money to cover the tuition for all children to go to any school, public or private, on this side or the other side of the border. While we could see the distant landfill out the window of our new home, it was simply a swath of land, overshadowed by majestic Jay Peak in the background, snow capped for seven to eight months of the year. The house looked west, so our sunsets dipped behind the nearly 3,900-foot mountain. The house lacked certain details including the square footage we were used to in Pittsburgh and flat walls on which to hang things (the logs took some getting used to), but it was still ours, and most importantly, we each had a room of our own in which to write.

The Northeast Kingdom is the most rural and the poorest part of Vermont, with the highest unemployment. Its cows far outnumber humans. While we found a dream home, the quintessential writer's abode, moving to the area was intimidating. We were out of our element, which was a bit scary, especially with what had just happened on 9/11. Being so close to the border with multiple border crossings, Vermont was on high alert. Everyone was on edge.

Moreover, civil unions had passed in Vermont the year before, and while the rest of the country looked at the state as a bastion of liberalism, some Vermont voters weren't happy. Huge signs were painted on the side of barns, road signs were graffiti-sprayed, and t-shirts were worn, all saying: *Take Back Vermont!* We had no idea what it meant at first and thought naively it was perhaps a slogan of state pride. Then we came to understand that the signs were saying Take Back Vermont! from the gays who could now be legally united.Shocked, we felt as though we had unwittingly moved into a homophobic backwater. Henry and I were both horror movie fans, so we had a whole catalog's worth of backwoods terror scenes that fed our imagination the first few weeks. We lived miles down a dirt road with the closest neighbor a mile away—a far cry from our life in Pittsburgh. At least in the city, you'd be able to hear a cry for help. Yes, we'd occasionally feared living as an openly gay couple in Pittsburgh, but thoughts of farmers with shotguns and pitchforks felt a little scarier.

The voice in my head once again did its job with its soothing and calm: you can do this, you are a strong capable man. Also, that fear of failure—that desire to prove our parents wrong, who'd fretted that our decision to start over was impetuous and poorly decided—helped block out the jumpiness from hearing oversized monster trucks barrel down the road.

In reality, it was the snow that arrived for Halloween that saved us and made those initial weeks of anxiety worth it. I loved the snow, feet of it on the ground for months. Eight unforecasted inches could arrive out of nowhere. Because it was a Tuesday or a Friday. Because in areas like this, snow was expected and embraced. I decided that if I was going to be taken out by a backwoods local because I was a proud open gay man, then at least I'd be buried in snow. But we soon learned that these signs were simply indications to avoid those venues. We learned to just drive by, to not frequent businesses that said "Take Back Vermont" in their windows. On our fifteenth anniversary, Henry and I got a civil union, partly just to spite those signs.

Chapter Four

⌄

We settled into our creative life. Henry continued writing poetry. I continued to believe in and encourage him. He had dedicated most of our years together to writing and had, for someone in their mid-thirties, accomplished much. He was a finalist for the Yale Series of Younger Poets and the Walt Whitman Award and was published in *The Paris Review* and dozens of other journals, reviews and magazines. But publishing that first book still eluded him. Throughout the nineties and early 2000s, the only route to publication for poetry was through university presses, usually through their contests. This was still during a time when becoming a poet meant having to go to an MFA program and, ideally, to date a professor who'd help you win a contest. The business was tarnished by too many stories of how so-and-so actually won their prize, who their professor was and how the fledgling poet landed their teaching job. It was done shamelessly, too. One of those people was our poetry professor at The University of Pittsburgh, who'd been chosen for her prize by the professor she slept with—thus establishing her legitimacy as a writer. It was her self-righteousness and arrogance that broke Henry and convinced him he would never go the MFA route. He'd do it himself, and he had. Except for that elusive book.

I, too, wanted to write. While most of my creative abilities were in music and theater, writing was my earliest creative desire. My first proclamation of wanting to write was on a ferry in the Aegean when I was nine years old. I glared at my father after a particularly harsh episode of his bullying and told him I couldn't wait until I was older so I could write a book and tell the world what a horrible father he was. I reminded him of that episode 15 years later on a phone call while in a psychotic split state of dissociation. That breakdown was just before I got clean, the year after I left teaching in 1996. I spent the next four years working at the Pittsburgh Athletic Association as a desk attendant, then as their spinning and water aerobics instructor and finally as their athletic director. I also did watercolor commissions by the dozen (having taught myself to paint as I was first trying to get clean and sober), sang jazz in a city club, and renovated our home. But I hadn't truly put pen to paper in any authentic way. Up to that point, the only time I wrote was when reading and following Julia Cameron's *An Artist's Life*. Or I was in a manic, psychotic or a drug induced state, times when my mind and personality would split and that voice, the normally comforting and encouraging one, would stage a coup and become a dictator of sorts, completely changing my personality and who I was. But now I was starting a new life up North and hoped to begin writing.

I arrived in Vermont happy, stable, clean and determined to live my best life. I was that kind of guy who said things like "I'm living my best life." I was so used to renovation and decorating from Pittsburgh that I was on autopilot once we moved in. I dove into making the cabin a home, cleaning up the property, building a bed, chairs and tables out of cedar branches, sewing curtains, reconstructing a retaining wall so our barn wouldn't fall down, climbing three-story ladders to power wash the logs on the cabin, and felling 100-foot aspens blocking our view of the peak. Alone, and a first-time chainsaw user, I powered through trunks 30 inches thick without a concern in the world because I could do it; that voice told me so. It was a time of solitude, of clearing land with a machete, suffering only one gash on my shin. It was a time of climbing massive glacial boulders in the deep woods, unzipping my pants and jerking off into nature.

Yet while much of what I was doing was creative, especially with the furniture I was making, I still wasn't writing. I figured I could take some time to wait for my muse, so I decided to build a website for doing watercolor commissions instead. In Pittsburgh, members of the athletic association including George Romero and Mr. Rodgers had supported me for years; I'd painted their houses and pets, which gave me a nice side income. So now in Vermont, I chose "apaintedlife.com" as my domain name, created postcards, and sent them out to local realtors encouraging them to give their clients a painting of the homes they either just sold or purchased. My life has always been filled with ideas, many of which I tried to bring to fruition. That particular one didn't work.

We started to run out of money within six months. There was no question as to who would find work and give up, hopefully just temporarily, his dream—me. Henry was actually writing—that's why we were there after all—and because I had yet to even try, I shifted my focus onto doing everything in my power to make sure he succeeded, which meant supporting him financially so that he could have the most important gift a writer can receive: time. Thus I would give up my own dreams of writing for the time being. (Since then, thankfully, I've come to understand that my definition of codependency is giving up your dreams for another person.)

I answered an ad for a tutor at the regional non-profit that implemented supplemental educational grants for the state: Adult and Migrant Education, Even Start, among others. I was a teacher by education, having received a Masters of the Arts in Teaching at Pitt. The year before Henry and I bought the house in Shadyside, I started teaching for the Pittsburgh Public School District in their Multicultural Education division, moving to a different high school each quarter to implement their initiatives. I may have been a white 24-year-old male at the time, but I was openly gay, something that wasn't brought up in teacher interviews in 1992. In answer to their question of why they should hire me, I came out to them—and noted that their initiatives didn't seem to include aspects of multiculturalism other than race. Perhaps that shamed or challenged them into giving me the job, because they did, widening their definition of "multiculturalism" during my tenure.

I burned out quickly, however, then had the drug-induced breakdown four years later, which landed me in Western Psychiatric Hospital. The city schools were tough. My first year of teaching I went to two of my students' funerals: one for a young girl gunned down by either the Crips or the Bloods and the other for a young girl whose boyfriend stabbed her and their unborn baby to death.

Months before my breakdown, while in my last school assignment in the same district where the gritty 1980s TV show *Hill Street Blues* was set, the teachers in the lounge told me to run for other hills, to get out before I was making the real money—at which point I'd never leave. They said I had too much going for me to be stuck in the failing school system. They didn't want me to become like them: miserable, overmedicated addicts. They actually said this to me not knowing I was already those things. I may not have taken their advice seriously had I not been. But I was high that entire school quarter on dextromethorphan, over-the-counter cough medicine, which had been my go-to make-everything-better pills since I was twelve. Take enough of them and you trip and, eventually, completely dissociate. Strangely, the drug made me a really good teacher for this particular school, whose students were either pregnant or coming back from the juvenile detention centers. It eliminated my insecurities, so everyone thought I was cool.

An hour after handing in my resignation to the district, the principal from the Pittsburgh Creative and Performing Arts (CAPA) magnet school, where I had taught my first year teaching, called me directly to offer a permanent position. It was a dream job for a kid who was saved by the drama club in sixth grade, who from the time he played *The Music Man*'s Harold Hill in eighth grade found solace on the stage, and who spent his high school years listening to the *Fame* soundtrack. But even though the decision to resign was in large part because of my less-than-stable mental state, a sincere part of me wondered if perhaps there was more out there for me. So I turned down the offer. I'd given up a music and theater major in college to go into education because my father wouldn't pay my tuition without a reasonable job opportunity waiting for me. This time, I decided that I was no different than those CAPA students—still full of hope for a life in the arts—so I stayed the course and left teaching to see what was waiting for me. In the end, the only thing waiting was Western Psychiatric Hospital.

In Vermont, the tutoring job at the Northeast Kingdom Learning Services was a perfect fit as it was part-time, flexible, and gave me the chance to explore our vast and desolate corner of the state. I traveled across the area into homes I'd never seen the likes of before, some of them with those same "Take Back Vermont" lawn signs that had earlier worried me. I quickly learned to leave the red Jeep Cherokee unwashed, to leave my Woolrich hunting jacket–the one made for style and not practicality—at home. I bought a pair of muck boots. I'd known how to blend in in Pittsburgh, but rural Vermont was different. In the city, I could just cross a city block and feel like I belonged again; in Vermont, the towns were all the same and my feeling of being an imposter was pervasive. I could change my outward appearance, but the defining difference between these families and myself was their poverty—true rural poverty. While I tutored some amazingly resilient kids, some were deeply troubled, leaving me to question whether the job was a good fit. I didn't know how to support them given I'd usually be tutoring at their kitchen table under the watchful gaze of often distrustful parents. It was one thing to teach troubled kids in the city, to be a support in a classroom and far from the oversight of a parent, but another to try to help kids in their home who were struggling in part because of those parents looking over our shoulders while I taught their kids basic math.

I was soon taken from field work, however, assuaging some of my discomfort, and given a position as their Workforce Investment Act coordinator. That soon turned into becoming the coordinator of the entire learning center and overseeing all of the educational grants for the Northeast Kingdom. It was in this job that I learned I was a good manager, a boss who listened and helped employees do their best. My looking for and finding a job, getting hired as a tutor and moving into this upper level role happened rather quickly. Here we were in the area with the highest unemployment in the state, and within months I was in an ideal job making a sustainable and decent salary in my professional field.

For years, Henry had had two distinct opinions of me, ones he often shared with others. The first was that I lived a charmed life, that opportunities fell in my lap and things just worked out, as they had with this job. He felt that I succeeded almost magically at everything I tried. And while I know his thinking was partly out of jealousy—because he hadn't had the same good fortune, especially with publishing his poetry—it was mostly out of bafflement.

It was perhaps also because of my looks. Henry was a handsome guy, but I always drew the attention away from him, and I suppose it's not unusual for people to think that good looking people have an advantage in life. I won't deny it, but I can also say that I worked hard throughout my life in order to prove I wasn't just a good looking guy who had it easy.

But besides the voice in my head that said I actually had to work harder than anyone else to prove my worth, I also had a voice in my head telling me I could accomplish anything I set out to do. I also had a deep sense of connectedness with the universe and with life itself. I had a spiritual foundation, which allowed me to see signs and messages in people, places and opportunities, especially those that appeared at seemingly fortuitous moments. I read those signs, took them to heart, made a choice and took action. Often without fear. Serendipity exists only with open eyes. You can't see or read the messages if you're not open to seeing them. Looking back, I can't help but think Henry was drawn to me from the start because of this, that in a sense he was along for the ride because, well, I wasn't scared of life. I went after it, and I got it.

The other thing Henry said was that if we weren't together, I'd probably go into porn.

Chapter Five

⌄

That he thought this, that I'd try my hand at doing porn if we weren't together, and subsequently sometimes shared it with people, was oddly intuitive for him. While future therapists would identify my former relationship as codependent and unhealthy by the end, one of the healthiest things I did was ensure that a week didn't go by without sex. My physical attraction to Henry had faded over the years, as it does for a lot of couples in a long-term relationship, but he was still a good lover who knew how to take care of me. It was strictly sucking and fucking, no rimming, no toys or gear, and—even after all those years—he still used a condom. Perhaps deep down he didn't trust me. Perhaps he predicted correctly that I would go into porn because, when he fucked me, I was such a voracious bottom. I loved getting fucked. I was long-limbed and flexible as hell, a power bottom who wasn't afraid to make noise or say what I wanted. The sex was great. But deep down, being fucked by someone for whom I felt I was becoming more of a caregiver than a partner wasn't enough. Perhaps he sensed this. After so many years of feeling this way, desires built and fantasies took hold. I started to want bigger, harder, and more.

It's not like we watched a lot of porn together or even had porn videos. Sex wasn't something we discussed for the first 14 years together, it was something we had and had on a regular, almost scheduled basis. I don't know what instigated it and why, but when we moved to Vermont we ended up purchasing several Titan movies which we would occasionally watch together. We'd jerk off, perhaps service each other, and that would be that. It's not like either of us was addicted to it or it had such a presence in our lives that his saying I'd go into porn was logical and based in something tangible.

But by this point we'd been together for a very long time; we watched each other grow up and were inseparable for over a decade and a half. Because of that long history, Henry knew my past. He resented much of my family because of my childhood and the damage that occurred, the damage with which he felt he ended up having to deal. For him, there might have been a list he compiled over the years of things I'd gone through that could be used as justification for my eventual landing in porn. Perhaps his comment was, in fact, more logical than it was intuitive. Maybe he knew me better than I knew myself in this regard or he saw things in me I'd yet to admit existed.

Neither Henry nor I knew how to talk about sex—and never figured it out over the next 17 years. During my drug and drink days, from 1987 to 1996, I strayed a few times and, under interrogation (because my clues were so obvious), I'd admit to having had sex with someone. He'd be justifiably upset; he'd let me know how much I hurt him, how much I'd risked in terms of our health, and I'd soon be tied up naked in his writing room. Then we'd never mention it again. I didn't understand fetish or kink and didn't enjoy being bound, because it only happened when I cheated on him. He may have seen it as a form of punishment play; I just saw it as awkward.

He sometimes caught me masturbating and would be furious. I was denying him sex. Guilt being my go-to emotion, I'd feel as if I had cheated on him. Associating shame with masturbation isn't unusual, but being made to feel shame from my partner only made me more secretive and resentful. Giving myself pleasure wasn't just because of hormones; it was lifting the lid off a pressure cooker. I saw myself as giving a disproportionate amount of energy in our relationship not just on the work I was doing on the house, but on the work I was doing in our relationship trying to lift and keep us in my world of optimism, faith and positivity. I fought hard not to let Henry's pessimism and darkness drag us both down. Taking five minutes to myself was a release from the resentments I tried so hard to quell. As years went on, those resentments grew, along with my sexual fantasies and desires.

The internet finally arrived in our house in the late nineties and I found a way to access porn. I wouldn't have dared bring a magazine into the house, for fear of Henry finding it and knowing I was jerking off to it. I was still a teenager in many ways, using explicit paragraphs in books as jerk-off fodder. But with the internet, I could find grainy clips to watch, cum and wipe it away, all within 60 seconds.

Then I got caught. One Thanksgiving, a holiday we hosted yearly for his family, his father was on the computer—and for some unknown reason in our browser history. Henry was standing there while his Dad scrolled through pages of porn history and said, "You know, you can delete these files so no one can see them." His father didn't think twice about what he'd said—obviously he took this measure himself after his own self-pleasure—but the flash in Henry's eyes signaled what I already knew: He was angry because I was denying him sex.

Thus I came to understand that with this new accessibility to porn, I'd have to become even sneakier. I wasn't going to give it up.

My history with porn was deeply rooted. In today's world, it's not unusual for even the youngest child to be exposed to porn in one way or another, whether by accident or by curiosity. It's everywhere and accessible and graphic. In so many ways, I'm jealous of the youth of today for their carefree attitudes toward porn. For most gay men of my generation and older, shame already ruled our lives. Unless you lived in a large urban area, the shame of being gay itself felt insurmountable. I felt ashamed even looking at a man, let alone a naked man, let alone a dick, let alone two guys with exposed genitals. I saw my first dicks when I was four, having found my dad's *Playboy* and *Penthouse* magazines. These magazines didn't normally have men in them, but they almost always had mainstream movie reviews, which had photo stills of sex as a part of their reviews—nothing overly flagrant. At that age, I suppose I didn't think much of the images outside of curiosity, but I did know I found them only by snooping in my parent's bedroom. They were secret. Porn was meant to be hidden.

When I was nine, I snooped through my paternal grandparents' house and came across my grandfather's porn. It was hardcore, with dicks shooting milky stuff all over and inside women who held open vaginas with ooze dripping out. The pages were cum-crusted, stained, stuck together. My sister caught me looking and explained what the white stuff was. I was hooked. And ashamed. Shortly after, I found my stepfather's porn neatly stacked on his bedside table and the illustrated Kama Sutra in my step-mother and father's bedroom. Then I found my maternal grandfather's copy of *The Happy Hooker* on a bookshelf. I spent a lot of time jerking off in both my grandfather's studies and my parents' bedrooms.

There was also the sexual energy around me as a child. Having moved from conservative Pennsylvania to Cape Town when I was six, there was a palpable shift in the energy to which I was exposed. I imagine our time there from 1973 to 1977 would have been similar to living near the coast in California in those carefree hippy free love days. Cursed and blessed with a Kodachrome memory, I recorded it all in highly vivid detail. My parents were 28, from rural Lancaster and barely urban York, PA, conservative in upbringing, and busting to break loose. I was a witness to it all. Unlike my older sister, who managed to find a best friend almost immediately, I was too awkward and weird to have a best friend or any friends for that matter.

So I watched my parents' raucous parties often behind a chair, with the knitting project my mother had started me on. Knitting was my secret cloak; if I just sat, watched, and wrapped yarn around a needle, I'd disappear from my parents' sight and minds and could stay within the party and feel like I belonged. Only after they finally remembered me and sent me to bed did their clothes come off. I still have the real photographs to prove that I wasn't making any of it up. My mother, her blouse nearly completely open in the front, throwing back a "blowjob" shot of alcohol, no hands, lips wrapped around the rim with her head tilted back. Then the photo of my father and two other male friends, naked, holding South African lobster in front of their genitals, my mother doing the same over her breasts.

In those photos, my mother oozed freedom and sexuality. The spark in her eyes was near wild, wild with drink, surely, but also wild with life. My mother needed to just exist to get attention, to have people stare. Her essential kindness and goodness, along with her looks, were a magnet. In the photographs, my father just looked awkward, like the kid hoping to fit in, wanting attention. From my parents I inherited internal warring halves. I had my mother's spirit, her natural kindness, sensitivity and compassion, but I desperately needed the attention I couldn't seem to get, especially from my father, unless it was the sort of attention I didn't want.

So it was the neighbor who filled the void between those halves by molesting me while my parents weren't looking. When I was seven, I learned I had something worth wanting, that I was worth something, that in order to get the attention and male affection I so craved, I just had to get on my hands and knees and do what I was told.

When we moved back to my mother's hometown of Lititz, Pennsylvania, after those three Sub-Saharan years, our family was broken. Something had gone wrong in South Africa. I didn't know what it was at the time, but I knew something had happened because from my bed at night I heard my mother's cries and my father's yelling. The anger, distress and pain I heard woke me up and haunted me for years.

Around 1980, my parents started hanging out with the couple two houses down the street in our development. They eventually engaged in a wife-swap, a soon-to-be scandal in our small town. At first, it seemed as though my parents had found some friends, a sort of relief to me because for the first time in years my father seemed content, if not happy. The two couples spent their time drinking, sneaking into the community pool to skinny-dip, partying with each other and going on sailing trips. With my father not being a constant source of fear, the reason to steer clear of him, I now seemed to have four adults who gave me, at least initially, some much needed attention.

Once again, my sister had found friends easily when we moved back to Lititz. She subsequently escaped having to listen to the goings-on happening in the basements of both houses, and depending on where the partying was happening with my parents, our house or the neighbors, I would either build model ships and planes in my bedroom or babysit the other couples' two- and four-year-old daughters down the street. If I was in my bedroom, I could look out my window across two backyards and see them having fun and laughing. If the wind was right and I turned down the Top 40 Countdown, I could hear it too. While I was glad the energy had shifted to where I wasn't always on edge, I was still alone and forgotten, literally sometimes, when the foursome would forget to pick me up from activities they sent me to at school so they could spend their evenings in our basement without me around.

Witnessing what was happening but not necessarily knowing the specifics of what was happening, especially the why, tricked me into believing my life was actually on an upswing. I wasn't the object of my father's wrath and that was enough to make me believe my life was somehow better. I could handle being alone. Being forgotten or ignored or dismissed was a little harder, but at least my father wasn't picking on me or bullying me. I had been taking piano lessons for several years by then and was already fairly good, if not accomplished for my age. I started to use the piano as a tool to get attention by playing music that seemed significant to other family members. For my sister I played Led Zeppelin's *Stairway to Heaven*, a song that seemed like an anomaly for a band whose other music made no sense to me; it was too rough and jarring. But more importantly, I decided I would conquer the *Theme from Brian's Song*, the movie that had made my father cry a decade before. My mother, an excellent piano player even after only having had two years of lessons in high school, had bought the sheet music shortly after the movie was released into theaters after it first aired on TV. Not only had I felt the power of the music myself, the power to elicit a longing and emotion I didn't understand, for ten years the piece was a sort of siren song for my father that could stop him in his tracks and entrance him into a dreamlike state. It was a difficult piece, one requiring all five fingers on the right hand, but after weeks of solitary practice, I felt I had learned it sufficiently to casually offer it up one day while the foursome was in another room. It did in fact work like a siren song, bringing my father next to me on the piano bench. His arm was up against mine. His eyes had tears in them, and for one very short moment I felt like I had some power, some magic which I could use in the future when things at home started to go awry again.

At some point things did, in fact, go awry; the galavanting took a turn and the couples stopped hanging out together, only the couples weren't the original couples. The switch had happened. My sister pulled me from my bed one night on my parents' anniversary. She dragged me down the stairs to listen to the grunting from my mother and father's bedroom. She turned and said, "You know that's not dad in there."

Shortly after, I locked myself in the bathroom and I tried to kill myself for the first time by taking all of the cold medicine in the medicine cabinet. I was twelve. I was scolded, asked by my mother how I could do such a thing to her and shuffled off to school the next day. She decided not to tell my father, and nothing was said about it again. In an ultimate act of disregard and abandonment, my suicide attempt was pushed aside and purposely forgotten. Eventually, like the sexual abuse, I dismissed the act as being yet another attempt at getting attention.

There was something else going on at this point within these two morphing households, something clearly more important than me and getting me help. I was so confused during this time, and while some might deem my attempt at my life as the whim of a child, I truly didn't want to be around anymore. I didn't know then that the sparks of divorce had been set in motion, that the acrimony of not just one breakup but two had started to infiltrate my short-lived sense of relative peace. There was a lot of whispering and too many overheard conversations about what the other couple did or were doing which might be used against them. There was yelling into phones, crying, and one couple trying to pit me against the other. There were questions by one parent about what was happening down the street with the other parent.

Outside of their interest in me as a go-between/middleman/spy, I didn't seem to exist at all. My father's anger and disdain for his loser son was back, but the primary feeling that pervaded this time was a sense of utter abandonment. The other couple's children must have felt it too, although being a decade younger than both my sister and I, they didn't know what was going on at all. I soon became a surrogate parent, spending a lot of time babysitting while our parents did what they did. Years later, at the start of high school, their children would become my step-sisters through two marriages. The wife-swap was eventually made official. My mother married their father, my father married their mother. My father moved two houses down the street, while my new step-father moved in with us. Interestingly, as if this isn't interesting enough, ten years later my father and my step-mother would again do a swap/remarry with the golf pro and his wife at the country club.

While I would reframe my parents' behavior as being the perfect fodder for a John Irving book, something to hold onto, file away and eventually share with friends in high school when we'd have our "who has the most fucked up parents" contests, the reality is that witnessing the experience cost me. It cost Henry, too. That instability fed my future drive towards stability in Henry's and my relationship. I had convinced myself Henry and I would last forever. Part of that vision was a drive to show everyone, namely both of our families, that our relationship was real, more real than my parents and sisters' attempts at marriage, that they were wrong in thinking Henry and I wouldn't last and that gay long-term relationships in themselves didn't last. I wanted everyone to know he was my soulmate, a word I presumed no one else in the family understood.

I was devoted to Henry because I loved him, yes, but I also loved him for a lot of wrong reasons. Maintaining and ensuring the longevity of the relationship became more important than making sure the relationship was healthy. It was always an unspoken goal in my mind to make it to 15 years with him, so that I could say we outlasted my parent's marriage. I didn't understand what codependency and enmeshment were at the time and therefore didn't understand the extremely dysfunctional aspects of our partnership. I didn't understand that my definition of a normal relationship had been skewed since childhood. Staying together at all costs meant Henry and I had stayed together through a lot of turmoil; I saw that as healthy. But because fucking around with the neighbors had been normalized along with the resulting secrets and lies, I relied on that normalization when I did go out and fuck around on him.

Henry knew all these stories. He knew everything about my childhood, so perhaps he used them as part of his reasoning as to why he thought I'd go into porn if we weren't together. He never actually told me why he thought this; my piecing it together is happening in real time as I write. He thought my family, or at least what had happened, was fucked up and utterly dysfunctional. While I wasn't aware of the extent to which my need for attention was based on early years of abandonment, he did. It was a piece of the puzzle.

I assume the final reason he said what he said about my going into porn had to do with my obsession with my body. By the time I hit my thirties, I had the body I'd always wanted. This went beyond having the model looks everyone had been saying I had since I left high school. During the decade of modeling I had done in Pittsburgh, even when I was a regular model for Dick's Sporting Goods (the irony of the name and the fact it was a sporting goods store is not lost on me), my body was slim and toned, but not athletic. I hadn't discovered the world of fitness yet.

I was a trim, healthy beach kid in South Africa, but once back in the states with no friends, a pre-pubescent with a father who shamed me for my increasing weight, my body-image issues started. One day in sixth grade, my four-year-old cousin said I looked fat—to which my grandfather chided him by saying, "Yes, Spencer has gained a lot of weight, but it isn't nice to say he looks fat." I started purging for the next two years until I finally started to grow in eighth grade, continuing to grow taller to the point that I could eat anything I wanted without gaining weight. I was tall and slim for the next decade or so, until my breakdown in 1996.

That psychotic break shook me and forever changed my life. I just quit teaching and was doing what I sought out to do when I made the decision to leave the classroom, which was to get back to theater. I was in several local musical theater productions; one of the largest companies in Pittsburgh cast me as Thomas Jefferson in *1776* while I was finishing rehearsals for *Forever Plaid* at a local dinner theater. I was also heavily using DXM, the cough suppressant, and was drinking hard.

Subsequently, I began to split. My personality was ripping in two, urged on by two voices in my head, the comforting and supporting voice, the voice who had always saved, soothed and encouraged me, and the other one, the destructive one that had been waiting for years to take over completely. Now was that moment. The night before opening in *Forever Plaid*, after consuming more DXM, my mind split completely and I had a psychotic break. My mind told me I was someone else; I called the director and said that my name was Simon, Simon Christ, and that Spencer was dead and couldn't do the show the next day. Then I called the production company for *1776* and told them Spencer no longer existed. Within several days I had an intake at Western Psychiatric

Hospital, the hospital's outpatient clinic for dual diagnosis (depression and substance abuse) patients, and committed to attending several group sessions a week along with regular sessions with a counselor. Within 2 weeks I decided that not only were the other patients too fucked up for my tastes, my counselor clearly had more issues than me so I committed to getting better by myself.

After my mind and body cleared, I was so horrified by my severe episode of dissociation that I promised Henry I would get clean. Getting clean and being unemployed meant having to fill once occupied days. I continued the renovations on the house, finally understanding how much easier it was to handle power tools without being under the influence of various substances. I also dusted off the Soloflex we bought on a whim in 1990 that had acted as a clothes hanger for the previous six years and started to work out. Eventually, I saw an ad in the paper for a job opening at the Pittsburgh Athletic Association, the PAA. It may have seemed an odd choice of a classified for me to answer, but this was one of those gifts of serendipity I immediately recognized as such. For years while going to both undergraduate and graduate school at Pitt, I was always drawn to the Pittsburgh Athletic Association building, which sat on the university campus next to the Masonic Temple and across Fifth Avenue from Heinz Chapel and the Cathedral of Learning. More than once I'd had a passing thought that someday I would be connected to the association, but I didn't know how or why. And now the PAA was hiring me.

Over the course of several years, I worked my way from desk attendant to spinning and aqua aerobics instructor to the athletic director. I'd never been athletic in my life, certainly never played any sports, but during these four years I turned myself and my body into a machine. I wouldn't have called myself obsessed with fitness at the time, but I was obsessed with my body and my need for perfection. This drive became so intense that at one point I decided to run the Pittsburgh Marathon despite having never run more than five miles in my life. After just three weeks of training and an injured back, I finished the marathon in just over four hours.

This was the magnitude of my drive, of my fixation on perfection, which led to an obsession with having the perfect body. I loved looking good, I loved feeling taut, being able to rub my hands on my abs and feel the indents. I can admit that I turned myself on. I felt sexy as fuck, so even after leaving the city for Vermont, I kept up a daily routine. I set up a gym in our weatherized but unheated basement porch, so even when the temperature was below zero, I was on my spinning bike and lifting weights to keep in shape. It helped me stay clean, sober and relatively happy. Once we left Pittsburgh, I missed being able to show my body off so readily to others. Whether at the PAA, running on the streets or dancing at the Pittsburgh Eagle, I was an unapologetic exhibitionist, but there was no one to show off to in Vermont. Unless I went on the hunt—the hookup website Manhunt, that is.

It's probably this exhibitionism on my part that most led Henry to the idea that I'd likely go into porn.

Chapter Six

⌄

J ust before Memorial Day of 2004, I took the easy way out of our
then 17-year relationship. I told Henry I fucked around on him,
knowing he'd leave me because of it. I'd fucked around the past
year in Vermont, from Manhunt hookups to bathhouses in Montreal to
rest stops along Route 91. I'd had opportunities to cheat in the cities to
which I traveled for Department of Education conferences.

But I knew all it would take to alienate Henry was a confession of
one infidelity, so I kept it to that. I didn't have the heart to tell him I'd
been so unhappy for so long that I thought killing myself would be the
softer, gentler way to leave the relationship. I figured he'd more easily get
over my dying than he would my existing in the world without him,
without our being together.

While I was fortunate to have the job I had, I felt like I was dying
inside. I had no creative outlets. Painting wasn't my calling—I could do
it, but it didn't excite me. I'd occasionally get to sing at a party around a
piano. I felt like I was way too young to be living in this desolate place
in Vermont, way too young to be "retired" at 36 in the Northeast
Kingdom. Henry might have been living his dream, writing in the

picture-perfect setting. But I was far from happy, and thus my plans on how to end my life started to come together.

It wasn't just the lack of creative outlets for me. My role in the relationship had become untenable. Even with my disposition toward darkness and suicidal ideation at times, I was still the energy, optimism, faith and drive in our relationship, always trying desperately to lift Henry from his own darkness and depressive attitudes. I was Pooh to his Eeyore, which essentially meant that there was no room for me and my needs. Like my mother, my tendency was to shine even when my spirit was being crushed.

Playing Pooh might have been bearable to me had we had an ounce of intimacy in our lives. The young sensitive boy in me had always dreamed of finding someone with whom I could hold hands, sit next to on the sofa with my arm around him or with my head in his lap, someone I could spoon with as I fell asleep. But Henry wasn't that guy—it just wasn't in his makeup. Forcing intimacy with someone like that only provides discomfort and disappointment, hence I'd given up that dream years before. My pleas had always fallen on deaf ears. He wasn't willing to change and didn't see why he should have to.

This isn't to say that we hadn't had, in many ways, a great life together. Our experiences were huge and life-changing, all for the better: London, renovating the house, the move to Vermont. We were soulmates, two boys meant to find and escort each other through the tail-end of adolescence and into young adulthood. Our families eventually accepted us, embraced our relationship, and helped make us feel whole. We were meant to be together, I firmly believed that. In some ways we both worked hard to stay together, with him forgiving my addictive behaviors and having to live with someone damaged by trauma and suffering from undiagnosed mental disorders. As for me, I'd put aside my own wants to support his needs and creative desires.

But this was a relationship of youth, of not ever having figured out who we were as individuals. In the end, without either of us having an individual identity, he became stubborn and I grew resentful and started acting out.

Ironically, though, it was the acting out sexually that started to bring me back to life, that gave me enough desire to live that'd I continued to rip up each suicide note I'd penned over several months towards the end. There was the addictive aspect of the cheating, the lying and sneaking around, and then the euphoria of the chase, the thrill, the release and all that. But those experiences also led me to the realization that there was more out there, that I had missed out on something that felt important, natural and, shockingly, spiritual to me. I wanted to fuck the world and have the world fuck me. I wanted that freedom, that power, that control. I wanted to be desired. I wanted more sex, but more than that, I wanted more life.

I was correct that only one confession of infidelity would end the relationship. After Henry slapped me the night I told him I'd cheated on him, he kicked me out of the house and made me go stay with friends. Within a couple of days, he said I could come back and stay while we figured out what was to happen next.

That first night back in the house, as I watched him make his normal happy-hour drink—a martini, up, dirty—I told him to make me one as well. I said to him that since we were no longer together, I could drink again. He knew I'd quit for him—that was the ultimatum he'd given me when I'd landed in Western Psych eight years prior—but in the following years, I'd embraced living without drugs and alcohol with the zealotry of, well, a true addict. I was righteous in my sobriety: My body was a temple, how could I ever put anything bad into it?

But splitting up with Henry meant that I was unleashed—and an unleashed animal is going to start exploring drinking again. I foolishly thought, having been sober for so long, that I'd be able to handle it. So I didn't think of that martini as a relapse. I considered it to be a toast to freedom, to change, to taking back my life.

After we'd each had two drinks, Henry brought it up again: If we weren't together, I'd probably go into porn. Minutes later, he brought out the camera. I can't explain it. I can't explain how Henry could go from being angry and in pain to taking photos of me naked. It could have been the alcohol. It could have been the desire to have post break-up sex. It could have been a need to prove to me that he was strong enough to get through what was happening to our relationship, that I hadn't actually hurt him let alone destroyed him. Perhaps he didn't think our doing so would lead to me actually sending them to a porn company. Only Henry knows, and while I'm not putting the weight of my going into the business on him, I have wondered whether my path might have been very different if that night of drinking and taking photos had never happened.

Regardless, after trimming my body hair and doing push-ups to get pumped, I was nude and working up a hard-on. We set up lighting. I rubbed oil onto my upper body to make it glisten and posed against the logs of the cabin.

Henry and I had ordered several videos from Titan from the TLA catalog while in Vermont. We both felt these videos were the ultimate in fantasy and quality. The films weren't just fucking. The settings were stunning and added an otherworldly quality to the sex that I felt enhanced the excitement. This was clearly a company that cared deeply about the artistic aspects of their films; they were creating art.

I became obsessed with *Gorge*, a Titan film that was shot in Arizona including at the Grand Canyon. The combination of naked skin, sand, huge boulders and cliffs limited the visual palette to just several earth tone colors against the blue of the sky. I found it stunning. Then, of course, there were the actors: Ben Jakks, Carlos Morales, Dred Scott, and Ray Dragon. Beautiful men, manly men, men who felt honest in their roles, like the sex was passionate as well as brutally masculine. But the one who caught my eye was Carlos Marquez. An uninhibited assertive bottom, he was the one with whom I felt a kinship. He had the unabashed desire to get fucked, and to me there wasn't anything sexier than a man who was man enough to show how much he enjoyed being topped. I could picture myself being him—and I could picture myself doing it on camera.

The morning following our drunken photoshoot, on May 21, 2004, I submitted several photos to Titan's website portal, then emailed Titan directly: *Attached, please find additional photos to the ones downloaded on your website application this morning. I didn't realize I'd only be able to provide four online. Thanks for your consideration. If you are interested in contacting me, please do——you won't be disappointed. Guaranteed.*

It's one thing to write an email with the same level of confidence needed to send photos of your raging hardon and another to believe your words will make any difference. I didn't think my photos would be enough by themselves, so with just a few simple words, 'you won't be disappointed,' I made an attempt to put forth an assuredness I had no idea would be one of my key attributes throughout my short career: confidence. Apparently it was both my photos and that confidence which set everything in motion. The following Tuesday, Titan offered to fly me to Palm Springs on June 8th to film with director Joe Gage. Brian Mills, Titan's coordinator and photographer, informed me that upon receiving my photos he immediately showed them to Gage. Joe had recently returned to the porn industry, working with a few lesser known companies whose production values were in line with movies made more than twenty years before. Now Titan had contracted with him to film a series of movies paying homage to his early classics of the seventies, but they would raise the bar on the production value. He was a legend in the business, having made *Kansas City Trucking, LA Tool and Die,* and *El Paso Wrecking Company*—movies which to this day are my favorites of all time. He saw my photos that weekend and decided to cast me as the passive role in *100° in Tucson,* his upcoming film project. I'd be partnered with an actor who would play the construction foreman. This actor oozed manliness, roughness and everything I wanted in a guy who would fuck me on camera. Midweek, however, they informed me that they were having a hard time reaching my costar-to-be, so Gage decided to put me, totally untested, in the role of the construction foreman. Titan would find me an appropriately younger bottom. It all happened less than a week after Henry took the photos of me.

Always looking for signs, I took this whirlwind opportunity as the universe telling me I had made the right decision with my relationship, that I was justified in all I had done, that my need to be free, to start a new chapter alone, to go explore who I was after all those years of losing myself in someone else, was all meant to be. Rationalization and justification is easy when you see only what you want to see. The fact is, I was looking for a new life, to live rather than die, and in order to do that, choosing to do something so crazy and absurd made the most sense because there would be no going back. I didn't want the choice of someday going back to the comfortable, to what I had known for 17 years, to the ease of being in a relationship, to being part of a whole instead of being the whole myself.

For Henry, his beliefs were once again confirmed: things just happened for me. I was charmed. The universe handed me things. He didn't know that for months I'd been contemplating suicide, and that perhaps the root of what was happening was deeper than luck.

While partially tempered by guilt over the obvious hurt I was causing him, the adrenaline rush I felt over what was happening was overwhelming. I'd felt like I was drowning in the relationship, and now I felt like I was getting my first big gulps of air just thinking about how much life I had to live. I didn't realize at the time that the breath of new life meant the death of what had been. Blinded by the exhilaration I didn't understand that it was the definitive end of an "us" after 17 years. I didn't realize that the loss of this relationship in which I spent half my life would be my first experience of true loss, the type of loss that forever alters you, that haunts every moment of your future, every reflective glance towards the past, and every emotion you feel, and have yet to feel. One can't spend half your life with a person and not feel loss even if staying in the relationship could be the death of you. Feeling loss and feeling regret are very different things. I'd eventually learn that much of the loss I was feeling was more a sense of absence. I may not have missed certain aspects of our lives and relationship, the ones that were stifling and killing me, but our daily rituals, our common language and catch phrases, our familiarity, those I'd miss for a long time.

The ten days before flying to Palm Springs were obviously easier for me than for Henry. In the martini-soaked moment of taking those photographs, he'd seemed to accept my leaving the relationship, but now that I was actually moving forward with filming a porn video, it was a different story. He decided that, while I was shooting, he wanted to be with his best friend from Pittsburgh, who now lived in Ocean Grove, New Jersey, with his husband. I was feeling a lot of guilt about the breakup, so I drove him there—a seven-hour drive. It was the least I could do, I told myself. I'd spent 17 years chauffeuring Henry because he didn't drive. It was part of my ingrained habit to take care of him. But all the while I'd built up resentments because of it, which turned into acting out. Every weekend when we lived in Vermont, I'd drive him throughout the northern part of the state so he could browse bookstores, while I'd end up cruising and having sex in parks, or meeting up for Manhunt trysts at the same time.

As soon as I dropped Henry off in New Jersey, I turned around and drove back home to Vermont, where I spent several days wondering what was about to happen.

The truth is, despite the confident initial email I'd sent Titan, I had major insecurities. Not about my body, but about the size of my dick. And the size of my loads. Neither were porn-size in my mind. My balls were also small and tight—they didn't hang like porn-star balls did. I had a hernia scar slashing across my pubic area. But clearly Titan felt that my dick and my balls were good enough to hire me. I comforted myself by saying they were body-appropriate. I wasn't a muscle guy but instead was slim, athletic, and flexible. Trim and lean. My dick, well, it was sort of the same. It wasn't huge, but it fit me.

My biggest worry had to do with cumming. I wasn't a shooter and I didn't cum a lot. I did realize that both holding off masturbating and being hydrated could help, and indeed, when Titan sent me an email with its pre-shoot rules, it included the request to not cum for several days before filming. I'd end up writing a blog about this the following year, which the gay porn mag *Unzipped* quoted in their "Say What" column: "I always envied those guys who would literally blow loads like a cannon, splattering walls and bed frames and faces. Hell, I'm lucky if it gets past my navel."

After seeing an ad in the TLA catalog for a product, Ropex, that guaranteed an increase in semen production, I went ahead and ordered it and started taking it before filming in the hopes it might do something for me.

And yet, with Titan deciding to switch me to the dominant position in the upcoming scene, my body insecurities were dwarfed by a new insecurity: I hadn't fucked anyone in over 14 years. I'd been a bottom my entire adult life. The guys I'd fucked were limited to my first boyfriends in my teen years, with only one or two after. It's not that I didn't think I'd be able to perform or wasn't going to be competent. It's that I wasn't sure if I'd be convincing enough. I'd always assumed that having a huge dick was necessary to be a top in porn. For me as a viewer, it had never really mattered if a top knew how to use his cock; I was focused on the size and how that made the bottom feel. I didn't have one of those massive dicks, so I imagined having to make up for that in the viewer's eye by being exceptional in the act of fucking itself.

I didn't share any of these insecurities with Titan because I'd learned long ago to push those things aside and dive into fear. That inner voice of mine said I could do it. Fuck fear! I'd come to believe that fear was merely a mindset. I'd spent a long time in states of fear as a child until one day I simply said, "No more." Horrible things had happened, but I'd learned how to float above the fear and dissociate. *I will no longer fear*, I told myself then, and eventually, with the introduction of addiction and mental health issues as a teen, that voice saying "no more fear" started to tell me to seek out fear in order to push through it. Fear could turn to excitement through the conscious decision to make it so. Fear was adventure, and I was addicted to adventure and the rush it gave me.

Having lived in South Africa as a child and traveled extensively through Africa and Europe before the age of 10, I've always had a wanderlust. But for my entire relationship with Henry, outside of the grand adventure of running away to Greece and living in London in 1987, we essentially traveled nowhere. We didn't have the funds; with a money pit of a home in Pittsburgh, we lived hand-to-mouth in order to put everything into the house to increase its value once we sold it. Once we were in Vermont, I traveled to the occasional work conference, which was thrilling in its own way.

The trip to Palm Springs to start my porn career was clearly different, however. This was a true flight to freedom and a new chapter, the new adventure I had been craving for so long. I had to drive to Montreal to catch a flight, it being the closest airport to get me to L.A., where I would catch my connection. Kelly Clarkson, having just won the first *American Idol*, came on the radio twice during that drive. As she belted out "One Moment in Time," an anthem for her and for all the other dreamers out there, I took it as just another sign that my own moment in time had come.

I cried when we descended into Palm Springs, it reminded me so much of southern Africa. I had a deep guttural feeling that, while I may have been leaving home, I was also coming home as well. I arrived with a week's worth of pent-up sexual energy, a ripped body, my bottle of Ropex, confidence and a script I had memorized. Joe Gage made movies, not just sex scenes. The scene I was about to film had been scripted carefully to create a slow seduction consisting of a construction foreman and a younger day laborer. There was as much dialogue and seduction as sex—it would be the ultimate fantasy. (After its release, the scene would become iconic for many gay men for that reason: it touched on a fantasy for so many who, even to this day, reach out and tell me it changed their life because it helped them come out and accept themselves.)

By the time Brian Mills, my original contact with Titan and the cinematographer for my first film, picked me up at the Palm Springs airport, I was already inhabiting my character to a certain extent, because the character had no fear. He knew what he wanted: he would win over the young straight worker. I needed to win over Titan.

Chapter Seven

⌄

The following day, I stepped into a new life. There were about a dozen guys milling about in the house that had been borrowed for the filming of *110° in Tucson*, half talent, half production crew. Joe Gage was screening the initial reel for his first film with Titan, *Back to Barstow*, which was in post-production, while several guys were building the set in the back guest room by the pool. I don't remember much outside of the initial introductions, those moments when I felt the stares of eyes scanning me to see if I lived up to my photographs. My chameleon-like nature, tendency to engage people, and easy-going demeanor served me and everyone else well during those moments, because I remember being immediately at ease. I also felt a collective sigh of relief in the house when they realized that not only did I match my photos but that I was a genuine person as well. I can be extremely social, even though I'm an equally extreme introvert who never truly feels like he belongs. But this felt like a low-pressure environment, with everyone busy doing their thing. I spent a little time talking Joe, then with my scene partner, Luke Pearson—the brief get-to-know-you-before-I-fuck-you chat. Luke was in his twenties, slim, classic looks. His most notable role up to that had been in a threesome in *White Trash*, which had been nominated for a Grabby, one of the two gay adult industry awards along with the GayVNs. While the crew was wrapping up its construction, essentially a fake wall that was going to be destroyed during filming, I was given a walk-through of the set and a talk-through of the scene. Then we started filming. The opening shot was me in jeans, black T-shirt and a tool belt, smoking a cigarette while using a circular saw. Luckily, I knew how to handle a saw, having spent nearly a decade using one in the house in Pittsburgh.

It was hot, Palm-Springs-in-June hot, in a closed space, only a door for ventilation, with studio lights beaming and a half-dozen people on set. I was drenched in sweat, the saw whining through a piece of wood, deep in concentration with the lit cigarette dangling from my lips. After capturing the initial shot in just two takes, it didn't take long for me to see in the faces around me an acknowledgement that I knew what I was doing, that what was about to happen was going to be good, at least in terms of creating a convincing character and the mood for the scene. Their risk in hiring me was going to pay off.

We filmed most of the day without even getting to the sex. This scene was as much non-sexual seduction as it was sex. The story was simple: I was a contractor working with a young guy who knocks a hole in a wall and finds a stash of vintage porn magazines. He calls me over, I see what they are, give Luke the once-over with an intense stare and say, "It's Harry," which was meant to sound like "hairy." After a pause, I clarify and say, "My name is Harry." To this day, I still have people who repeat that line to me.

I soon convince him that it's too hot to work and we should go to my place for a beer and to cool down. After leaving him on my sofa and encouraging him to look through the magazines he found in the wall, I go to shower and come out naked with a towel around my neck. But in a clever and funny twist, Joe Gage wanted to play the next part like the famous Austin Powers movie. We carefully had to film as I moved here and there so that you couldn't see my dick. First it was behind a lamp, then a chair, then something else, while I slowly crept my way to the couch for the reveal. It was a blast. I immediately fell in love with what I was doing: being in front of a camera and acting. I also loved being naked in front of people, something I didn't realize would bring me such a sense of ease, comfort and validation.

I don't need to go into the full description of all the sex. It's out there to watch. But it worked. The level of confidence and command I felt pouring out of me felt honest, real and authentic. I was the contractor, the foreman, but I was still me. It was a role, and it wasn't a role. I realized while filming that, while I was creating a porn persona, it wasn't far off from my own personality, that perhaps a porn persona could exist along-side me rather than in contrast to me. I sat on the sofa next to Luke while we paged through the magazines. I asked whether he liked what he saw, eventually revealing my dick to him and asking him if he liked what he saw again. I seduced the fuck out of him, getting him to lean over and taste the tip, then eventually getting him to suck me.

In two senses, porn scenes aren't done with just one shot. First, the cameramen will cut the scene several times, reposition, get different angles and close shots all the while with the actors holding the action until the filming begins again. Secondly, an actor is typically paid for two cum shots—one oral, one anal. It was time for my first cum shot, what I felt was my first true test on the journey. I passed with flying cum. Whether it was the seven days of abstinence, the Ropex, or the sexual build-up of the past several hours, I managed a healthy load, something I could be proud of in the moment. But I immediately worried that I had literally blown my load and wouldn't be able to get another out of me for the anal action.

But first it was time to show everyone my asshole, perhaps the most vulnerable thing I'd ever done in my life. I'd never been rimmed before, even though I'd essentially been a bottom all my life, and a voracious one at that. No one on the set knew this, and I wasn't about to tell them. They likely wouldn't have believed me given how well everything else was going. Again, no fear, I dove in—or rather, Luke dove in. I played the coaxing but assertive top, telling this "boy" what to do, encouraging him in a gentle way, smiling, then smirking while he explored my ass with his fingers and tongue.

Clearly I enjoyed the sexual act, but in all honesty, the most exciting part was the feeling of control I had, knowing that, even though this was a scene and Luke was supposed to enjoy it, the fantasy we were creating felt real. Again, I could sense something on the set. I'd catch a glance and a smile from one person to another, an acknowledgment that what they'd captured wasn't just good sex, wasn't just mechanical, it was hot. Something special was happening.

Thankfully Viagra had been provided, my first time trying it, so I was rock-hard throughout the scene. By the time it came for Luke to sit on my cock, I was at ease in terms of performance, if not with the impending second cum shot. If you know how to fuck, it's not hard to get it right when your dick is engorged with the help of the blue pill. There were no worries about going soft and struggling to keep it inside Luke's hole. In fact, being able to slam-fuck (a new term for me), pulling out completely and slamming back in, was easy. My insecurity over my size was fading, but the second cum shot still had me worried.

But it happened. Abstinence and the Ropex seemed to work, and while those shots weren't geysers, load size no longer seemed like something I'd have to worry about.

So I'd conquered a few things: first film, first time being rimmed, first time topping in 14 years, first double shot—all the while sensing that something unusual was happening for those watching. The energy was electric and the crew and director felt the same thing: This was the start of something special.

⌄

With Titan, it took two full days to complete a 15-minute scene along with all the necessary still photography. This wasn't porn by today's standard: arriving in someone's living room or hotel, pulling out an iPhone and filming unedited sex for fifteen minutes to post online. This was a professional film set, just like any commercial shoot I'd done during my ten-year modeling career in Pittsburgh. Throughout the filming, from start to finish, including wrapping up the last details, the last missed shot or close up, I couldn't have felt more proud. This was why I'd chosen Titan to begin with. My belief that they were the best at what they did was confirmed, and added to that was relief and gratitude that almost every single person on the set was kind, down-to-earth, outwardly appreciative and caring. These were really good people, people with whom I thought it would be possible, if given the chance, to create a community of friends.

Before I flew out of Palm Springs, Brian Mills took me to a quiet room to do a post-scene interview. Most of Titan's movies had a personal interview at the end with one of the stars, along with behind-the-scenes bonus material. It was an interview with Jon Galt in a movie in my collection that inspired me and got me thinking that porn was something I could do. He was a professional, had a job in a very legitimate tech business, and clearly knew who he was and what he wanted in life. I'd later work with him and tell him that he was part of why I went into the business.

Brian asked a short series of questions including, "how did you break into the adult industry," "do you have any acting experience," "what was the most difficult part?" I remember simply being me: a wide-eyed, somewhat innocent newbie from the woods of Vermont with hopes, dreams and ambitions. That's who I still was at that point. Fans would later tell me it wasn't just the sex in *Tucson* that made my scene so important to them, it was the interview. I struck them as being real, just a normal guy exploring a part of himself he hadn't yet tapped into. I suppose I reminded them of themselves.

I thought, after the last question in the interview, "why did you choose Titan," that my experience, already one of the most exciting and rewarding of my life, was over. But Brian indicated he wanted to talk after. We continued to sit and he proceeded to tell me what he and what the others saw and experienced on the set, what they saw in me and experienced through me on camera. I don't remember the exact words, but he explained how he had contacted Bruce Cam, the owner of the company, who'd given him permission to ask me to be an "exclusive" for Titan. He expressed their appreciation for the work I'd done, the preparedness, the professionalism and energy, both natural and sexual, and the passion I'd brought to the set. He said I could go far, that I had "it."

Being exclusive meant that, instead of trying to get jobs with other companies, I would be under Titan's wing. I'd make just four movies a year, per contract, and they would make me a star via a well-planned strategy. I could be the new face of Titan Media. The thing those outside the industry don't understand is that porn isn't necessarily lucrative for a model by any means, at least it wasn't back then and certainly not for a newcomer. The value of the exclusivity contract wasn't in financial compensation, it was in the promotion of and the publicity for me as a model. For most, it could take years before a model could be touted as a 'star.' Titan was offering to get me that status after a single movie. And there it was. Henry's belief was again confirmed: I was charmed. Just twenty days after taking photos in the log cabin, I was now a full-fledged porn star with an exclusive contract with Titan even before my first movie was in post-production.

With the filming of *110° in Tucson* completed and my exclusive contract signed, I now had to fly back east to tell Henry what had happened and what was about to happen: it wasn't just one movie to get out of my system, it was the start of something bigger. But once on the plane, I began to go dark. I realized that what I'd just done couldn't be brushed away, like a line in the sand, but was in fact more like a score across wet concrete that would dry, solidify and remain permanent. I had ended my seventeen-year relationship, thrown it away, and within weeks was doing porn. I couldn't help wondering what kind of person would do that. It all felt right but completely wrong at the same time. Had I just become the person I said I never would be—an unkind, cruel, selfish and deceitful man about to further hurt the love of my life, the person I'd committed to take care of and protect? Had I been a coward and made the easier choice when the healthier one would've been to learn how to communicate with Henry? After all, we could've gone to therapy. I could've gone to therapy. I could've learned how not to sacrifice my own needs for his and learned what codependency and enmeshment were.

But instead, here I was, going back home to tell him that my life had changed completely, that I was already officially a porn star and that he and I were now truly over.

The night before I drove back down to New Jersey from Vermont to pick Henry up, another 14-hour round trip, I went to the video store and rented a movie called *Circuit*, about the hedonistic, sex- and drug-filled world of muscle-bound gay men who travel the country from one massive, orgiastic rave to another. I'd seen it on the shelf before and never had the nerve to tell Henry I wanted to watch it. I think part of me didn't want to share it with him because I knew from the cover and synopsis that it would tap into a desire I wanted to keep private. But this time, I took the video home and fell into its world of sex, drugs, parties, the ups and downs, the exhilarating highs and the devastating bottoms. In the film, a midwestern boy finds his way to L.A. and lands in this hypersexual and ultimately toxic world. I knew that I could become that main character in real life if I wasn't careful. It was a vision of the future, of what might be, but for some reason it didn't scare me. In fact, it seemed exciting, dangerous, and enticing.

That's probably because, even though I'd been clean and sober for eight years, I was an addict. I wanted the sex, the parties, the friends—perhaps even the drugs, if it meant truly experiencing what it was like to be single and gay in 2004. Just 48 hours prior, I'd been telling my story to the camera in a post-film interview about being on a soulful sexual journey. Now, a sound was going off in my head that should have felt like a warning, but instead it was more like a siren beckoning me with its song—a song with a deafening dance beat, promising me all I wanted.

I knew that following this voice might lead me to self-destruction, because I'd spent much of my life following songs like this and, in fact, self-destructing. I knew these promises of pleasure would lead to pain, and when faced with hurt and pain, whether mine or someone else's, I'd always resorted to hurting myself. Now I was about to really hurt Henry—and along with that, I couldn't help but question who I was as a person. I'd never been gentle with self-criticism, a gift from my father, and in those moments, my darkness was on call. I think that's why *Circuit* held such an appeal. Through it, my darkness was calling and coaxing me, a lotus eater beckoning me to a feast. In the bounty it was offering,

I'd find both pain and pleasure—pain I deserved because of what I'd done to Henry and what I'd done to us.

But something else was also starting to work itself loose from the shadows, from the plot of earth in which it had been buried long ago. A memory, something fuzzy, something confusing, something so current and present in its emotional effect but out-of-reach, like a dream you can't recall. It started near the end of the filming in Palm Springs.

Chapter Eight

⌄

The senses have remarkable memories. A smell, a sound, a touch can trigger feelings one hasn't felt in decades. It was during filming of *110° in Tucson* that I was struck by a moment of recall that set the ball rolling for the next two and a half years.

There's nothing quite like sucking a dick you don't want to suck. And I don't mean because you're in a role play, in a mutually agreed upon sexual encounter where you're being "forced," but because you're actually being forced, physically or psychologically. Because you have no power. Because it's assault. Because it's molestation. Even if you're young and curious and mysteriously drawn to the idea or the image of a penis, having no choice but to put it in your mouth isn't fun. It isn't hot. Even if while doing it you realize you're getting something in return, perhaps attention or perhaps you see it as affection. Even if you now realize you have something to give in order to get a form of attention and affection you've never had from an adult male, including your father.

It's still not hot. And it isn't, or at least shouldn't be, a right of passage for underage gay boys. Especially if you're seven-years-old.

I had buried the memory only to have it resurface on the set of *110°*
in Tucson. Even the few times of my life when I'd happened to remember
the incident, it had been just a passing recollection that would then fade
back into the volumes of interesting things that had happened to me as
a child. I'd think, "Oh that's right. That guy molested me." I couldn't
even think about it as having been traumatic because, well, I thought it
was just something that happened to a lot of gay boys, that right of passage. No big deal. I got what I wanted, actually, and so desperately needed
at that time: male affection.

Yet, a fleeting moment on the set, just two days into my new career,
all the suppressed pain and shame of that buried memory suddenly
awoke. Beneath the soil, in the dark, this living thing, a seed, that memory, started to absorb its surroundings, started to take in energy that
would eventually allow it to crack the surface.

It was becoming clear after two long days of filming that we weren't
going to get a necessary second cum shot from Luke. There is a lot of
sitting, waiting, stroking, and coaxing on a porn set. When it's time for
the cum shot, they cut, change the lights, resituate the camera, and wait.
I wasn't exactly sure what the problem was other than performance anxiety. Perhaps Luke hadn't followed the three-day abstinence rule. It was
getting a little awkward. The last thing a porn star wants, given what he's
being paid to do, is not be able to cum. It's called the money shot for a
reason: we were being paid for two of them. I would witness this a few
times over the years, and while it may be part of the agreement with the
performer, Titan was always kind and patient. These were decent, empa-
thetic people who would never say anything to humiliate or disrespect a
performer. The performer would beat himself up enough in more ways
than one.

But after an hour of waiting for Luke to cum, the director called it
quits and decided to take a break. My scene partner was given time to

relax and eat and try to get himself mentally prepared to give it a go, while Joe and Brian decided whether they should waste any more time waiting when it might never happen.

On the set, my gut told me I could and should say "no" to sucking the director's dick when it was revealed this was to be the solution to the problem. Everything else about the shoot was completely professional. Telling me the director was going to step in as a "dick double" for my scene partner, 30 years his junior, gave me pause. It felt rather seedy. Was this for real? A hazing joke to see how I reacted? How could Joe's dick and cum shot possibly be used as a fill-in for young Luke? It was clear Joe desired me from the beginning—that's why I was hired. I thought Brian was going to step in and tell me they were just pulling my leg. Yet my initial moments of uncertainty as to whether the situation was really happening quickly melted away, along with the choice I briefly imagined I had in terms of whether I would go along with it.

I suppose I still could have said no. But on the other hand, I couldn't say no and wouldn't say no. I would prove to everyone that I was a professional. Joe essentially held what could be a potential career in his hand. Sucking the director's dick on camera in front of the crew in some lame attempt to fill in for the missing cum shot—well, I'd asked for it, hadn't I? I was now a sex worker. What right did I have to want to be a porn star and yet think I could say no to something like this? Sex workers didn't really have rights, did they? Perhaps this was how it worked after all, perhaps being a professional porn star meant you had to suck a director's dick in front of the crew once in a while. So I did it and I did it well. I performed; he came.

During those few minutes with him in my mouth, though, a sensory moment of taste and smell mixed with old emotions and a recollection of being in another time and place rippled through my body. A memory briefly came into focus of another dick long ago that I hadn't wanted to suck but did anyway.

In my mind, performing this act hadn't been a question asked of me even though the question had been asked. It had been asked by Brian, but in another way, it felt like a given; it was now part of the scene, and I would do it. I got on my knees, and with the help of my natural coping mechanism of making sense of confusing situations, I quickly told myself it definitely had been my choice. It was my choice and therefore I actually had the power in the situation. Throughout my life, this switch of perspective worked for me: take the feeling of powerlessness and turn it into a feeling of being in control. That cum shot didn't make it into the film, it's possible it was never intended to. (This scenario with a director was also completely different when, two years later, upon meeting and shaking the porn director Michael Lucas's hand for the first time, I was immediately on my knees in his office sucking him off. That I wanted.)

In describing the how and the what above, I need to be very clear that I do so with no judgment of anyone other than myself. There's no blame, no criticism of the director or anyone from Titan there that day just like I don't blame the neighbor who molested me. It "was what it was," a platitude I used to hate but which, with years of recovery and healing under my belt, has become key to accepting the past. It may have felt shady at the time, and in reality, it probably was. But it was what it was and I moved on.

These recollections, reflections, and memories I'm sharing will continue throughout the story because my journey was, as mentioned in the beginning, a journey of cause and effect, an explanation of why everything does actually happen for a reason. In describing an experience that triggers a fleeting memory causing a seed to grow, I'm not judging but instead getting to the root of the cause, the root of what happened next.

We seem to bandy about the term "triggered" now, as though it's a funny thing that happens when your friend casually brings up an Instagram post and you both break out in laughter: "I'm so triggered!" But as a victim of trauma, any trauma, which so many of us are, being triggered is something that can happen both as an immediate explosion or as a simple seed that gets planted and cared for in your subconscious. Until it then explodes to the surface to live in the light. It could be a sound, a smell, a feeling, an expectation.

Fifteen years after my porn career ended, when I found a therapist who knew how to deal with trauma, I finally understood what my experience at seven years old meant and how it had affected every behavior, sexual and otherwise, for 45 years, how it was one of many root causes of why I ended up in the porn industry and how being triggered happens on a cellular level. It has been a piece of my last decade of recovery that hadn't been examined initially, because six of those ten years I had a therapist with whom I'd never discussed the issues of early childhood trauma. I had been dismissing it, minimizing it, disregarding it and misunderstanding it for a very long time—and continued to do so even in the therapeutic process.

I believe, in part, some of the gay community was helping me do that. In today's world, sexual trauma is trauma. "Me-too" happened, Harvey Weinstein happened, the Catholic Church priest scandal happened. We've collectively come to an understanding of what molestation and sexual abuse are and mean (it's sad we actually had to clarify the definitions) and how it affects those who suffered.

But years ago, and still to this day, some gay men I know think back to their own sexual experiences at early puberty with adult men as something positive. Some think of it with fondness. I've been told the stories: A friend who was 12-years-old and having sex regularly with a married man. He shared that with me because he thought it would be as hot to me as the memory was to him. I've been asked a lot about whether I had sex with older men when I was a kid, how young I was, how old the men were. Even in recovery, I've shared with an older man in his seventies, a former mentor and sponsor, about my experience and the trauma work I was doing at the time with my therapist—only to have him ask me to describe the molestation. He asked me if I liked it. There was no "I'm sorry that happened to you." He wanted details. He wanted to know how many times we did it, as though my molestation was a consensual act where I went back for more because I enjoyed it.

I don't judge anyone who qualifies their early sexual experiences with adult men as something positive or titillating. I don't judge anyone's sexual behavior—period. I did a lot of crazy, terrible, sad and hurtful things sexually; I'm not in a position to judge those who look back or fantasize about these sorts of experiences we now definitively categorize as abuse. Because I certainly did; I looked back at that memory with the neighbor and edited it in my head so that the young child willingly engaged and perhaps even instigated it. The incident simply became another story to tell about what happened in South Africa as though it were as scary but exciting as the time we camped on the Zambezi River on a vacation in then Rhodesia (now Zimbabwe) and awoke to lion tracks outside our tent.

I first shared the story in a poem I wrote for Henry's and my senior poetry seminar at Pitt. It shocked the class with its detailed images and its language because I wrote it as a fairy tale. That's what trauma does: it rewrites the story so the child can survive. As much as the idea of child porn and sexual abuse is utterly devastating to me, my own fantasy life is about being used and abused. I get sick to my stomach with any reference to sexual abuse in movies or books, but I used to use the memory of my molestation as fodder for masturbation. Abuse of others is one thing, but being abused myself? When I dig into a fantasy, when I'm in the act of self-pleasure, it's about servicing, submitting, being forced and of having no choice.

The experience as a child seeped into my cells. I still remember the smell of body odor, of genitals ripe with sour sweat and dirt. It's why I can't have sex with anyone who has any kind of smell: They have to have showered. That smell will be forever a trigger for me. That encounter became the foundation of my sex life, of my life in general. It defined me and my relationship to myself and to my body. I associated sex with getting the love and attention I never received from my father. Sex became the only thing I felt I had that was worth anything.

My decision to go into porn was in part because, in my mind, all anyone ever wanted from me was sex. From early childhood, to teen years with friends and a particular older female who manipulated me and forced me into sex in high school by repeatedly getting me trashed to the point of blacking out, my formative years twisted my perspective of my worth. There was the adult theater "mentor" in my junior year of high school who was clearly a predator, and my two best female friends in freshman year of college—all of whom coerced me to have sex. I cried through that last experience. I was so distraught, not wanting to have sex but not wanting to hurt their feelings. I didn't know how to say no.

But with sobriety in my late twenties and the transformation of my body into something crafted of marble, internally I started to believe I had a power I hadn't had when I was younger. I entered the world as a newly single gay man for the first time at 36 years old. I thought I was going to have the opportunity to say no. I could show off what I had, I could ooze sex from every pore, and I could still say *No. You can't touch this. You can't have this. I want your desire, but I will not give this away. You have no power over me or my body. If you want it, you need to pay.*

This is why porn seemed like such an amazing option to explore sexually. Otherwise, trying to exist out on my own and experiment in a world of gay sex, I had doubts as to whether I'd be able to say no. Porn would give me the validation I craved, the need to flaunt and be desired, but I would be protected by the boundary of the TV or computer screen.

So it's ironic that in what I thought was the safety of that first porn set, I ended up not saying no when I was asked to suck the director's dick.

After we finished shooting *110° in Tucson*, Brian told me I would be filming one of their *ManPlay* videos in several weeks. These videos were exactly what they sounded like: men at play, group sex, no talking, no script, no costume. Just fucking and sucking. Titan told me that even though I was already an exclusive and about to be launched as a new star, they wanted me to do the *ManPlay* video because the series was usually their testing ground for talent. They would bring in a group of guys who had sent photos to the company and let them go at it to see who piqued Titan's interest. I'm not sure why my involvement in this was necessary given that I'd already passed an even bigger test as a lead scripted role in a Joe Gage film. I suppose they were just checking a box on the traditional path to exclusivity.

But I also admit I was excited. This wasn't just sex, it was a gangbang. What better way to catch up on all the dicks I'd imagined I missed over the years?

Before flying to San Francisco to film in early August, I stayed with Henry in our home and started the process of leaving Vermont and leaving the only life, as a couple, I had known my entire adulthood. I had to quit my job with the nonprofit, but fortunately the State of Vermont's Department of Education offered to hire me as a consultant which I could be from anywhere. Charmed again. The contract with the Migrant Education Program gave me the initial financial security I needed to start over. Financial security was something my father had drilled into my sister and me from as early on as I can remember, and while I turned those lessons into a comfortable living, there was never much left over after paying bills. We'd used most of our gains from the sale of the Pittsburgh house on the down payment for the Vermont log cabin and the first months of living without working.

Henry was now feeling the full force of what was about to happen, and he was understandably in a place of fear and anxiety. I was leaving him in the middle of the woods in a house he didn't know how to maintain, without a job or a driver's license. My life was changing by choice; his, not so much. But the fact that he'd chosen all those years not to get a job or a driver's license, or to learn to do anything practical around the house, didn't alleviate my guilt.

Much to my family's dismay and frustration, I decided to walk away from everything, including our financial investment in the house, most of which I had built over eight years of labor on the house in Pittsburgh. We split our dwindling savings, my portion being about $12,000, and I gave him the house, the car and everything we owned. I asked for $10,000 in return for my half of the house, which for the time being we would keep in both our names; he'd just start paying the mortgage. He wanted to stay there, and I'd help him do that until he got on his feet. Eventually we would have to get a divorce—it was required in Vermont to end a civil union—but that too would have to wait so we wouldn't legally have to separate ownership of the house yet.

We spent those six weeks together preparing for my leaving and his staying. That meant I had six weeks to teach Henry to drive, which he learned rather quickly, leaving me to wonder if I should have insisted he learn years before. By the end of July I felt that we both seemed prepared for my moving out. I'd do so after I filmed *ManPlay*, after which I would pack my stuff and head south to my parents.

It was during that summer I reached out to Ropex, the company from which I had ordered "cum pills," to explain that I was an exclusive for Titan, how well the pills had worked on the set, and that I would be ordering more in the future. It was a small company, so my call was answered by the owner. I gave him my positive review and ordered more. He called me back a week later and asked if I wanted to be a spokesperson for the product. He'd use my name in print ads, like the ad I had found in the TLA catalog, and I'd have the opportunity to be an affiliate for the company. It was surreal; suddenly the boy with cum insecurity was now representing load size and strength as a spokesperson.

San Francisco was as magical to me as any mythical Atlantis. It was the legendary place of gay freedom, the iconic safe harbor for those coming to terms with their sexuality in the seventies and eighties, but also full of danger and death in the form of the monster that was the AIDS epidemic. Voracious reader that I was, I'd read *Tales of the City* in high school. I had a second cousin who had lived in the city who had co-founded RazorMaid records, the source for gay club music in the eighties, records that were sent to me in high school and that I'd play at the parties I held senior year. That second cousin died of AIDS in the early nineties.

I told myself that San Francisco could be my new home, and when the taxi took me from the airport into the city, I felt like a character in one of the many books I'd read throughout my life. This was my book, however, still unwritten, but happening nonetheless in real time. This is what I would write. Imagination meets reality. When the two are balanced, it can be magic, so I soaked up every sight and sound, every piece of architecture, every unique smell that wafted my way.

Manplay 18 was going to be a quick shoot. It didn't take me long to realize that I was completely out of my element—not with the crew or the production, but with the other eight guys having sex. I was at least a decade older than most of them and certainly the only one who'd just left a 17-year relationship. Conversations on set were awkward; even defining them as 'conversations' is pushing it. But overall, everything was okay. *Manplay* was the other guys' testing ground, and I was going to do what I could to make it as hot as possible. I knew I'd succeed when, after squatting and riding this young beautiful Black guy while he sat on the edge of a five-foot-high stage, I managed to keep my balance without falling forward and off the platform and shooting a geyser in an arc into the air.

As I climbed off him, I saw two other actors who'd been watching me describe what they'd just seen to someone else. For a moment I thought they were judging me—until I realized that the looks on their faces were more along the lines of awe and respect. That's when I realized that my limber body could become one of my promising assets in porn. Little did I know that I'd end up winning a GayVN precisely because of that.

But then, just as I felt I might be holding some sway, one of the young guys pushed me aside when I tried to fuck him. This wounded my quickly growing ego. Didn't this kid know I was an exclusive? Didn't he realize he was being paid to fuck whomever wanted to fuck him on camera? I was self-aware enough to feel a slight tinge of hypocrisy, because he was a young man confident enough to say no, the precise thing I didn't say on the set of *Tucson* with the director. Perhaps my indignation was towards myself—but, as would so often be the case in the coming months, I focused outward, blaming others. Later, in an email to Brian, I expressed my frustration with that moment on the set. Whether or not that kid had the right to push me aside, it *was* his audition, after all. To my knowledge, he never worked for Titan again.

Chapter Nine

⌄

Upon my return to Vermont, it was officially time to leave. Since I was giving Henry our red Jeep Cherokee, I was happy to find a used forest green VolvoS70 for sale. My very first car at 16 was a late-seventies version of the same sedan, so it felt like another symbolic piece of treasure I happened to come across on my journey to the unknown. I packed it with what I could fit in the trunk and back seat, leaving at least another carload of my personal belongings in the second story of the garage, and headed back to my parents in Lancaster. While my driving away from Henry might have felt definitive, it wasn't yet the official end of the relationship. We promised to try to be friends and to continue to be in each other's lives, because neither of us knew how to walk away from the love we still had for each other. They say it takes at least half as much time to get over a relationship as the length of the relationship itself, and indeed it would take us five years to divorce and 12 years to stop calling each other, but to this day my dreams of him have yet to end.

My mother and stepfather knew about my consultant work, which helped alleviate some of their concern for my reckless financial decision regarding the separation. They both knew divorce, so the idea that Henry and I were not dividing our assets equally was confounding to them. What they didn't and couldn't understand was the depth of my guilt in leaving him. They certainly didn't know about my infidelity and my going into the porn business. Instead, with my next film coming up soon, I'd told them a yarn about having several necessary conferences on the West Coast to complete the report I was tasked to do for the Vermont DOE. I was already working on this extensive project for the state, spending hours in my stepfather's den, so it wasn't too far a stretch—and in at least one instance, I did go to D.C. for work.

My father lived in Lancaster's sister city of York, Pennsylvania, a 40-minute trip, so, with a gutful of anxiety, I visited my dad for the first time in eight years. But in fact, not only was I visiting him, but we were planning on making our first return to South Africa in 28 years, just the two of us.

Let me start by jumping back a bit. Several weeks before I'd confessed to Henry that I'd cheated on him, my father called out of the blue. This was during my dark days of hopelessness, those days I was drafting suicide notes and ripping them up the next day. My father and I had been estranged for eight years at this point; we had had no communication whatsoever during those years, which turned out to be just the first of two eight-year estrangements in our relationship. I remember standing in our dining room in Vermont with the phone in my hand and his voice at the other end, looking out at the vast expanse of snow and forest and being frozen, not from the winter cold, but from the shock of his call, his voice. I couldn't breathe. I was choking back emotion and there was silence on the other end as he did the same. It was a short call because neither of us could put enough words together to make much conversation. My father was never much of a talker to begin with, and I was completely caught off guard, so we simply acknowledged that with his calling, we'd call a truce and end our estrangement. We promised to talk in a few days to catch each other up on our lives and to forge a new relationship.

Over the next several months, we spoke regularly as we tried to piece together for each other an outline of our lives, the events that had taken place during our lost years, where we were now, where each of us was going. I told myself this phone reunion had nothing to do with what was happening with my inner life and my personal relationship at the time, but I did allow myself the acknowledgment that this reconciliation seemed timely in the same way everything seemed timely in my life. Serendipity and such. My father and I had built a foundation on the phone so that when I finally saw him and my stepmother in person in York, we had something, not quite yet solid, on which to move forward.

I shared with him that I had decided to go back to South Africa. My brief stay in Palm Springs had awakened my desire to return to Cape Town after nearly three decades; the truth is, there hadn't been many days in my life since we'd left in 1977 when I didn't dream of going back. Now a trip back suddenly became my number one priority besides my film commitments.

My father hadn't been back either, and before I knew it, in our first face-to-face encounter in eight years, he invited himself to go with me. I didn't say "No, this is my trip." I didn't set a boundary by telling him that three weeks alone with him seemed extreme after such a long time apart. I could have said that I needed to go back on my own. But in my typical caretaker fashion, I didn't want to hurt his feelings, which was ironic given that we were about to go back to the place in my childhood where my father's emotional and mental mistreatment had spiked to new levels—a primary and unresolved reason for our estrangement in the first place and a root cause of my addictions including self-harm. My inherent fear of hurting people and my willingness to sacrifice my own dreams and even my own well-being led me to agree to his joining me on the trip. It would essentially be a journey down memory lane with the man who had never been willing to admit he had done anything wrong as a father.

Since I was unable to say no, the romantic in me instead framed this trip as a mythical stage in the quest for my future self. It would be a time for healing, of letting go of the past and rebuilding a father-son relationship. I thought to myself that this was the book I was going to write, that this was a journey worth capturing on paper.

The thing about trauma is that it can sometimes be paired with unbelievable beauty. The pain isn't beautiful, but the world around the pain can be. This is why our years in South Africa haunted me. It was a time of amazing adventure and excitement, moments so cemented in my memory and core being, that the pain became secondary and, in some cases, completely forgotten. There was nothing to forgive, I told myself, because it hadn't been that bad, because the opportunities we'd had over our three years there were so incredible, especially for a wide-eyed child. The pain was easily numbed by my awe and wonder.

In those long-ago years, we'd spent Saturdays at the beach surf-skiing in the Indian Ocean, diving for crayfish in the Atlantic, scouring ocean cliffs for abalone and spelunking in caves and enormous whale-mouth caverns that flooded with water and captured us inside. We spent vacations on safari, camping along the Chobi River, being awoken at night by the elephants splashing 100 yards away. (Afterwards we spent the weekend at the Chobi Game Lodge where Elizabeth Taylor and Richard Burton were renewing their wedding vows at the same time.) We spent weekends at farm houses in the bush, rappelling cliffs in the Drakensberg Mountains, hunting for poisonous snakes (in one case a pregnant black mamba, the deadliest of all African snakes that needed to be killed before its babies were born, babies my sister and I took to school in bottles for our science teachers). We regularly hiked both the back and front of Table Mountain to have picnics. We sought out hidden waterfalls and their untouched pools. We drove through Rhodesia to celebrate my mom's 30th birthday at Victoria Falls, only to have our car's transmission fail in the bush miles from anything.

On the way back to America when I was nine, we drove alone through Kenya and were chased by spear-wielding Maasai after my father started taking their photographs. (He'd tell me years later it was the scariest moment of his life.) We climbed inside the great pyramid of Giza and ferried through the Greek islands, then on to Italy, Austria, Germany, the Netherlands, and Great Britain, with Frommer's Guide in my mother's hand. Much to my parent's surprise, in London, *Europe on $10 Dollars a Day*, the bible for frugal travelers at the time, got you a room in a brothel on a night when it was closed and the girls were gone. Frommer's guide book recommended a lodging which actually turned out to be a brothel. We were the only people in the entire building; the name placard decorating the door in crushed red velvet said it was "Juliette's" room we were staying in.

All that adventure and wonder, all that culture and opportunity to understand how other people lived, helped to develop and nurture feelings of empathy, compassion and gratitude in me. It was a gift my father had given our family, perhaps one of the most significant gifts I have ever been given. But most of those adventures happened on weekends and vacations. During my dad's work week in Cape Town, meaning most of the time, my father was someone I tiptoed around just like I had learned to do from the time I could stand on my feet.

As I've explained already, I learned long before that being funny and goofy was the best way to neutralize my father's rage, but now in South Africa—as his rage increased toward not only me but my mother, it no longer seemed to work. I'd once made him laugh with my Donald Duck impressions, but now he told me to never talk like Donald Duck again. Whereas once I'd learned that being clumsy and cutting or scraping myself might get me a bit of attention or affection from him, now he began to threaten me with the dreaded 'or else' if I fell or hurt myself. My lack of coordination and athleticism suddenly seemed proof to him that I was pathetic, not worthy of his respect or love. My ability to with-draw from the scene, to sit knitting behind a chair, to become invisible while the adults played hippie-like, getting naked and drunk under my watchful gaze, now only got me condemned as being a loser with no friends, with nothing better to do, as though an already shy seven-year-old who never had any friends before should be able to make friends after moving half-way around the world and going to a school of which he was deathly afraid.

Yet as I stood caught in the headlights of my father's inviting himself along with me back to South Africa, a lot of these vivid memories had not fully resurfaced. I had left my wounds in South Africa in 1977 choosing in all the years since to only see those three years as the adventure of a lifetime. That's what everyone called it. From friends to family, I was told it was the opportunity of a lifetime and how lucky I was, and how one day I would write a book about my experiences there. The scabs had fallen off years ago, the scars barely visible to the naked eye now.

When I initially decided to go on the trip by myself months before, I was seeking and planning on adventure, the rekindling of the excitement of my youth; I was already high on anticipation and the adrenaline of my new life outside of my relationship with Henry. As I thought about it now, I convinced myself that my father and I returning to South Africa could be what was supposed to happen. In my head, *The Return* might be the name of the book I'd write about the upcoming experience. I'd finally be able to rise above all that may or may not have happened when we lived there in the seventies. I would show my father how strong I was now, show him the kind, decent, caring and compassionate man I had become despite him.

Perhaps, I thought, I could also take back some power in the relationship through means other than choosing not to be in his life like I had for the previous eight years of estrangement. Perhaps I could actually have the majority of power in our future relationship; after all, that's what happens in all the stories of fathers and sons. The son must kill the father—figuratively or literally, depending on what myth you're reading. Perhaps the opportunity to travel together was karma putting in my path the precise challenge I needed in order to evolve and become a better person. After all, it was in South Africa where I first recognized I was different, that I had a place in the universe and that what I was experiencing at that time, the good and the bad, was simply a test. A test to determine which would win—the good or the bad.

There were two film soundtracks of our time in Cape Town in the seventies: *The Rocky Horror Picture Show* and Neil Diamond's *Jonathan Livingston Seagull*. My father loved them equally, and both started to define how I saw myself in the world. I didn't necessarily know what sex was yet, even after having seen my father's porn or actual naked adults—including my grandparents, who would skinny dip along with my parents when they visited us. Skinny dipping wasn't necessarily a sexual thing for my family, perhaps a bit taboo, but not sexual. For me, it was something else, another moment of awareness that the naked human body meant pleasure.

Knowing all the words to "Sweet Transvestite" by the age of seven allowed me to explore this thing, the energy I felt around me: sexual tension whether it was overt or subtle. My father would sing it along with me with his surprisingly pleasant and soothing voice. I sang "toucha, toucha, toucha me, I wanna be dirty," questioning years later whether singing these lyrics had given the neighbor permission to molest me, that I had literally been asking for it. We'd also duet to "Dancing Queen." ABBA was his favorite group but the song wasn't 'gay' to anyone in South Africa in the 70's. It certainly didn't have the connotation it ended up having as a gay anthem in the States. ABBA became the voice of our years in South Africa. But I also knew the songs and all the words to *Jonathan Livingston Seagull*, a different soundtrack on the opposite ends of musical genres. There were moments I'd catch my father staring off in the distance and singing the lyrics to Neil Diamond's "Be," and I'd feel something for him other than fear. I could sense there was good in him; I could see through his darkness and find shimmers of light. There was gentleness, perhaps even compassion in there somewhere. Even through the tortuous nights at the dinner table when he'd decide to ridicule me in front of his friends and colleagues, I still sensed he had some good in him. The witnesses to his mistreatment may have felt sorry for me, but I, in fact, felt sorry for him. Sure, I was angry, in pain, and scared but this man could also laugh with me on weekends while we both sang along to *Rocky Horror* and then cry to himself while singing *Jonathan Livington Seagull*.

My father's behavior confused me. Why was it okay to sing and swagger through *Sweet Transvestite*, albeit with just a minimal understanding of what the song was about, and yet not be okay when I dressed up in our landlord's, a surrogate grandmother, clothing and jewelry? Who was this man who would smile and become contemplative when my mother, who had purchased the piano music to *Brian's Song*, played it in the evening with me on her side wishing I could play it too, wishing I could have the power she seemed to wield over him with her fingers and notes. Why would he berate me for being unathletic and clumsy when we'd trek up Table Mountain but then be gentle and almost fatherly when we reached the top? How could his voice singing softly about a seagull become angry and cruel when directed at me?

Sometimes we're not just given genetic traits when we're born. Sometimes we're gifted with things less scientific, things like awareness and insight, or perhaps intuition. I knew early on in my childhood that life was more than my pain and joy, more than my suffering and more than my dreams. I was there to endure and to survive, not an uncommon belief among those abused at a young age. There's a story told in the spiritual recovery circles; the last time I heard it was from Richard Rohr. It's about a toddler, a boy, who liked to go into the nursery and talk to his new baby sibling. The parents decide to listen in on the "conversation" one particular day from outside the room and they hear their child say to his young sibling, "Remind me who I am…I'm beginning to forget." The story is likely just a fable made up to prove a point, but it's a significant one for me: we're born with endless potential and an untouched and perfect spirit until the world immediately starts to strip us of both.

I could write another book about my beliefs on spirituality and my place in the larger realm of things, but an important point to explain here in the retelling of my porn quest is that I've always believed there was something more to me than my experiences. There was something more to me than the fear of my father's belt, the one he used on our dog we had to leave behind. There was something in me that triggered my father's anger, something other than my feminine qualities and my goofiness.

When I sat at the kitchen table being constantly told I was less than, I knew deep down I was exactly the opposite. My father could see it too, I believe, and when I would look at him in response to his tirades and hold his stare, I saw something close to fear and shame in his eyes. He knew he was beating down someone he didn't understand, someone, his child, who in many ways he recognized as being more evolved than he was. I knew throughout these painful experiences that I was to learn from it all. I could use the hurt to remind me who I truly was not knowing that in years to come, I'd end up self-inflicting the hurt in order to call upon my slowly fading memory of who I really was.

At times when I would start to forget, when the onslaught of disparaging remarks, the ruthlessness of his barbs, made me question whether I was wrong, that perhaps I was worthless and deserved his wrath after all, the voice in my head would tell me it was okay. The voice would bring calm. My faith in being a larger part of things might wane, but it was the voice, another Spencer, who would pull me through in those moments. "You got this," he'd say, encouraging me forward, telling me to walk into the fear. It was the same voice from Pittsburgh telling me it was okay while I stood before a wall I was about to take down or the voice in Vermont who coached me while standing before a 100-foot aspen with chainsaw in hand.

So at this moment, standing in my father's home all these years later with his genuine look of affection and a voice full of excitement,

I told him that of course we should go back to South Africa together. This father and son trip was going to be a spiritual journey, a return, and another quest.

Chapter Ten

⌄

The trip wouldn't be for another three months, with a departure date set for December 26, but in the meantime, in early September, I needed to fly back to San Francisco to film *Horse: Fallen Angel 5* for Titan. I also needed to come up with a porn name—and quickly. I'd already shot two movies: *100° in Tucson's* release was being pushed into 2005, but *Manplay 18* had a quick turnaround (not much post-production needed for gangbang action) and Horse was slated to be out before Christmas. There wasn't much time to decide on the nom de porn that would carry me into and through my career, but it was an important decision for me, one that carried the weight of creating a new identity. I wanted it to be significant.

I tend to ascribe meaning to most things in life, and while I didn't know whether the choice of a porn name really mattered in the porn industry, it mattered to me. I knew there were all the classic manly "stud" names and the double entendres, but, for me, going into the business wasn't just about having sex on camera. I'd also never felt like a manly stud in all my life. With all those insecurities about size, load, topping, etc., there was no way I was going to pick something that made me uncomfortable, even if it was for a persona.

I could have picked a name via the tried-and- true method: use your middle name and the name of your first pet, or the street you grew up on, or use your first pet's name and the street you grew up on. They were all ridiculous (i.e. "Bongo Woodland"). I just wanted to be me, and honestly, I'd always loved my first name. There was no question as to whether I would use it. I wanted to be as authentic as possible on this journey, and nothing could be more authentic than using my given first name, especially one so unusual.

But what should follow? It took me two hours in the car driving to the Baltimore- Washington airport to settle on it. This was a journey, an adventure. It would have meaning. I was following my bliss. I called upon one of my gurus and asked myself, "What would Joseph Campbell say?" He'd call it a quest; he'd confirm that I was on a true heroic quest, no different than anyone else's mythological journey to the self. With the upcoming trip overseas, I immediately thought of the Hardy Boys, my only friends in South Africa, on some wild sexual escapade, and then, of course, there was Johnny Quest, adventurer extraordinaire. Having stepped into my car as Spencer Keasey, by the time I reached the airport, I stepped out as Spencer Quest.

I arrived in San Francisco and again fell under the caring wing of Brian Mills. He quickly became not just my connection to Titan and the man who made me look incredible on film but my mentor. He was also becoming my first adult gay friend. Brian was on his own journey as a photographer and was fortunate to be able to connect his creativity to his work, to a job that let him express himself and pay the rent. He wanted more beyond photographing sex and skin, and during our conversations off the set we shared a common interest in the creative journey. He listened intently as I described my life, what I wanted to write, and what going into porn meant for me. I immediately felt he believed in me, in my creative aspirations, and during our times together, we seemed to inspire each other.

Brian also believed in me on the set; he'd seen what I could do in my very first scene and had offered me that exclusivity contract. One of the benefits of now being an exclusive for Titan was that they proactively asked me, then gave me, what I wanted in each film. Over the course of my time with the company, Brian would usually ask: What do you want to do or who do you want to have? For this movie, Brian acknowledged in a planning email weeks prior that he knew I was exploring and that, at this time, size was at the top of my wish list. He affectionately called me a size queen and sent along photos of a model with a dick that frankly shocked me. It was nine by seven inches. The guy used not a Redbull can for reference but a regular 12-ounce soda can. I had no idea if I'd be able to handle it, but my rallying cry of "no fear" turned worry to excitement. I was ready to charge forward in the face of any warrior's sword, no matter what length or girth.

He also informed me ahead of time they wanted to sell me as versatile, that being versatile was the epitome of a Titan man, and that they wanted me to be the aggressor in this movie. This wouldn't be seductive like *Tucson*, but pure aggression. *Horse* was a leather movie, the fifth in the award-winning *Fallen Angel* series, but unlike the more traditional black leather used in the first four videos in the series, *Horse* would showcase, as the title suggested, a different vibe with brown leather, gladiator meets horse ranch. That distinction between black and brown leather would become an interesting one for me because while I had never pictured myself in a more traditional leather movie, the brown leather allowed me to enter the world of master and slave that black leather wouldn't have at that time. For some reason, my comfort level and confidence hinged on a color.

I didn't necessarily know what Brian meant by "aggressor," given that this was an unscripted sex film. Then, when I arrived on set, Bruce Cam, the president and owner of Titan, confused me even more when he told me that he had his doubts as to whether I should even be in the film. As I stood in front of the production team seated behind a folding table, as though it were a regular audition, Bruce told Brian that I was too all-American to be in a leather movie. He didn't think I had it in me. He thought a nice guy like me couldn't do it. Even though they'd flown me across the country to be in the film, I still had to prove myself to them. What I showed them would determine what sort of role I could play, if any. Cam could maybe picture me servicing, whether on my knees or in a sling, but there was no way he thought I could be a master. They all knew I could seduce. They knew I could be an aggressive bottom—I'd done that in *ManPlay*. But an aggressive top? Truth be told, part of me thought I was way in over my head and part of me wanted them to explain their definition of "aggressive," but the rest of me was smirking inside; they had no idea what I was capable of or what I could do or who I could be.

I was fitted in brown leather assless chaps and a harness and put on the stage. Troy Anicete, Mr. San Francisco Leather 2003, designed and hand-made all of the gear, which made putting it on feel all the more special and spoke to the care with which Titan approached their productions. This was my first time in any sort of leather, and I quickly realized why it was a thing. I immediately felt powerful, in control, and sexy as fuck. The stares coming from behind the production table told me I looked the part—but could I pull off the action? What they didn't realize was that I could become someone else in a heartbeat. It'd been a coping mechanism all my life, fine-tuned by some decent acting chops, a desire to please, and a need to succeed. I could turn on a dime—or in this case, with a riding crop in my hand.

Bruce told me to take control of the other actor they put before me. I clenched my jaw and cemented my role; I owned the man in front of me. He did what I told him because the sound of my voice and my clenched jaw gave him no choice. He was mine and knew exactly what I wanted from him. I spewed orders, grabbed his head, forced him onto my dick, and made him beg for more. There was no doubt I was his master.

I continued for a few minutes before stopping our short scene, turned around to my audience and saw a jaw dropped and wide eyes on Bruce and a big grin on Brian's face. He'd never doubted me. Now the others didn't either.

I also now had a glimpse into what leather was and what it did, or could do, to and for a person. It involved all the senses: the smell of it, the look of it, the feel of it, the sound it makes, even the taste of it. But more than the sensory, there was a deeper connection to a part of me I hadn't even begun to acknowledge sexually. Power dynamics had confused me as a child, especially as it related to men, sex, abuse, etc. But with this, whether making someone gag while they sucked me, slam fucking an ass brutally (in the best sense of the word), or ruthlessly riding a dick, the power was intoxicating. It was this movie that made me tap into an inner pig that had been penned inside me for a very long time. I tackled that nine-by-seven dick, somehow managing to get it down my throat without gagging. I left that set with an insatiable hunger. Apparently it showed; the scene in which Joey Russo and I fucked each other, me in my powerful 'frog" position, was my first official release with Titan and was nominated for Best Sex Scene at the 2005 GayVNs.

Chapter Eleven

⌄

I flew back to the East Coast, to Lancaster, where I was to finish work on the Vermont Migrant Education project before flying to South Africa. Since leaving Vermont, Henry and I had been in regular contact by phone and email, the latter often filled with gut-wrenching honesty on both sides of how we were feeling. When I told Henry about the trip to South Africa, he offered nothing but support and encouragement, suggesting that the trip with my father could indeed be just what I needed to heal my past. Henry understood who I was, how I was made, and what were likely some of the root causes that brought about the end of our relationship. One of those was the relationship, or lack thereof, I had with my father.

But it was the phone call I got from Henry the day I returned from filming in San Francisco that threw me: he had, while driving the three miles on dirt roads from a party at a friend's house, flipped and totaled his Jeep, and apparently, from the photos he sent me, was lucky to be alive. We'd had a core group of friends in Vermont who occasionally got together, all serious drinkers. I was always the sober one, however, the safe ride home. Sadly, without a thought, these friends had let a brand-new driver get into his car after drinking. Hearing the story, I was furious with the friends and angry with Henry, but mostly devastated because I felt that somehow I was to blame. Henry was an adult, of course, but I still felt that sort of anger and responsibility a parent might. And guilt. This was the first reality check since May, the first serious repercussion of leaving my old life—a repercussion I was willing to own. I was more than willing to take on the hurt I felt I'd caused, to allow it to fester.

Yet, along with the shock of Henry nearly dying, all I could think of now was having sex. This was the heyday of the gay hookup website Manhunt, and while Amish country didn't offer much in terms of the number of guys online, I hooked up with a few men. Those usually quick sessions were fine, but I was beginning to want in real life the kind of intense sex I was having on the porn set. I wanted that level of excitement and hotness on a regular Monday afternoon. But hours-long porn sex with the hottest guys around isn't real life, and certainly not in Lancaster County, Pennsylvania. The only other time I'd had that same level of intense sex as I'd had on set had been ten months earlier, in San Antonio during a conference for Migrant Education. Although I never thought of it as such, I'd actually broken with sobriety not with the martini I'd had the night Henry and I broke up, but months prior.

For it had been during that work trip to Texas when I'd hooked up with a guy who introduced me to crystal meth, which I'd thought was a gift from the gods. Instead of attending that conference, I'd spent two days in a bathhouse, also a first for me. I'd had the best sex of my life, which is why when I came home to Henry I'd told him, not that I spent the weekend in a bathhouse, but simply that I'd fucked around outside the relationship at some point in recent weeks. If the sex in San Antonio was what single gay life was like, I was game. That sort of excitement, lust, and raw sexuality had been what I'd seen when I'd watched the movie

Circuit. I'd wanted that kind of sex—the uninhibited, overwhelming baseness of it. I could have that sort of sex while sober and filming for Titan, but the only way I thought I could have it in real life was to find meth again. So my search began.

While living with my mother, it didn't take long before realizing I'd have to drive at least an hour east towards Philadelphia to find guys who wanted to party and play, or PnP—the code for those looking for meth. Those who have used crystal meth understand its attraction. Unlike other drugs that provide their variety of chill or speedy effects, a drug that enhances sex to levels you can't even begin to comprehend was instantly addicting. As an addict, I am wary of glorifying anything that destroys lives, but it's important for the uninitiated to understand that for me, discovering and using meth was all glory. Almost like a gambler who might risk everything and in that risk chance untold riches, the reward of a drug that sexually stimulates you for hours and days on end was a revelation. Imagine the bounty of an endless orgasm. Imagine tapping into a base and insatiable need that turns fantasy into reality with one puff of smoke. With that puff I'd turn into someone whose desire for dick immediately led to me offering up every orifice. Even though I'd only tried it once, nearly a year before, the first experience was so powerful and Pavlovian that a simple memory got me hard.

By this point, back in Pennsylvania, I'd had months to process the end of my relationship and I was starting to feel the deep loss, unlike anything I'd ever felt before. I was also processing Henry's car accident, as well as the pending trip with my father. Just the idea of using meth again was enough to help me forget the pain, guilt, and anxiety of all these things, to avoid sitting with those feelings. Before Henry and I split, I'd spent endless hours jerking off over mental images of what had happened that weekend in San Antonio, and I now began to conjure them again. To this day, scenes in my head from the two days in the bathhouse seep into my fantasies and can get me hard immediately.

Scouring Manhunt, ever increasing its location radius, I found the drug and a group of professional men, lotus eaters with real houses, jobs, and nice cars—an important distinction between the guys in that bathhouse, where I had no idea who I was sucking. Using meth in a three-story suburban townhouse actually seemed harmless. Taboo, yes. Intriguing, perhaps a bit dangerous, yes. Smoking out of a glass pipe and immediately falling to my knees or onto my back with my legs spread didn't feel wrong. It felt incredibly right, and it made me forget. The sex I'd sought out on the porn set in front of the camera, in that secure and safe environment, suddenly was shoved to the mild end of a very wide continuum of behavior. At first, with my new suburban meth buddies, I still used condoms. But as I worked my way from those professional men in townhomes who talked about their most recent HIV tests and cleaned their sex toys with bleach, to men in basements and barns where the meth was endless, where names weren't exchanged and the letters "HIV" were never spoken, safety stopped being a concern.

With one particular group I was in a sling; I asked a positive guy to use a condom and he actually did. Then there was more smoking and my first experience with ketamine. The older guy, perhaps in his 60's, someone who eventually went to jail for dealing, dosed me since I had no idea what ketamine was, what it would do, and how much a first dose should be. I remember little, very little.

I came to hours later being barebacked by this guy who dosed me. The drug had completely knocked me out; I had gone into what they call a K-hole and my mind split from reality. Ketamine is a horse tranquilizer used as a party drug that has dissociative effects. The last thing I remember was being in a sling with a group of guys and then coming out of it in a bed with no one else around but the man fucking me. When I initially came out of it, I struggled understanding what was happening. I couldn't even grasp that I was having sex, but I have this powerful image in my head that when I was looking up into the face above me, I saw the Devil. The Devil was fucking me. I was terrified. As he pounded away, eventually cumming in me, his face slowly changed back into a human and it began to dawn on me who he was.

Of course I should have known that would happen. Correction: I knew it would happen eventually, I just didn't know it would happen that night. I started out the night with a boundary (condoms) and woke realizing I was essentially being raped. I'd lost hours of time, but at that moment, it didn't matter. I was still high and by the end of the night, after it was no longer an evil entity fucking me, being taken forcibly felt good. The neurons were firing from the meth, but my deeper pleasure came down to understanding that I deserved what was happening. I was worthless except for the sex I could offer. I deserved to be used. One lesson did come from this experience: I never used Ketamine again.

This wasn't the same as being on a set clean and sober and embracing the power of leather and domination, like on the set of *Horse*. Being forced this way was familiar in a different way. It was similar to my being on the set of *Tucson* and sucking that dick I didn't want to suck, but on a different part of the power spectrum. For me, that spectrum of power ran from "don't use me, I don't want to be used, I will not be used, I choose to be used therefore it's not being used," to "I want to be used, I want to be abused, I need to be used, abused and hurt, rape me." I went back to that man I found on top of me multiple times. He was a drug dealer after all.

My partying happened a half-dozen times over the course of a month, the last experience being the most seedy, just days before getting on the flight to South Africa. Once I recovered from that group scene, I panicked. Although I think I remember the guys using condoms with me, I didn't really know. I couldn't be sure. I knew I needed an HIV test quickly before I left the country.

I took myself to a clinic, but rather than describe the exact circumstances (drugs/bareback group sex), I lied and said I went to a party and was drugged and gang-raped, somehow thinking that scenario would get me sympathy from the clinic workers rather than judgement. I was thoroughly horrified with myself. The guilt and shame I felt for being so reckless, for making decisions that clearly weren't healthy, for wanting to do it all again, were too powerful for me to articulate truthfully that I'd let a bunch of guys fuck me while I was high.

They tested me for everything. I wasn't sure if I'd get the results before I left for South Africa, but what I did get before I left was an incredible burning in and around my asshole, with accompanying open sores which hurt like hell. I was in the Atlanta airport with my father when a call came in. I stepped away from him and was told over the phone that while I was HIV negative, I did have herpes.

And believe me, there is nothing quite like getting your first herpes outbreak on your asshole before boarding a 16-hour flight halfway around the world.

It's taken years of therapy for me to understand that I am capable of having more than one feeling at the same time. Those feelings can be completely contradictory, diametrically opposed, night and day, dark and light. The confusion of not knowing this for the first 40 years of my life was exacerbated by an already existing tendency to dismiss feelings or to minimize one feeling over the other in order for one to stand tall and take center stage. When attached to memory, these contrasting feelings and the feud between them led me to look back and classify an experience as having made me feel one way but not the other. Even though both feelings existed at one given moment or across a span of time, my propensity would be to shut one out, throw one off the stage, or simply tie that feeling up and hold it hostage for later use.

It bears repeating that for decades, I remembered our short time living in South Africa and our subsequent travels across Africa and Europe as a chapter of wonder and excitement. I acknowledged the experience with gratitude and accepted that it made me who I was, not just in terms of my adventure-seeking, but also in how, decades later, I dove into fear, took risks, faced challenges head on and accepted opportunity. Those years provided me with a worldview and an empathy for those living with less, sometimes with nothing and under oppression. With the decision to take our family to the tip of Africa in 1973, my father had given me the gift of perspective. But given that it was paired with my father's emotional abuse, it came at a cost.

I now believe that my father and I were both chasing the story of South Africa we each had been telling ourselves for years, that it had been the best experience of our lives. All my life, I'd been looking at those three years as a sort of storyboard for a nostalgic movie or an outline of a book. But our time there hadn't been a movie or a book. It wasn't just a series of still images depicting high adventure and beaming sun-kissed smiles. It was real life, and with real life, we experienced all sorts of things, all sorts of emotions, creating a wide range of memories which, again, just like feelings themselves, can be contradictory.

The Return actually does need its own book, but for this book's purposes, let's say that our trip was just that: a contradiction of memory and feelings, not just internally within each of us but between us as well. He remembered this, I remembered that. At any given moment, our moods could be polar opposites as we experienced feelings neither of us could explain to the other. My father stayed three weeks; I stayed on another three weeks before needing to get back to film my next movie. The trip was life-changing if not necessarily healing.

I spent much of my time trying to impress my father with the man I felt I had become, the one who had risen out of the ashes of the boy he had so callously rejected and burned. I was at the top of my game physically, mentally, and emotionally; at least that's how I played it, never mind the fact that since he'd called ten months prior, ending our long estrangement, I'd started drinking again, left a 17-year relationship, gone into porn and started a nice budding meth addiction with its first token gift, herpes. I'd always felt the need to portray myself to him as having survived his treatment of me: "See, Dad, you didn't break me, see how well I turned out in spite of you?" The irony is that because I portrayed myself to my father in a certain light, often hiding wounds and bad decisions, and because I had "turned out well," he used the same point to assuage any guilt he might have had over his treatment of me as a child. Years after our return, right before our next eight-year estrangement, my father would throw a counterpunch to an offensive jab I made while on the phone suggesting he was a less than perfect father: "At least I didn't beat you. Look how well you turned out. I couldn't have been that bad of a father."

For three weeks, we stayed with family friends we hadn't seen in decades and traveled along the coast to Cape Agulhas, the southernmost tip of Africa, hiked Table Mountain, traveled to Zimbabwe, safaried in Botswana, and visited vineyards in Stellenbosch. I bungeed off the Victoria Falls bridge and fell backwards 230 feet into the Batoka Gorge on a swing—my most blatant attempt to get validation from my father.

It was truly a beautiful time, and my father and I never felt closer. Shortly before he left, we went to the top of Table Mountain at sunset with our friends and had a picnic. One of the most tremendous sights I'd ever encountered as a child was dusk on top of that mountain, the sun splashing oranges and pinks across the ocean, the stars of the city lights below shining with the ones above, which began to slowly appear as darkness fell. I was dumbstruck by the beauty back then, the beauty that made everything else okay, that covered the wounds and hurt and told me there was more out there than my pain.

Now, almost three decades later, I experienced that same sight and was suddenly that child again. I was overwhelmed by emotion and cried into my father's shoulder. It was the only time I remembered him comforting me that way in all my life. He certainly had spent enough time making me cry, and while it doesn't take much to get me crying (a simple sunset or a Hallmark commercial will do), this was a guttural, deep-in-my-soul cry which, unbeknownst to me, was all those contradictory feelings rising from within. They had started to gather inside me over the previous months, feelings I couldn't name, but their gravity and density were real. It felt like something dark was growing, reaching up from my gut through my body. I told myself it was a healthy, cathartic cry, me with my head against my father's chest, but, as the subsequent weeks and years would reveal, it was really a cry of anguish—of remembrance, the cry of a child who just wanted the pain to stop.

My father simply let the tears happen. While no words were exchanged in the moment I felt an energy from him that was palpable. It was compassion. My father was comforting me, and it felt like a breakthrough. I have no idea what he was thinking, whether his recollections of our time in South Africa had jarred memories of behaviors toward me for which he felt badly, but in the moment it simply didn't matter. All that mattered was that here I was, a 37-year-old, finally getting the affection and attention I had wanted from my father all my life. While it could have been a step towards a healthy discussion and a true breakthrough in our relationship, we never spoke of the incident.

Immediately after my father left, I planned to do two significant things. My father and I had already sought out the first house we rented, in Claremont, because that's what you did on these sorts of trips down memory lane. We stood outside the high gate around the house, which hadn't been there before. Since we'd left in 1977, the entire country had put up gates and high walls around their properties—tall, imposing fences clearly meant to keep people out. My father and I stood sharing memories while looking through the bars and standing under the same grand White Stinkwood tree that always dropped the newborn squirrels our landlady would then nurse in her bedroom. Standing in front of this house, with my acute memory I was able to recall and share with my father clothes I'd worn then, food we'd eaten, and who had been there during certain events. We smiled and laughed, while I pushed away the feelings of sadness that were fighting their way to the surface. I didn't know why I was feeling so incredibly sad.

I returned to that house the day after my father left and stood looking, but this time at the ground-floor apartment next door. I believed I had already processed most of what had happened in my life, to the extent I convinced myself much of it wasn't abuse. It was actually my fault, I'd always told myself, that the guy next door, the guy who lived in the apartment on which I was now concentrating, forced me to have sex. Dismissing that experience had allowed me to focus on the beauty of our return, and that's what had happened during the weeks with my father. But when he left, I was left with the trauma that I didn't know was trauma, all the emotions the trip was evoking, and the memories of things I had forgotten and suppressed. I was left with a feeling of the loss of my childhood and innocence—neither of which I knew at the time were lost.

The other thing I did the day after my father left Cape Town was to go to the only bathhouse in the city. It's not lost on me that I went from revisiting the site of my molestation right to a bathhouse. It was the middle of the day, dead, but I still managed to end up bent over in a room with an incredibly handsome Afrikaner fucking me.

Even though I was only to remain in South Africa for three more weeks, we started dating—my first experience with rebounding, which, looking back, made sense. Within six months of being single for the first time in my adult life, I quickly lapsed into needing someone to distract me and to help me forget. He was in finance and was a professional violinist, and within two weeks I was actually thinking of moving to South Africa. It was a fleeting thought, although a very appealing one. But I had obligations with Titan, and it didn't take me long to realize that I'd jumped too quickly into the relationship, if you could call it that. I was taking something back, trying to regain ownership of something I had lost. All I knew then was that I was being courted and entertained, which was precisely what I needed. We made plans for him to come see me in the States when he visited his sister in the spring.

Chapter Twelve

⌄

When I returned from overseas at the beginning of February 2005, I began to prepare for the next stage of my journey. Once I wrapped up the consulting work in the following weeks, outside of filming porn, I had no plans. I was already feeling the weight of it. Freedom was beginning to have a cost; left to my own devices and without a commitment to others, I began to feel lost. I needed to start over somewhere, and because Titan was out West, that's where I was going to head. I'd drive across the country to find a place to land. Henry had emailed while I was overseas saying that my emails to him, mostly updates of my travels with my father, seemed to reveal how unaware I was of the damage I had done to him and to our relationship. He also told me he didn't want me to write to him anymore.

But I needed to go to Vermont before crossing the country because I still had some things there that I needed to take with me. I decided I'd drive through Canada and come down into the United States on the other side of the Great Lakes on my trip to California. It was a short, cold visit to a place that was becoming less and less my home. I could now see clearly in Henry's face the pain, anger, and resentment that hadn't seemed to exist six months prior. I suppose he was correct. While he was clearly going through the normal stages of grief, I was trying to ignore them by filling my life with adventures and new things.

But now, leaving Vermont again felt like yet another ending, an even more powerful and definitive one. Coming back to what still felt like my home, to the man I still loved, was like my rubbing salt in both our wounds. Functionally, he seemed well, having gotten a job and a new car. He was proud of his new used SAAB. Perhaps he was trying to prove how well he was doing, but regardless of the stoicism with which he handled my brief stay, when we hugged just before I drove away, we both broke down.

I sobbed the first half of the road trip while listening to k.d. lang's *Hymns Of The 49th Parallel* and Annie Lennox's *Bare* over and over again. Both albums had their emotional appeal for obvious reasons, but it was Annie's, supposedly based on her own relationship breakup, that tore me apart. She'd written on her blog about calling the album "Raw," also a perfect title for a collection that included a track called *The Saddest Song (I've Got.)* I listen to it constantly, hoping to feel and even exacerbate my pain. There were warning signs that pain was coming, but nothing could have prepared me for the profound enormity of the loss that filled my gut for those 3,500 miles. I was being eaten alive by it, and by the shame and guilt that mixed so easily and smoothly with everything else growing in me. My Volvo was constantly filled with the heat and steam of endless crying, and it was somewhere near the border crossing at Sault Ste. Marie, Michigan, that a whispering voice appeared in my head and I thought about dying.

Explaining my life-long struggle with thoughts and hopes of dying and subsequent attempts to die is futile. Most people experience thoughts of dying at some point in their lives, but they are usually fleeting. For me, though, I have an actual relationship with these thoughts. They are an old friend, a warm blanket or briny body of water in which to swim that releases me from pain. For me, these moments can lead to a sense of comfort that is almost spiritual, and that's what I needed in the moment. Like someone dreaming of their favorite place in the world, perhaps a beach on a desert island which can calm and relax them during moments of crisis, this is how I have always thought of dying: it would bring a sense of great peace.

Fortunately, endless miles and hours of driving through the Canadian wilderness and several stops of significance along the way broke through my desperation if not my sense of loss. I stopped at the University of Wisconsin-Madison, where my cousin Emma was working on her graduate degree in writing. Emma had lived with Henry and me on our third floor for her sophomore year at Pitt. It was during that year she'd started taking her writing more seriously, mostly due to Henry and his own dedication to the genre. But unlike Henry, she went the MFA route.

I hadn't seen Emma since Y2K, when our whole family had gathered in the mountains of Central Pennsylvania. She had struggled with some mental health issues since leaving home for college, and while I hadn't been diagnosed yet as bipolar, I was the addict in the family, so we had a connection. She also knew Henry and had experienced our relationship first hand, so she could understand the breakup to a certain extent.

She was also the first family member I told about my porn quest. Her response was casual, as though she wasn't surprised, and after that we simply changed the subject. I'm not sure what I was expecting in sharing it with her; we weren't especially close since she left Pittsburgh. I suppose more than anything, I wanted to get some affirmation as I started this new life, even if it only meant someone telling me I was crazy, good crazy, because being crazy in our family meant you belonged. Our family wasn't literally crazy as in awash with mental illness; they simply acted crazy as in 'fun crazy.' She didn't affirm this directly, but simply being with her and sharing a beer in a bar reassured me.

I also stopped in Boulder and saw one of my two stepsisters, Laura, and her soon-to-be husband. Somewhere between Madison and the Colorado border, I decided to change my music and listened to the debut album of Maroon 5. Their songs, along with my excitement at spending a few days with Laura, pushed the clouds away. Once my step-sister through two marriages when my mother married their father and my father married their mother, now she was just my step-sister via their father. Their mother, my once-stepmother, and my father had since divorced and swapped partners again, with the golf pro and his wife at the country club in York, Pennsylvania. During those original wife-swap nights with Laura's parents and my parents, if I wasn't in my bedroom listening to top 40 and assembling my model Boeing 747 together, I'd take care of my soon-to-be stepsisters. I was young to babysit, just twelve, but I was only two houses away from my house, where the alcohol was flowing and where I could easily break up their galavanting if something happened with the girls I didn't know how to handle.

My sisters grew up being watched over by me, the ideal sensitive brother they looked up to who could do no wrong. Now Laura was 26, just starting her new life, which she was excited to share with me. Having no fear over whether I would shock or disappoint her, I told them both my porn plans. After her jaw dropped, Laura smiled, laughed and said that if anyone could go into porn and stay just as they were, it was me. They both joined in my excitement, asking questions—serious, thoughtful questions, because they knew that when I did something, I would give it my all. I told them about writing a book, which Laura said that she knew I'd end up doing. She wasn't surprised at my new choices, because that's how she'd always seen me, as a taker of chances. Her reaction was just the boost I needed to get me back on track emotionally and mentally.

After visiting Laura, I headed south to Pagosa Springs, Colorado, as my plan was to go through Sante Fe then catch Route 40 toward Los Angeles. While my life had been filled with times of self-care, being sober and working out, I was never one to treat myself to things like a spa retreat. And while this was only a short stop at the famous hot springs, I had a massage which ended up being another message, a spiritual and mystical experience, and another sign I was on the right path. While the masseuse had her hands on me, I felt something happening, as though sparks were flying off my body.

When we were done with my massage, she sat quietly for a moment, then spoke to me gently, saying I had an energy she didn't often experience. She said she'd felt the sparks too. She then became a soothsayer and told me that I was on a journey, a wild adventure that would bring both pain and great success. She told me I would teach, comfort, that people would feel drawn to me and that I would have many followers. The more she spoke, the more the tears streamed down my cheeks as I laid on her table.

In a way, her words, this recognition, and the energy that had shot through my body into her hands as she held my head, felt like an end and a beginning. I felt renewed, reborn even, as though I were escaping my cave of self-recrimination, releasing something I needed to let go as I heard my future being told by a mystic in a magical place of healing waters. What was different about this experience as compared to future ones on my quest was that I thought I was in a stable place mentally, if not emotionally, at this point in the trip. The closer to California I was getting, the more I was separating myself from the pain that had so tortured me for the first half of my trip across the country. I defined myself as being clean, having not used meth in a while. I was beginning to feel a growing purpose with a rekindling of hope. It was like I was the best of me again, and at times like this, I couldn't have felt more connected to a higher power, to the energy I so often tapped into throughout my life.

Unfortunately, I had too much time to think as I took a longer route to L.A., backtracking a little so I could go through Taos and Santa Fe, not realizing some of the smaller roads were closed due to the mountains of snow yet to melt by the spring thaw. By the time I got to California, I was at war with myself yet again, as my depressive side once again took up arms against the part of me whose hopes and dreams had been briefly revived. I felt half-dead in one way, but in another, I felt sparks of life arising and regrouping in formation as I found myself on I-10 getting closer and closer to L.A., another magical place that had lived in my youthful fantasies. I could feel my blood coursing through my body on the highway snaking into the city, turbulent then calm, rough then smooth like a river offering both deep pools and rocks and rapids.

Titan suggested that, before going on to San Francisco, I attend the GayVN Awards in West Hollywood. They were sponsored by *AVN* magazine, the *Billboard* of the porn industry, according to *The New York Times*. Titan scored 27 nominations for the 2005 awards, the most of any porn company, with one of the nominations being mine, for Best Sex Scene with Joey Russo in *Horse*.

Filming a porn movie is one thing, but arriving in the heart of WeHo for an event as large and crazy as the gay-porn Oscars was another. It was here that I realized I would never feel like I belonged in that world. Granted, 37 years-old may not seem very old, but in this environment, between my age and my life experiences up to this point it felt like I was generations apart from the energy around me. It was an energy of youth and a certain type of flamboyance of which I'd never been a part. Having come out in the mid-80's, I had years of adulthood, of creating a life far from the maddening crowds of the bar scenes. It wasn't that I was critical by any means. I was jealous. I had been in a 17-year relationship with very few outside friends and didn't know what it meant to be a part of an urban gay community. While I know how to be sociable, standing at a bar and striking up a conversation had no appeal because the likelihood of finding someone with whom I could relate or someone who could relate to me seemed doubtful. I was grateful for a small team of Titan people who came from San Francisco to L.A. for the event so I could at least pretend to feel a part of what was happening around me.

It took all of two hours after arriving at the hotel to justify why I didn't belong. I suppose I never really gave myself a chance. I could have made an effort by hanging in the hotel lobby, soaking in the atmosphere, or tracking down someone from Titan. But I arrived late in the morning in WeHO and had an entire day to kill. By the time late afternoon came, I convinced myself it would be okay to seek out friends the easier way. It'd been three months since I'd used meth in my December gang bang, and I wanted it again. The only way I knew how to find it was on Manhunt. But for me to be an effective prowler online, I needed my inhibitions to fall to the wayside. I needed vodka. So I got myself a bottle, sat down in my room that first night, the night before the awards, and went fishing.

First cast, I caught Andrew. Hot, masculine, a lawyer, an enormous dick, a top and fully supplied with party favors. After having partied with guys along the continuum of sexual experiences from bathhouses to suburban developments to basement gang bangs, finding myself in a hotel room with someone who seemed like a nice guy with good energy—a professional, stable, funny man who just happened to use meth—was even more appealing. Seediness was hot, but having a sense of stability while drugging was hotter, even more taboo. I know that may sound ridiculous, but, as an addict, I've always convinced myself that as long as I could manage the rest of my life, my usage was in control. Why couldn't two stable, level-headed, highly educated men party and use meth occasionally? Certainly if Andrew could manage being a lawyer for a large entertainment company, I could do what I was doing. I could film porn, write a book, and occasionally use meth. Andrew and I partied all night, flip-fucking. (He said he didn't bottom, but he made an exception.) After we assured each other that we were both HIV-negative, we decided not to use condoms. Overall, we had fun. We talked, fucked, laughed, fucked some more. Then the next day, having not slept, I went to the hotel gym, felt great, napped in the afternoon and went to the GayVN awards party where I again immediately felt like an outlier. It felt like I was walking into a convention, similar to those education conventions I had once gone to, where everyone knew everyone else. They all seemed to be friends with a shared history. The noise was deafening not just in volume but in intensity, and I immediately felt claustrophobic. Fortunately Titan had a table, so I sought it out and found people to talk to. I didn't win, begged off the afterparty hosted by porn-making drag queen Chi Chi LaRue and went back to the hotel to crash.

The next morning, I drove up the coast to San Francisco to film *Spy Quest*. Titan imagined doing a James Bond-esque series created especially for me, using my porn name for the title. If the original *Spy Quest* did well, there would be a *Spy Quest 2* and perhaps even a third. From what I understood, this had never been done before, creating a character around a specific porn star. Titan went all out: the set was incredible, the filming intense, and, after asking me in advance what I wanted for this particular movie, they delivered. They wanted me happy and so they found Markus Ram, whose name explains it all. We had a shared energy, being similar in age, and a self-awareness and self-esteem that comes from having lived lives outside the world in which we found ourselves in. Doing porn wasn't a career choice or even a job for either of us; it was an adventure. It seemed like this was perhaps a bucket-list item for Markus, a meaningful one which would ensure he would have no regrets later in life. We certainly had a sexual connection. The fucking, sucking and licking were on a completely different level than anything I had ever experienced up to that point while clean and on the set. He was my fantasy; sex with Markus Ram was an explosion of pure lust. I couldn't have been more turned on by him, and I believe he felt the same towards me.

Our first scene, the oral one, had me riding an industrial elevator to the lower levels. I was the Bond character, the man in charge, the one who controlled all others. But when the doors opened and Markus, having just swum into the underground cavern, a secret lair, stood there in a wetsuit, dripping, cock pressing against the rubber of his suit, I pulled him into the elevator, dropped to my knees and serviced him like I was drowning and there was oxygen in his balls. I was the man in charge who kept his men happy.

During our second scene, the fucking scene was on industrial large scale shelving, the kind with "L" bars with holes in them. He rimmed me, tongue-fucked me and slammed me so hard I had cuts on my hands from holding onto the metal supports. "Stigmata," I joked on the set, after we stopped shooting to tend to my wounds. When asked if I was okay, I confirmed that I was more than okay. How could I not be? It was the most intense sex I'd ever had. This wasn't the drug-fueled intensity of partying when I was only half present, when my pleasure circuits were firing not just because of sexual stimulation but mostly because of the chemical alteration in the brain. This was clean and sober sex where the intensity was real. I was completely present in the moment and I felt comfortable allowing an inner drive and a desperate need to be taken over. I wanted him to ravage me, and he did, but he did so with passion. Passion made the difference.

As I've explained, videos of this quality took a lot of time and were, as my bloody palms could attest to, hard work. Typically, each scene in a movie has both an oral cum shot and an anal cum shot. It could take several hours for each to be completed, with all the light changes and the adjusting of camera angles. Then Brian would come in with a regular camera to get the still shots. Those stills you saw weren't action; they are literally stills, where we posed pretending we're having sex. It was a lot of starting and stopping, but not so much that it detracted from the sexual energy. In some ways, the anticipation between shots actually enhanced it.

It felt like Markus and I were extremely compatible not just sexually but when the cameras stopped as well. Had we met at a different time in my life, we might have been compatible off the porn set, as friends or more. Markus left a lasting impression on me in terms of just how much pleasure someone could get out of rimming. The act was still relatively new to me, and I hadn't quite gotten used to it in terms of the level of vulnerability I felt when I spread my legs and let him go to town. I didn't yet fully understand how eating someone's ass could be so erotic and impossible to resist. His passion and insatiable need for it drove me crazy.

Unfortunately, I left a lasting impression on him as well: a week after filming, he called to tell me he'd caught a parasite from eating my ass. I was horrified, embarrassed, and did my best to deny it was even possible. As much as he clearly enjoyed eating my ass, I wondered whether he thought it had been worth it. I was filled with shame, and from that point on, I was always anxious when someone ate my ass. I'd later learn for myself just how sick one gets with a parasite feeding off you, but I'd also come to accept that, just like shit, parasites happen.

Spy Quest was also when I met porn star Owen Hawk, who was to be, Titan and I joked, my Pussy Galore. At this time in his career, Owen was still a small guy, a twink, well before he worked himself into a mass of man muscle. He clearly knew his way around a porn set and within the business. In a way, I found him a little intimidating because he knew a lot about the industry, and I, over a decade older, was still naive and new to it. Much of what he said about the porn business circled around the need to have a union of sorts, because he felt the porn companies didn't compensate the models well enough. Having only been in the business for less than a year myself, I found what he said interesting.

He was a a spitfire, a little rough in the best way, which made me want to fuck him hard when the time came. That helped keep me in character and feed the plot line: I was in charge, he was a minion, I put boys like him in their place. Funnily enough, though, I distinctly remember thinking, at a moment with him bent over and my dick inside him, that he seemed a little bored. It was perhaps the least enthusiastic on-set fuck I'd had up until this point. It felt like he was just going through the motions, as though getting fucked was work. I thought he might soon check his watch to see when his shift was over. He was going through the actions of having sex, but that was about it—at least that's how it felt from my perspective.

In that moment, his passionate discourse prior to filming began to make more sense. This was how he made a living, it was a job, it was rent and food. About a year later, when I saw that Owen had started his own company, I had to smile. He said he'd do something like that on the set of *Spy Quest*, and he had. Perhaps it was my age, feeling like a big brother to all these young guys, but I actually felt proud of him. He took his work seriously and, instead of allowing the industry to have power over him, struck out on his own. He knew what he wanted, and he went out on his own adventure to seek it.

Chapter Thirteen

⌄

The timeline of the next three months is difficult now for me to piece together, outside of knowing specifically when my next movies were filmed; I still have all my emails with flight information. A lot happened between shoots, much of it in a meth-induced fog. On meth, days became one big blur, causing even the clean days in between to go out of focus. Having no home anymore, no specific place where I could say I was living even temporarily, I journeyed from the cities of San Francisco and Los Angeles to the forests along the Russian River to the deserts surrounding Palm Springs, each its own island of mystery and danger. I was lured by siren calls, pulled by currents against rocks, grateful for the moments of beauty and joy when they came, and relieved when the distractions kept my growing sadness and darkness at bay. Instead of seeking, I now wandered, aimlessly at times, with my purpose slowly fading.

Trying to understand this particular time period was what sparked me seven years ago to try to write the story of my porn career. I thought, after a few years in therapy and in the rooms of AA, I was ready to write the book I said I would write when I first went into porn in 2004 and when I came out of rehab in 2006. But after finishing a chapter or two, I broke a blade out of a razor, made a shiv, tucked it inside my bathing suit and swam into the middle of Provincetown Harbor where I was going to cut my wrists. By the time I got out to where I couldn't stand, the alcohol I'd drunk had worn off enough that my inhibitions came back. So I swam to shore, got home, drank the rest of the bottle and cut my wrists in the bathtub. In the hospital, I then managed to open up my wounds with a plastic straw and quietly drain two pints of blood into the pool I created in the crook of my arm before the hospital staff discovered what I had done. A locked psychiatric hospital followed. There were a few factors involved in this episode including the fact I had started drinking again, had gone cold turkey off of Wellbutrin, and still wasn't ready to look at these difficult years.

The second time I tried to recreate on paper those weeks from Spring 2005, I fared better. It's what you are reading now. But writing about those days meant living through them and once again I spent a lot of time in my darkness.

Nonetheless, in Spring 2005, I think I still appeared to most people as healthy, happy and in control of my destiny. But for three and a half decades, I'd honed an acting ability allowing me to walk through life as though nothing was wrong. It was a finely crafted coping mechanism in itself, but when I added the other coping mechanism of escape through drugs and alcohol, I'd start to lose my balance on the seesaw between depression and mania. Still, at that point, no one knew what was truly going on in my head. My parents thought I was doing grant writing and my sisters knew about my new career and were unfazed. (Even my brothers-in-law thought it was cool.) They thought of me as a well-adjusted, if no longer sober, adult who always succeeded. If this was what I wanted to do, they supported me. Titan and Joe Gage obviously believed in me. I'd even convinced myself that everything was okay. Yes, I told myself, I was hurting from loss. Yes, I had left South Africa feeling a little off-balance with a sense of growing sadness. But I was also on top of the world, so I pretended I was handling it all as well as I could. I certainly didn't think I was on the verge of spiraling.

Several of the guys I'd already partied with, knowing I was new to meth, advised me to limit my usage to once a month. They warned me of its dangers. I had seen it in the movie *Circuit*, but while that character didn't seem to know what he was getting into, I thought I did and therefore could control it. It'd only been the previous week since I'd met Andrew and smoked meth, but my itch for it was present and strong. I was still focused on writing and had the idea that I'd go to Joshua Tree to do so. While I knew I was going to eventually scratch the itch, I also thought if I could just get to the desert, get settled somewhere and write, I'd be okay.

But I had to start making some regular money if I was going to really go deep and hide myself away with the elusive book. I had started a basic website in the previous weeks and was getting requests to be hired out as an escort. I also firmly believed that having sex for hire was something I could do. I'd end up doing it perhaps eight times in total over those years, but trying to make money having sex when all you really wanted was to do drugs and let people use you for free wasn't the easiest thing to manage. That's where my darkness was taking me.

Immediately after I finished filming *Spy Quest*, two different gentlemen hired me out. After both appointments were over, the next thing I did was find a small party in the Castro where I stayed for three days. After three days, when you're exhausted, dehydrated, depressed, raw, red, chafed and spent, it's pretty easy to want to find some semblance of normalcy—with a little help of course. So I bought a small stash of meth from the guy who'd spent the previous 12 hours fucking me and headed north to the Russian River.

My final destination was south towards the desert, but after my interactions with guys in San Francisco, both on the set and in my drug fueled encounters, I'd learned that many gay men sought vacation refuge north of the city in Guerneville. I had all the time I wanted, so I took the detour and drove up and into a wet, cold and empty shell of a town. It was the middle of March, off-season, and the town was deserted, but I found a room in the gay resort that was open and appeared to be the center of off-season activity.

When I say it was raining, I mean the kind of soaking, bone-chilling, dreary and depressing rain that can affect you deeply. While driving, I'd already snorted the small amount of meth I had and was in a mental panic over what I was supposed to do without any more of the drug in this dreadful place. It was at this point I learned about the residue left in a glass pipe, because I had now become a drug user who owned a glass pipe. The guy in San Francisco gave me his extra one. I scraped the bottom of the pipe with tweezers and got high enough to pass the time jerking off to porn until happy hour. Then I sought refuge in a bottle, my steadfast friend.

I was determined to learn how to be a part of a community, determined to explore what it meant to be single and gay. But I had no clue what that meant outside of porn and drugs. I'd always been the type of person who was friendly, able to be social, who knew how to focus all my attention on the other person in order to draw them in. But not in the gay community and not in bars. I still exuded confidence, but I couldn't broach people or engage in the sort of banter one normally hears in a bar environment. People might talk to me, but they lost me quickly because it was like they spoke another language. It had nothing to do with me feeling superior or above the topics of conversation I was hearing. This was literally about not knowing what they were talking about in terms of cultural references, a large part of which included location specific talk about this place or that place in this town or that city. I suppose it would have been no different for a born and raised Californian being transplanted into a gay bar in Boston.

I was grateful when I got to the bar and saw they were having karaoke; I would have something to focus on. Put me in front of a camera or on a stage with a microphone and I could really shine. I sang a standard, "Bewitched, Bothered and Bewildered," and I got the typical reaction of whispers and looks. Yes, the good-looking guy could actually sing. I also downed vodka martinis, loosening up as the night went on; I was chatted up by a few customers, one of whom turned out to be either the owner or manager, someone in charge.

The next thing I knew I was waking from a blackout with him fucking and cumming in me. I couldn't remember how I'd gotten to his room, but I remembered the part of the conversation in the bar when he told me his partner had died of AIDS. No big deal, I told myself as he pulled out. I didn't ask him if he was positive; I assumed, from what I remembered of our chat the night before, that he would be the type of guy who'd only fuck someone raw if he were negative. But underneath my rationalization, which I didn't want to admit as being a rationalization, I was scared as hell by what had happened. I realized I'd have to test again, but the growing dark part of me actually didn't care and felt I deserved everything coming to me, not just the good.

This was my new normal, I started to think, it being the second time in three months where I woke up from a blackout with a guy barebacking me. But this was, as far as I remember in my adult life, the first time someone shot into me. Even with all the partying, even waking up the previous time with the old guy on top of me, guys always pulled out. At that time it seemed like cumming in someone was still the last boundary most men wouldn't cross unless given permission, even when high.

Cum. Semen. Jizz. Man juice. As a teen in the eighties, cum equaled death to me. It was way beyond taboo, it was toxic. Cum in the eye, nose or an open wound could infect you, we believed, never mind in the ass. We were either scared or shamed into making sure semen didn't enter us. Gay men were responsible for all the deaths happening, those in charge said, and while condoms were still part of the straight world's pregnancy protection strategy, condoms weren't necessarily used or promoted in the heterosexual world as a safety device as necessary as a life jacket when drowning.

But in the gay world, you were a pariah if you even thought about having sex without a condom, and considering how the world looked at gays in those decades, the last thing we needed was more judgment— from those outside our world or from one another. Of course condoms were necessary during the epidemic and saved countless lives. But by the late nineties and early 2000s, condom fatigue was a thing, guys were tired and angry, science started to change, new treatments were being discovered, and bareback movies were entering the porn world. Swallowing and taking loads was surreptitiously creeping back into the sex lives of the few who dared, even though this was often among men who all knew they were positive. Yet no one spoke of cum, for to do so would be to dishonor all those who died because of it. For 17 years, even Henry had used a condom when fucking me.

But all that was changing for me now.

One night in Guernville was enough. I couldn't leave, however, without at least seeing some of the old-growth forest and the mythical redwoods; somehow I felt that doing so would put me back on track and help me erase the anxiety and growing guilt with which I woke up that morning. The trees were awe-inspiring, yes, but I was still hungover. I accepted that I'd ruined what could have been a moment of serenity and reverence in nature. So I started the nine-hour trip to the desert. I really believed I was heading towards some sanity, towards a period of time where I could have a clear head, towards a place to write and to work on my porn persona by building a new website that would honor what I still saw as my epic journey.

The blog I wanted to start would not just be about porn but also my struggles along the way. Even in my haze of growing shame, confusion, and sadness, I still thought there was a purpose to what I was doing and I felt compelled to share it. It was time to put myself out there, to be vulnerable, and also to try to take control of my porn career and now my compulsive need for drug-fueled sex. Led by my ego and naivete, I assumed that somehow I should be able to make money simply through my porn name and what I expected would be a growing fan base. An interactive website where I could show another side of myself to those fans made sense. This was a quest, a spiritual journey. I was a child imagining himself as Johnathan Livingston Seagull flying high into the sky and then diving at full speed, trying to stay in control. I wanted to be known as the soulful porn star, because that's who I still thought I was, hoped I still was.

I'm not sure what I was expecting prior to arriving in Joshua Tree, but it wasn't the complete desolation I saw when I drove the dusty stretch through town looking for a place to sleep. I suppose I thought it would feel less deserted than it was—more like a smaller Palm Springs, where people actually lived. Instead, the desolation I saw seeped in and mixed with the desolation pooling in me. I drove straight through town looking for a place to stay the night and headed to Twentynine Palms to the Motel 6, my favorite no-frills, inexpensive hotel choice on my travels. I was still my mother's son, frugal as they come.

I had barely been able to stay awake on the trip. I was physically exhausted after the days of partying in San Francisco followed by a night of black-out drinking in Guerneville, but I still managed a fantasy of finding a hot soldier on Manhunt from the Marine Corps training base. The next morning, after a fruitless online prowl, still exhausted and starting to crave meth again, I made my way back to Joshua Tree into the National Park.

While my brief hour in the redwood forest was tainted by a hangover, even my exhaustion couldn't prevent me from having a complete spiritual awakening as I drove into the park. I'd spent my life searching for and experiencing moments of deep connection to the environment, to nature, with the resulting deep sense of belonging to something greater. I'd felt it in South Africa, Kenya, Greece, Vermont, the woods of central Pennsylvania, the Amish farmland across from the house in which I grew up. I found it in the simplest of things. This connection had always been there to provide solace, comfort and a deeper meaning to my childhood troubles. I'd heard it in Neil Diamond's soundtrack for *Jonathan Livingston Seagull* when I was seven.

Through most of my experiences in life, there was always something deeper. I intuitively knew it would happen in the park when I made it my destination, and while I may have been in the throes of growing addictions and darkness, somehow I thought that if I just got there, to this place, I was going to be fine. I would find peace and healing from the loss of my relationship. I would find that voice that would allow me to become the strong and creative seeker who understood his deeper purpose in life: to write, to help people, to let them know through my writing that they were not alone. That's what I was told I would do and be by the soothsayer masseuse in Pagosa Springs.

It took only a few short hours before I knew my next step: to find someplace close by, near the park, and commit to staying for a month to write. There weren't many choices, but I did find what initially looked like an abandoned motel and struck a deal with the owner for a month's rent. It was just outside a side entrance to the park, so my plan would be to visit the park daily and to use the energy there to guide me through the commitment to write. I asked for a room in the back so as not to be disturbed, but it wasn't necessary because, with spring having barely arrived, only three rooms of the 20 were even occupied.

The next day I set down a daily schedule and proceeded to sit outside by the half-full green pool, one not fit for humans, with my tiny travel laptop. I didn't know what I was going to write. How did one start the great American novel? I was a trained English teacher and educator, so I thought about what I'd tell students and quickly revamped my expectations, breaking down my goals into more manageable tasks. Just start with a short story, I told myself. A paragraph in, all I could think about was crystal meth.

Any addict understands that once the mental obsession kicks in, all bets are off. My mind could think of nothing else. Unbeknownst to me, it had taken no time for my brain to become addicted to crystal meth. My pleasure centers had already gone haywire. This drug and its corresponding connection to sex had hijacked me well before I could recognize its danger. It happened way back in San Antonio at that conference, when I tried it for the first time and spent the weekend in a bath house. The mental obsession may not have found its voice for many months after, but the whispers started immediately.

While I knew I was now on a slippery slope, having engaged with the drug and other users too many times for me to even count or admit to, I was still drawn to the idea of allowing myself time to experience everything as a single gay man. I convinced myself it was manageable. I was a well-adjusted, mature, capable man who had been responsible his whole adulthood and knew how to take care of himself. I'd been sober for eight years; there was no harm in blowing off some steam and in turn having something to write about. This quest would be about the pitfalls and all, even the most dangerous ones, the pits I willingly dug myself. Danger was a part of adventure and adventure was part of this journey.

Succumbing to my itch, I scratched by reaching out to Andrew from L.A., the one-night stand from WeHo before the GayVN Awards. The next day, he arrived at the motel with his dog and a stash of meth. We partied for days, hid the dog from the management, fucked in the park on rock outcroppings, fucked more in the motel room. He told me he had some time off from work, so there was no reason to wonder how a respected lawyer might find himself in the desert midweek partying in a dark hovel of a room. But nothing really matters when on meth, at least in the romance period of the drug relationship. It's everything and all. Life outside of cock meant nothing, even while I was convincing myself this was a chapter that would have an end. I'd have these drug-fueled experiences, put them aside, and live the rest of my adventure. Andrew had said he was negative the first time we were together, and while we hadn't swapped cum then, I let him let cum in me now. The door had opened in Guerneville, and now I wanted more of it, more of the feeling of being taken, of being owned, of being marked by a man who equally wanted to mark and own me.

It took three nights of not sleeping to finally break up the play date. He needed to get back to L.A. and I needed to write. He could always come back if his schedule allowed. I crashed for 18 hours and awoke surprisingly refreshed. That's what happens when the body gets a chance to sleep after days of partying but then wakes up with the drug still in the system, providing the energy needed to let go of your dick and move into your real life. I took my laptop and my camera into the national park with high hopes of connecting to the energy I had initially felt days prior when I drove into the park the first time. Having tried to write with little success for a whole hour my first day arriving at the motel, and now still tweaking, my attention shifting here and there every minute, I decided to first focus what little concentration I had on my website.

Building a website in those days was more than plopping photos and text into a template. It meant building from scratch and learning HTML, something the voice in my head said I would be able to do, even if it meant starting by having to look up what HTML was or stood for. Thus, gathering photos seemed like the only task I was capable of that day—and what better place to project the image of myself as someone on a heroic journey than in Joshua Tree with its magical rock formations? Three days of no eating and profuse sweating meant that my body was without an ounce of extra weight. I was ripped, rippled, tan. Having fucked ferociously for days, I felt sexy and desirable. I found a private parking area and climbed into the rock formations to find the place where I could be nude and work myself hard. The photographs turned out well. I was feeling happy with the ideas forming in my head as to how I wanted my website to look and feel, the color palette, the fonts, but my happiness faded along with the daylight as I began to crash. I somehow still managed to write my first blog entry.

Chapter Fourteen

⌄

The defining events of my life have always been large, providing tectonic shifts of perspective: moving to South Africa at six years old, running away to Greece and being a boytoy in London at 19, buying a dilapidated old Victorian to renovate at 24, moving to remote Vermont to live a creative life at 33, and a few years later ending a 17-year relationship and going into porn. Each shift in perspective changed how I then continued to live my life moving forward. The shifts continually taught me how big the world was, how endless the potential for new beginnings and growth, and how numerous the opportunities to explore. I believed these large moments helped me evolve into a more compassionate, understanding and giving person.

Smaller defining moments had also happened that initially shifted my perspective, sometimes on a daily or even hourly basis, but those things changed me in other ways, leaving just scars—some small, some ugly. I learned to live with and accept them as part of my shell, which continued to grow harder. Scars, while often ugly, can leave the skin stronger. My father bullied me daily and relentlessly. The neighbor forced his dick into me. My parents swapped spouses with the neighbors. I popped cold medicine like it was a daily vitamin before puberty even arrived and continued for the next 15 years. I cut, burned, and tried to kill myself. I chugged from the liquor cabinet and then went to school. I looked in the mirror with disgust and puked after meals to try to change what I saw.

All of these large and small things happened before I got to high school. They were the hows of how I got to Joshua Tree. They made their way into the anecdotes of my life story and provided the "wows" one might read in a John Irving book. My life was no less bizarre and interesting than *The World According to Garp* or *The Hotel New Hampshire*. The crazy stories got me through those difficult high school years; my friends were in awe and convinced me I was lucky I had such a backstory. But I never realized how the small and large events actually defined me and my decisions in life until I tried to write. I had once tackled writing with Julia Cameron's guidebook *The Artist's Way* by my side. I had tried writing while in a drug-fueled psychosis after making the decision to quit teaching. I wrote my first memoir during that time, while in a personality split that ended with the declaration that I was the messiah. I deleted that manuscript just like I did twenty years later, seven years ago, when I landed in yet another psychiatric ward.

Sitting on the massive boulders in Joshua Tree with a laptop resting on my knees, I was convinced it was different this time, that I was ready and it was time to capture my life with the written word. This was my *Canterbury Tales*, my *Odyssey*, my hero's journey. I was no less arrogant than a knight in search of a holy grail, no less determined than a seafayer trying to get home. I had purpose, a goal, faith—and now, as a newly liberated gay man, I could show the world how soulfulness, kindness and caring could be wrapped together with desire and sexuality and make the world a better place. I wanted to make sure people knew they weren't alone. I wanted to share my life, to share the pain I had felt on a daily basis as a child in the hopes I could make a difference for someone else. I wanted all those gay boys who grew into gay men to know that I understood their pain and to know that they were beautiful and deserving of love.

When I was eventually diagnosed as bipolar years later, my severe bouts of grandiosity, weighed against my equally severe and life-threatening depression, helped make sense of this desire to help and heal. Sometimes naming it, diagnosing it—whatever "it" is—is a first step to healing, whether it's mental health, trauma, or addiction. Eventually knowing something was amiss in my brain would help me understand that when I "split" during a drug-induced psychosis, a messiah complex arose. It would help explain why I desperately wanted to care for people, to heal them, to tell them they were okay, that they had it in them to also change their lives, that no matter what they had been told, what negativity had been forced on them as a child, they were loved. It explained much of my relationship with Henry.

It also helped explain why I had tried, so many times, to die. When I found the right therapist, after the bipolar diagnosis, I would also come to understand that while I'd started tripping on cold medicine at twelve-years-old, and continued to do so for more than a decade into young adulthood, my brain had still been growing. Subsequently, because I had these psychotic breaks in my personality while using, my brain was forming permanent altered neural pathways that made it all normal. I was literally being rewritten and programmed the whole time to have a side of me who believed I was a healer, the savior of man. Believing I was special, that I had the power to change lives, to make everything better, that I was gifted with a higher energy, that I sometimes even thought I had special supernatural powers, was as natural a part of me as any other healthy programmed behavior from childhood. It was also an amazing coping mechanism: Move the focus from my hurt and my unacknowl-edged traumas and turn that focus towards helping others.

Therefore, I told myself my website would be different from other pornstar websites. My blogs would be different. My career would be different: I would be the soulful pornstar. A pornstar who sucked, fucked and ate ass but who would also help change the world in whatever small way I could. They were grand ambitions, but par for the course for some-one who used to try to revive dead flies with drops of water as a child. So I initially wrote about change, how everyone could change their life, that my decision to go into porn was multifaceted but that the primary reason was that without changing my life, I wouldn't be living my life, and therefore would be dead, either figuratively or literally.

One of Henry's and my favorite movies was *Another Woman*, a brilliant Woody Allen film (there was a time when he was revered) packed with stars. The incomparable Gena Rowlands was the lead character who, along with Mia Farrow and Sandy Dennis, was faced with a monumental shift in her life. The signs and messages that followed her all clearly stated she needed to shift with the events that were causing such disturbances in her psyche. At one point in the movie, Rilke's poem "Archaic Torso of Apollo" is recited with its poignant ending line: *You must change your life.*

That purpose, to change your life, was no different than the message I'd heard from *Jonathan Livingston Seagull* as a child. It was the same message I heard from Joseph Campbell freshman year of college: *Follow your bliss.* It was the same message I could hear from Oprah every day I watched her. That was the message of my first blog: I was changing my life, and others could do the same.

However, with my ability to act, to play a role and be chame-leon-like, and with a returning sense of a growing imposter syndrome in this gay world I now found myself in, I was struggling with a creeping feeling of hypocrisy, starting to wonder if I was a fake. The liar and cheater with good intentions. I was an addict fooling himself into thinking he wasn't back at it again. I was preaching health, awareness, and insight, all the while digging myself deeper into a hole, often without caring. Self-destruction was always right around the corner in my life, especially when I was trying to heal others. At times, however, I was capable of using that hypocrisy as motivation, as the impetus to actually listen to my own message to others. Preaching to others without following my own advice wasn't the path of the seeker.

After finishing the inaugural blog and launching a basic homepage for my website, I realized that if I didn't leave Joshua Tree, if it didn't go somewhere else, I'd call Andrew and spend yet more time getting fucked in a meth-fueled binge. Much to the anger of the motel owner, I broke my agreement to stay for a month, left three weeks early, and escaped being caught in a whirlpool of self-destructive behavior.

I arrived in Palm Springs singing Kelly Clarkson's "Breakaway." Kelly started my journey with me, sharing my own moment in time, and would continue to be with me for the next two decades. Her songs "Because of You," "Breaking My Own Heart," "Stronger" and "Piece by Piece" all brought comfort during years of recovery. When one of her songs came on at just the right time, I'd smile even if I was crying, know-ing someone else was with me. Just like when Kelly sings in "Breakaway," I too had grown up in a small town and had stared out the window with rain falling down. That song always made me think of our last days in South Africa, listening to the "Theme from Mahogany" as a young sen-sitive gay boy wondering about his future, wondering where he was going (to). Now, driving into the gay desert mecca of Palm Springs, I hoped I'd feel a warm breeze and possibly sleep under a palm tree (also as Kelly sings in "Breakaway.")

I was pretending I didn't know the town could lead me in different directions, up or down or further down or to my bottom. We addicts can convince ourselves of anything. There was a resort on the far side of town willing to negotiate a short-term rental that I could afford. I was running out of money and starting to live exclusively on credit cards. I assumed that once my website was launched, I'd be able to make a decent living escorting, so my growing debt didn't bother me. For now, it was really important to commit to getting back to the book, that elusive book, that holy grail of words I couldn't seem to start. Palm Springs would be different. Being around people would inspire me; I'd be living in a *Tales of the City* complex, ripe with anecdotes and quips and lessons on how to live in a gay community. My hope was high, my spirit lifted from the hazy dregs of drug-fueled need, and my path felt clear and relatively unobstructed. I was the only thing standing in the way of writing. I knew that. I'd spent half my life with a writer; I understood the process and how it did or didn't work. So I set aside the cravings, the doubt and insecurities of being alone for the first time and the loss of my relationship.

I started the work of writing, but a few days into my stay, I received the phone call that Jessie, one of the dearest friends of my youth, had finally succeeded in killing herself. After all those previous attempts, all those dark moments in her life through which she emerged, scarred but alive, she had finally done it. And I knew she'd done it, in part, because just six months earlier, visiting her en route to picking up Henry in New Jersey after shooting my first Titan film, I had broken her heart.

Chapter Fifteen

⌄

I didn't know what to do in the first hours after my mother and grand-mother dropped me off at the University of Pittsburgh to start my freshman year in 1986. Nervous, scared, intimidated and uncom-fortable behind my stoic facade, I clenched my jaw, trying to look serious and confident. I knew I was doomed to be an outsider in what felt like a straight jock school, but I was also in a city with the potential for finding my people. I just needed to find the singers, the glee club and theater kids who would respect my voice, along with the fact I was gay and out.

What I found, however, while I explored the campus and sought out what I perceived could be a potential safe haven in the student union, appeared between the opening doors of an elevator. She was wearing an Orchestral Maneuvers in the Dark (OMD) concert shirt, black make-up and spiked-out hair, like the Cure's Robert Smith, that made her already 5'10" height meet my 6' 1" frame. Our eyes locked for a moment, then shifted away as I stepped into the elevator. There we were, preppy me, punk her, alone in a steel box where we began our conversation over how the elevators in the building were Art Deco and so cool. We were in love with each other before the doors opened on the third floor.

When two soulmates meet for the first time, it's a revelation. Richard Bach's *The Bridge Across Forever* got me through my love-longing in high school, so I was ripe and ready to be plucked by someone who immediately fell in love with me, like their life was meant for that moment. It was just how Bach had described it in the book. I was lost, alone, a deeply romantic and sensitive boy who lived a life of books, so in that first eye-lock, I felt everything she ever felt. I knew her story, I knew her light, and more significantly, I knew her darkness, because it was my darkness. Our coming together within the first hours of stepping onto campus was the gift of my lifetime thus far.

While I loved Jessie immediately, Jessie fell in love with me as only the deeply, deeply wounded can. That dynamic would never change during our decade-and-a-half-long relationship. Even while our future lives unfolded, during which we shared our moments of happiness and days of darkness, our connection never broke. She understood why I burned myself with cigarettes and hot metal objects in my dorm freshman year when she went with her punk friends to a concert I'd never wanted to go to in the first place. I had felt deserted at the time. I understood her trying to kill herself while she temporarily lived in my first apartment with Henry. Perhaps it's ego to think she never stopped being in love with me, but I could see it in her eyes no matter how long we'd been friends. I could hear it in her voice when we sometimes spoke on the phone over the years when we shared updates on our lives.

Since our reunion of lost souls on that elevator the first day of school, over the next decade she rose from being a dark and traumatized child of eighteen to becoming one of the top chemists in the country. She married in a fairy-tale wedding on Cape Cod, where I sang both "Ave Marie" and Depeche Mode's "Somebody." She then divorced but was seeking her own answers in life and in love, trying to settle on a next

chapter, when I saw her on my way to pick up Henry after I filmed *100°
in Tucson*.

On that visit, she'd shared with me her desire to leave Merck, the
drugmaker where she worked, and become an ornithologist, because birds
were all she cared about. She told me about spending her weekends in the
marshlands of New Jersey with binoculars and a sun hat. Jessie was fair and
freckled with gorgeous red hair that, when pulled back, gave her the stature
and looks of one of the dancers in Robert Palmer's "Addicted to Love"
video. She was breathtaking and utterly stunning both inside and out.

Sitting with her on that visit in her New Jersey townhouse, I could
still feel the intensity of her love for me. Soulmates never lose that love.
But when I started to encourage her to change her life, that she could do
it, that she should follow her bliss because she now knew what her bliss
was—birds—I saw the doubt in her eyes. I felt the trembling of her soul,
and I could hear the sadness in her words. Her darkness was back. So
instead of simply being there for her, which I was physically, I shifted the
focus onto me and shared my own excitement for life, my changes, my
quest. I thought it could help, that it could encourage her to seek her
own change.

But with one simple sentence I broke her heart. She knew that I'd
left Henry; we'd been corresponding via email since my decision to insti-
gate a break-up. She offered unconditional support and love, for Henry
as well as me, because she'd known Henry almost as long as I had and
had come to accept, all those years ago, that he was to be my person in
this lifetime, not her.

She was not ready, however, to hear that I was going into porn.
She was not ready to hear that I was going to give away what she'd
always wanted, something I had given her once freshman year, that
time I ended up crying during the act and telling her I couldn't be what

she wanted me to be for her. I was now going to fuck men on camera for all the world to see.

Her reaction wasn't about the sex; she was far from a prude. I'd helped her do her laundry freshman year after she got crabs from some low-life wannabe Sex Pistol. It was what my doing porn meant to her—that I was offering the world the intimacy that she had always desired and wanted from me, and I was going to do so in such a carefree way, as though intimacy were a commodity instead of a life force. I explained the decision like it was a simple job change—the very thing I was encouraging her to do. I saw it in her eyes, in the seconds it took her to process. I saw the devastation. I saw the last remaining hope of love die in her eyes. The energy in the room shifted, cracks started to appear in her facade, and I realized I had done something irrevocable. She had just lost me and I had lost her.

It's important to understand that I'm not using the word 'soulmate' as a cute, throwaway term to describe our relationship. Jessie and my definition of soulmate was rooted in a deep belief that we had literally found each other again in this lifetime. Richard Bach again changed my life my sophomore year in 1984 with the publication of *A Bridge Across Forever*, a book about finding his wife, his soulmate. It was my first exposure to the term 'soulmate' and I knew deep down that this would eventually happen to me. I say 'finding' instead of 'meeting' because just like with Richard Bach and his wife, the actress Leslie Parrish, Jessie and I were two souls who once knew each other in another life and now had found each other again in this life. Neither of us ever believed it was a chance meeting. We both believed in a hierarchy of souls, that in each life we are meant to evolve and that you do so by interacting with other souls you've touched or that have touched you in previous lives. These people come in and out of our lives providing opportunities to heal and to grow. While it may seem like arrogance to think I knew what Jessie thought about me, that she loved me, that I broke her heart, our relationship operated on a deep spiritual knowing. We knew each other through a look, a touch, and an intuitive sense which might not make any sense to someone who doesn't hold the same beliefs.

At the end of our visit, we promised to stay in touch. I promised myself I would reach out to her when I got back from South Africa in February. I thought that, with a few phone calls, I could still possibly help her make the change she wanted and clearly needed, to go back to school and become an ornithologist. But for six weeks upon getting back from South Africa, I was too focused on myself. I was busy, filming, getting high, trying to write, making excuses.

It was Henry who called me, while I sat having happy hour on my Palm Springs lanai, that Jessie had done it—that with a balcony railing, a bungee cord, a bottle of pills and a bottle of booze, she'd done it. No mistakes this time, she'd made sure of it, and she'd already been dead for three weeks. The services, burial and memorial were already done. Her parents didn't even bother to tell their daughter's best friends that she had died until weeks after the fact. Only then did Henry find out, and now I sat with the news.

In the light of the falling sun with a bottle of vodka, my computer to my side, I forced myself to cry. The alcohol helped me do so, through the night into the next day. Crying felt appropriate, but in reality I couldn't come to terms with how I actually felt. I'd never lost anyone to death before. No one. I was 37 years-old and everyone close to me, including all my grandparents, were still alive. I'd made it through the worst of the AIDS epidemic, before the advent of effective treatment in the late nineties, without losing anyone close to me. Now here was the ultimate significant death, a soulmate, and while my cheeks were wet, my eyes raw and my body numb, the only thing I actually felt in that moment was jealousy. I was jealous she had the strength and guts to do what had to be done to end her pain and to start over. Suicide is not for cowards; it is painful, sad and tragic, but it is far from an act of cowardess, and in her succeeding, a large part of me judged myself as not having her strength. She had excused herself from the darkness of life, and I was still in it.

The second day after Henry's call, I drove to Joshua Tree because I needed to talk to Jessie and I knew I'd be able to speak to her there. While sitting on a rock outcropping 30 feet above the ground and conversing in a combination word/chirp to any bird that showed itself, I painted the sunset. *Jessie's Sunset*, I called it.

At that point in my journey, after Jessie's death, going down was the only direction I could go. Once you're in a hole, it gets easier to dig deeper. You become one with the dirt. There's an excitement in finding yourself going deeper, a challenge in trying to burrow further and further below the surface, to dig far enough that light becomes faint and you can finally welcome darkness as your long lost friend and blanket of comfort. Down was where Jessie had gone, both literally and figuratively. With the end of Henry and me and the resurfacing memories of my childhood trauma, I was already caught in the grasp of my own Cyclops and Scylla, monsters who wanted me dead.

That darkness Jessie and I shared, the life we found in pain, in hurting ourselves, in all those suicide attempts, wasn't something we feared. It was something in our core, something we shared in an otherworldly way, and something we never judged each other for. Our desire to simply stop this life, our understanding that stopping wasn't an ending but a new beginning and a starting over, had always remained an unnamed and unspoken belief between us. Instead it was expressed in deeds, in all those moments of self-harm we couldn't help but inflict on ourselves. Upon finding out what either of us might have done to our bodies in our early years together, our reactions weren't necessarily of concern or worry. Our reactions were more like a casual shrug, a knowing half smile that said, "I get it." Inside we'd simply take that deep breath of relief a cutter feels when they draw blood. We would share that breath even when the blood wasn't our own and we didn't do the cutting.

Finding another dark soul in life with whom you can truly relate and can share the peace that comes from hurting yourself is rare, especially as you grow older, when you are supposed to have moved on from what the general public would call an adolescent phase as though living with darkness was the same as wearing black makeup or a mohawk as a rebellious teen. Now my one person was gone; no one existed out there anymore who got it.

I called my mother and my father and Brian Mills from Titan, and I cried to them for obvious reasons, the tragedy of it, but also for reasons I couldn't possibly reveal to them. The loss of Jessie wasn't what others thought it was to me. They didn't understand its full and powerful meaning.

She had done it without me.

I wasn't just feeling the loss of her death but also a betrayal, as if Jessie had tossed aside our unspoken pact that each would let the other know if one of us was going to kill ourselves. And I had caused this. It was my betrayal—a betrayal that must have seemed flagrant to her, of telling her I was giving my body away for money—that made her finally do it. Of course nothing I did made her do anything, but I know I did, in a small way, contribute to her state of mind that led to taking her own life. She was in a vulnerable place, and hearing my news didn't help just like hearing the news of her death didn't help me given my own vulnerable state at the time. So it seemed natural to want to take a portion of the blame, to use it against myself.

Given I was still going through the end of my own long-term relationship, my family might have wondered if Jessie's death would be too much for me. They might have heard the warning signs in my voice, recognized that I was changing, eroding, that my attitudes and optimism were evolving into uncertainty, that I was valiantly putting up a facade. But I actually think they appreciated that I was showing them a facade. They were the ones, after all, who had shuffled me off to school in sixth grade the morning after I'd first tried to kill myself, as though I had just had the sniffles.

Knowing well my history of self-abuse, my parents had reason for concern, at least my mother did. She and my step-father were the ones who'd received the hospital bill indicating I'd gotten stitches on both wrists freshman year; they paid the bill without questions. My father had seen the cigarette burns on my hands when he came to visit me that same year, and while he reached out to my mother afterwards, nothing was said to me. They were raised on facade, which was all they wanted to see—and by this time in my adulthood, I knew how to create that. Gently and with love and support, they did their best to comfort me in the loss of Jessie, for which I was thankful. My father encouraged me to move forward step by step. So, in my need to appear strong and stable, I picked myself up and grabbed my sword and shield and tried to prove just how stable I could be in the face of adversity.

The folks at Titan didn't know me or my past beyond what I had offered them in those anecdotal John Irving tales. They knew me as a professional, as a dedicated and a serious performer. Brian saw a deeper side of me, the creative side, but not the dark side I so vigilantly protected others from. To him and to Titan, I had it all together and was someone who was thriving. My energy and attitude was all positive. Even in the shadow of Jessie's death, I knew that's what I would have to muster and continue to give them. They needed me in three weeks on the set of another Joe Gage movie, *Alabama Takedown.*

In the meantime, however, I needed destruction, and alcohol wasn't cutting it. I needed escape and I needed to be debased. I needed to be punished for what I did to Jessie and what I did to Henry. I also needed to worship and serve. I needed meth.

Back on Manhunt, using the "PnP" key word, I found a few users willing to share. One older guy, dressed in some serious leather, showed up at my door, but I was in such a sorry state of boozy crying that he gently told me to take care of myself and left. Realizing I might not find the escape I was looking for, and also realizing I needed more of the gentleness the online trick had given me, I reached out to Andrew again. After a phone call, I made a less than safe drive from Palm Springs to L.A., cracked out of my head and offsetting my manic energy with vodka—the perfect combination.

Within a couple of days, it felt like Andrew and I were dating. He was a huge support as I processed the loss of Jessie. We picked up where we had left off in Joshua Tree drug-wise, but now I was crashing in his apartment and living within what I thought to be his normal life as a successful lawyer. He had very flexible hours, which I didn't question at the time, not knowing that he simply wasn't showing up for work. I was looking for someone to take care of me, and Andrew seemed willing, so I pushed aside any passing suspicions that something was amiss. I also really liked him. He was a good person. And our sex was mind-boggling. We hung out for a few days, and then, feeling like I was stable enough (stable in meth-head language simply means you had a few good nights' sleep), I headed back to Palm Springs to once again try to do what I kept telling myself I was supposed to do: write.

Writing is already the hardest thing in the world to do under normal circumstances. Add to it the distractions of uncurbed and growing addictions, trauma and guilt, shame and depression, and the process can easily become like entering a maze which leads to endless deadends. On top of that, you feel like there's a minotaur breathing down your back. But I pretended to write, convincing myself that staring at a blank computer screen was what all writers did. I drank, and I tried not to think of Jessie, Henry or South Africa. I'd end up working on my website instead, getting caught up trying to teach myself HTML and subsequently thinking that using just a little meth would help me focus or maintain some creative discipline.

I also focused on the plan Andrew and I had devised I left: I'd stay in Palm Springs for a couple of weeks, he'd come spend some time with me, and then, after I'd completed filming *Alabama Takedown* in San Francisco, I'd go back to WeHo and move in with him.

All of life's travails come with a priceless accompanying gift, coping mechanisms needed at the time. Those you learn and master, then store away because they worked so well, then eventually dig out of the dusty chest you tucked in the closet for safekeeping. You can occasionally—out of need, boredom or no reason at all—drag that box of treasures out from beneath the shelf in the closet upon which you store your yearbooks, photo albums, and the nostalgia you felt obligated to keep but didn't necessarily want to remember. You can dig around, pull out one of those gifts of survival and shine it until you see your reflection—a reflection that shocks you and confirms that you really do need the coping mechanism. You are a witch in the window and you need to break your own spell. Like reviving a bottled genie, the coping mechanism works for you at first. Until it stops working for you because you've pushed it too far, gotten greedy. All along, the genies in your trunk are laughing at you, wondering when you'll realize you're not in control of them but that they, instead, own you.

Dissociation was my favorite treasure. As children, we're born into a world of magical thinking. As we slowly start to make sense of this and that, our natural need to make believe should lessen as reality sets in. But some of us need to hold onto that magic. Some of us become addicted to daydreams. Some of us are ripe and ready for the dissociation that can come from living in a mystical world of book and fantasy. Thankfully some childhoods are blessed with the gift of security, safety, attention and respect, so the need to dissociate never arises. But some children, quite early in life, whether through nature or nurture, feel the need to split, to separate, to shut out one side of themselves and create another self, because the original self too intensely feels and experiences things.

Originally, dissociation helped me survive those pieces of childhood I didn't want to acknowledge were happening. I learned to turn the key and lock away my hurt as my father bullied me. I could turn into a different kid when the words flew and the threats cannonballed, or when there simply wasn't anyone around and the loneliness of being disregarded and forgotten was too much. Once I discovered alcohol and drugs, they exacerbated my splits. DXM, cold medicine, was my go-to pill. I could pop it and suddenly switch and split. Sometimes I could just tell myself that the hurt Spencer was gone, and that the invincible one would step into his place. I could will my other self into being.

But Jessie's death was too much, so I didn't just go into the closet and grab the bottle to release the genie. I shattered the bottle on the floor and stepped onto the shards.

I needed to forget, I told the genie, but I still wanted to feel the pain.

Chapter Sixteen

∨

I hadn't seen Joe Gage since filming *110° in Tucson* nearly nine months before. This would be my second of his films, another tribute to the hypermasculine porn of the seventies. It was a wrestling movie, more sex than script this time, but enough of a story line to raise the film into a classic Gage plot: two brothers running a wrestling school. Enough said.

My "brother" was Cliff Rhodes, who was tall and had a chiseled chin and enough of a natural Southern drawl to make me nervous. Because we were siblings, I'd need to match that drawl—and if there was one thing I didn't feel comfortable doing, it was an accent. Cliff felt like another version of me: someone not quite willing to admit that they were in the midst of a midlife crisis. He had just left his relationship with a woman, with whom he had a child. Like me, he was starting over—with porn as the first chapter. We connected and were both disappointed we wouldn't be fucking on camera. This wasn't an incest movie, however hot it was to both of us to picture that scenario. I did manage to ride his enormous dick on set during a break between filming. We could barely call it sex; I think we did it after jokingly complaining to Joe Gage that we didn't get to fuck. So I plopped down on Cliff off to the side for all to see more as a "we'll show you" and a joke than with the intention of getting off. I think Brian and Joe just rolled their eyes.

We first shot the opening scene for the title sequence, which had no sex. It showed Cliff and I speeding down a backcountry road—guffawing, being bros, trying to set the movie up for the Joe Gage mystique. We were two Southern boys hitting the road in *Dukes of Hazzard* fashion. Imagine Bo and Luke Duke fucking guys in a wrestling ring. That was going to be *Alabama Takedown*.

Starting with a non-sex scene was a nice change to the normal first day schedule of arriving on set, shaking hands, and then sucking dick. Cliff and I got to build a rapport and I had the chance to listen to and practice his accent. That time together allowed me to jump into the dialogue with more ease during my scenes, which then allowed me to focus on the character and the sex.

Our first scene was with Blu Kennedy—a name I'll never forget. He was the young wannabe wrestler whom Cliff and I needed to "interview" and induct into our school. Blu, the boy with the fiery red hair whose entire raison d'etre seemed to be to service daddies. With every film a few key moments always stuck with me. With this one, it was that initial moment when Cliff and I had Blu on the massage table. It was also that moment when Blu had me on my back, fucking me like his life depended on it, as I commanded my boy to go harder and deeper. It was then I realized there were young guys out there who needed to not just get fucked by daddies but that wanted to fuck daddies in return. (Years later, I learned that Blu was in jail for child pornography.)

Down the line, there would be that moment when Jon Galt, the performer who had inspired me to start this journey after I watched his post-interview on another Titan video, nearly had his hand completely in my ass—prompting shock from the Titan team, as they realized that fisting might be something I would consider in the future. Another moment was when a different young actor had a meth meltdown, a tirade of drug-fueled aggression, and was quickly thrown off set.

As sexy as *Alabama Takedown* was, it wasn't going to give me any iconic scene like what I'd had in my first Gage film, nor would it yield me award nominations. On the other hand, it did allow me to participate in a fully staged Gage orgy—a wrestling ring full of guys fucking. I got to check that off my fantasy fucklist, and I also pulled the accent off to boot. I believe Joe was happy with the work, and while I never ended up working with him again, we left the set having had an initial discussion of whether I'd consider doing a bisexual movie. I said I would—and, believe it or not, I regret not ever having made it. Nothing turns me on more than watching porn where a guy goes down on a woman, something I haven't quite come to understand even today.

By this point, there was little I wouldn't do on a set, or at least be willing to try. I saw it all as an adventure, an opportunity to try something different, a challenge. There was a moment, however, after filming my first scene with Cliff and Blu when I heard the word I actually feared, heard the thing that I knew I wouldn't be able to do: watersports. All the confidence, all the positive self-talk, the suppressing of my fears and the determination to overcome them, couldn't save me from the thing that had defined me as being "less than" much of my life: I was pee-shy. Titan wanted all the actors to stand on the edge of the ring and piss on someone—and they wanted me to be one of the pissers.

I've been pee-shy all my life, horribly so. That's how I would describe it years later to a therapist who helped me rephrase the personal judgment contained in the word *horribly.* It was serious, deeply rooted, permanently imprinted and likely will never go away. If I had one tangible physical manifestation of something I was able to categorize as abuse by my father in my childhood, it was the fact that I couldn't pee in front of anyone. Any guy who can be in front of other men and simply let a strong stream go can't understand that some of us who have childhood trauma are blocked this way. And being told to just "get over it" wasn't ever helpful.

I've never been able to successfully relieve myself at a urinal unless I was alone in the bathroom. Starting a stream was impossible, and even if I was alone and had started, the second I'd hear footsteps or the door creak, the stream would automatically stop. Using a stall with a door was sometimes worse, because people outside could see my feet facing the toilet but would know I wasn't peeing, because there was no splashing sound. I could pee by sitting, but that always triggered yet another inhibition, of people thinking I was shitting.

I'd spent my whole life making decisions based on what bathrooms looked like, where they were located, whether there was a clear view of the path leading to them so that I could monitor whether anyone was in it. I'd track who went in and who came out, to make sure the bathroom was empty, before briskly making my way there before anyone else.

All my life, I'd based my decision to go to events that lasted longer than a couple hours and where there would be lines, solely on whether I'd have to use the bathroom. I'd not drink anything for hours beforehand. If I did go to such an event and eventually had to go, I'd hold my bladder for as long as possible to the point where the pain became so extreme I'd be almost incapable of walking. Eventually, if I couldn't stand it any longer, I'd find myself standing next to someone at a urinal, completely unable to go. I'd stand and stand with multiple people coming and going next to me, trying to appear as though I were peeing by holding down the flush handle just enough to get a trickle of water into the urinal, so that it sounded like pee. I'd assume whoever was standing next to me was laughing at me, questioning my sexuality, wondering if I was trying to look at their dick.

Then my body would suddenly trick me: Even though my bladder had been beyond full and the pain had been excruciating, the pain would stop. I'd think I was okay. I could actually manage a little longer, I'd tell myself, so I'd head for the door, only to be struck by an even stronger pain. I'd think about finding a corner or a bush outside somewhere.

I was a bedwetter, not unusual for young boys. Most grow out of it. At four years old, however, I wasn't growing out of it fast enough for my father. Having to experience his disgust and impatience over my peeing the bed added a new dynamic to our relationship. My father actually decided I went to the bathroom too much. Even when I'd tell him I needed to go, he'd sometimes say "no" which of course makes no sense in terms of helping a child and his bedwetting. I often felt I had to sneak to the bathroom.

Unlike lying, cheating, and stealing, all of which can become coping mechanisms for children with trauma, it was sneaking that helped me the most in terms of navigating my father. While I learned to tiptoe even earlier on, tiptoeing is different than sneaking. With tiptoeing, you can still exist while you are being careful not to be heard or to rock the boat. With sneaking, you can become invisible. But along with sneaking is a side effect, a powerful one that can be both helpful and debilitating: hypervigilance. The obsessive attention to my surroundings dictated the level to which I needed to sneak. Even now, I still scan my surroundings before going to a public restroom. Hypervigilance creates enormous amounts of pressure, stress and anxiety which, while useful for scanning your environment, isn't helpful with standing at a urinal and trying to relax enough to pee.

On several occasions I had to go outside and shit behind the bushes along the front steps of the apartment building in which we lived because he simply wouldn't let me use the bathroom. No one knew, and I was too ashamed to tell my mother, but someone certainly must have found the evidence. For years, and to this day to some extent, I was hypersensitive in terms of where I would defecate and even more vigilant in terms of cleanliness when having sex. If I'm even remotely dirty, even if there is no evidence other than a slight smell, I get overwhelmed, shameful, and apologetic. The logic that shit happens and that it is bound to happen during anal sex doesn't make sense to me emotionally. While it may seem surprising, then, that I chose to be an eager bottom on camera, it's only because of a meticulously crafted routine in terms of the foods I ate, my liquid intake, how much imodium I used which allowed the confidence that comes across on camera. I never had an issue with needing to stop and clean up in any of my films. This internalized fear, though, the fear of humiliation around natural bodily functions did eventually play a part in a descent into hell over a year later when a messy incident was described in detail in *The Village Voice*.

These were the rules my body integrated on a cellular level at a young age. Once emotional scars and neural pathways are formed, the body owns them. You've been programmed like a computer. It is one thing to be afraid of something like spiders or great heights. Those can generally be avoided. Going to the bathroom can't be.

On the porn set, I told myself I wasn't a child anymore. I wasn't an insecure teenager or a confused and unindividuated adult. I was on the path, walking towards and through my fears. So while I could have simply told Titan I couldn't do the watersports scene, I climbed up on the edge of the boxing ring and stood next to the five other guys. I had drunk what felt like a gallon of water beforehand in the hope it would make a difference, and I strategically put myself on the end so that I'd at least not be in the middle of the pack. I focused, I concentrated, I relaxed and I felt the loosening of my prostate, felt a slow easing of the muscles, and then I watched as the other guys flooded the actor on the ground. Beautiful thick dicks let go completely, releasing heavy streams at full force. Suddenly, that bursting bladder of mine didn't feel full. Just like every other instance in my life when I thought the flow was about to come, I lost focus and froze. I stood there shaking my dick and telling myself it was okay. No big deal. I'd put myself on the end so they could cut me out; the scene didn't even have to have me in it.

No one said anything about it, because they probably didn't even realize I hadn't pissed. They were focused on the scene, on themselves and on the reaction of the receiver, not on me. I felt some amount of embarrassment and shame, but ultimately I was humbled and perhaps that's exactly what I needed at that point—an acceptance of imperfection. Part of my split, of my needing to feel invincible, was built on arrogance. All gods and heroes have hubris, and my coffers were being filled with it. While I'm the first one to look back and berate myself for my growing righteousness and pride, I also believe that a tool as sometimes necessary as dissociation comes with arrogance. It's arrogant to think one has the power to lock away darkness without darkness getting resentful and very angry.

Despite my continued grief over Jessie, I managed to make it through filming without a breakdown, tears or mention of what had happened to her. In order to block out the tragedy of her death, to do what had to be done, I split. I turned that key, locked away the hurt, and was left with an incomplete, yet what I hoped was still an authentic, self.

Authenticity has always been important to me. It's hard to describe the complexities of someone who can be in a dissociative state and yet also be an authentic self. Drugs, trauma and acting all aside, there was always a core piece of my identity I could bring forth to portray a stable, healthy, well-adjusted person. But most importantly, I tried to put kindness, compassion and caring first—those were my authentic qualities. When I stepped onto a porn set, I was able to show the best of myself. I was not only everything they wanted me to be sexually, I was also the Spencer who didn't have drug problem, who didn't go to dark places, who wasn't thinking about death, who hadn't just lost the two loves of my life, who hadn't just reopened wounds of sexual abuse. But for most of my films, as soon as the cameras stopped rolling I'd find the key to the closet and be reunited with my darker half.

⌄

Once again, with my Volvo packed solid with all I owned, I headed back to Los Angeles to try living with Andrew. We had more time together now, so he introduced me to friends, gave me a list of L.A. sites we'd visit together, and fucked me.

At some point after I'd arrived—I forget exactly when—he told me he'd just been fired. The law firm had said he wasn't working enough. Suddenly, it all made sense to me: He wasn't using his vacation time or working from home, he was just absent from work. He wasn't the put-together lawyer after all who could handle some harmless partying while maintaining a successful career. As he told me, through all his tears was genuine shock and confusion along with a healthy dose of denial. He couldn't accept what had happened and certainly wasn't going to accept he was on the verge of losing a lot more. And he also wasn't going to admit that it was due to meth.

Sadly, while I really cared for him—as much as one can really care for another in a context of meth-fueled sex—I decided I wasn't going to fall along with him. He was a lesson I was meant to learn, a warning I was supposed to heed. Even through my own meth use and growing death wish, I convinced myself that I wasn't even close to becoming him. I had to escape. But instead of simply saying a definitive "Goodbye, it's over," I let a certain phone call serve as my excuse.

Henry and I had stayed in touch, especially in the days after the news of Jessie. He was a tremendous support. We held each other up during that time. But this phone call from him was different. It was clear that he wasn't doing well. Our split and Jessie's death had been too much for him and he was drinking too much. For the first time, I truly worried about his safety. I felt that whatever might happen to him was going to be my fault.

So I told Andrew I had to go back to Vermont immediately. It wasn't an official goodbye. I didn't have it in me to hurt Andrew when he was still reeling from his job loss. But I knew it was the end of the two of us. Distance would end it. Going forward, not answering his phone calls would be easier than seeing the hurt in yet someone else's eyes when I said goodbye.

Armed with a small amount of meth, I started driving. Henry seemed better on the phone the next day. I'd made it to my sister's place in Boulder after a 15-hour first leg of the journey. I then drove another 12 hour day so that I could take a side trip south of Davenport, Iowa, for an escorting appointment. It was with a sweet man who happened to be rather overweight and who just wanted me to use dildos on him. He also just wanted to talk. He let me crash for the night, something I needed because I'd been going non-stop with the help of my nearly exhausted supply of meth.

When I got back onto I-80 early Sunday morning, I was flying again having used the last of my meth in the car. I was also flying in terms of my speed and was pulled over by a cop. He asked whether he'd find anything if he searched my car; my empty baggie of meth was in the glove compartment. My Volvo was still packed with my life including bins full of Migrant Education documents, so I quickly explained that I was crossing the country having been at a conference in case he did start looking. I guess the story seemed unusual and plausible enough that he let me go with a warning. When I finally arrived in Vermont, Henry greeted me with a sheepish smile—his apology of sorts for asking me to drive across the country for him.

Outside of not sleeping in the same bed, Henry and I quickly fell into our old domestic roles. During the day, I'd work outside, puttering around the property doing chores that he hadn't been doing, while he was working his new job for the local mental health agency. The only difference now was that I was also drinking and could share in his happy hour every day.

He seemed fine, well-adjusted even, and we were both genuinely glad to see each other. As much as he was home to me, I was also still home to him. Half of our lives had been spent with each other, an intense and remarkable period. Regardless of the hurt I'd caused, love still seemed to prevail on those evenings when, martinis in hand, we watched the sun dip below Jay's Peak on the horizon. We then sat by the woodburning stove, him occasionally reading me a line from the book he was reading, me with some knitting I'd purposely left behind, as a kind of bookmark for our life together.

My coming East also meant that Henry and I could drive to Pittsburgh together for a memorial our friends were holding for Jessie. None of us had had the chance to grieve together; her parents had stolen that from us. Our gathering was to be simple: a get-together at a bar in the Squirrel Hill neighborhood of Pittsburgh, far from Jessie's Aliquippa steeltown roots. It's what Jessie would have wanted from us: drinks at a bar. She would have rolled her eyes at anything else.

It was also a reunion of sorts. Henry and I hadn't been back to the city since we'd left four years earlier, in 2001. Because he and I had been in a cocoon of domesticity since we were in our early twenties, we'd really only shared a couple of friends with Jessie whom we'd see at a party once or twice a year. Yes, I knew everyone—we'd all gone to college together—but we didn't really have much of a relationship with anyone other than Lori. She, Jessie and I had been a trio our freshman year in college and she was the only other person from Pittsburgh I could really call a close friend.

Despite all that, the trip did little to help either Henry or me grieve. I suppose neither of us, having ever lost anyone close to us prior to Jessie, actually knew what grieving was. I was hoping for some sort of catharsis—and as much as Jessie would have hated it, perhaps something more than drinking at a bar would have helped. Perhaps we could have had an actual memorial, something with a bit more soul and spirit than drinking Rolling Rocks around a table and sharing stories.

Laura would have liked more too. I knew Laura as Jessie's friend via a different group of people Jessie hung out and lived with in college. She and I found ourselves talking alone together at the bar, and soon we'd made tentative plans: I would visit her that summer in Provincetown where she lived, and we would do something special for Jessie and for us. We would try to find some closure together on Cape Cod.

I had no idea at the time that Jessie's greatest gift to me wasn't just her love but that, via Laura, it would also be Provincetown.

Chapter Seventeen

⌄

After returning from Pittsburgh, I yet again left Henry in Vermont, almost a year to the week I'd originally left. I tried to focus on the fact that he was okay, that he was moving on, that he drove, had a job, was paying the mortgage himself—and that perhaps he was even happy in his own life with his new responsibilities. I forced myself to believe that he may even have been happy for me in my new life.

Of course I hadn't really built a new life yet—not like the life we'd built over our 17 years together. As much as I still wanted to consider Vermont and Henry home, as much as my heart and every cell in my body staked their claim in those Green Mountains, my only home at that time was the forest-green Volvo that held most of my possessions.

I was also living on credit cards—despite the fact that one of the lessons my father had drummed into me all my life was the importance of establishing good credit.

I'd worked since I was fourteen. By the time I was a high school senior, bussing tables at The Loft in Lancaster, I could pull in more than $300 in tips on a weekend—a substantial figure for 1985. I'd established good-enough credit in my early twenties to help secure a mortgage. By my early thirties, I had a $45,000 line of credit available to me across three different cards. I rarely carried a balance in my early adulthood, because I thought of being in control of my credit as one thing I could do to make my father proud—even during the eight years we weren't speaking to each other.

But during times of upheaval in my life, maintaining good credit had often fallen to the wayside. That was certainly the case after leaving Henry, and after the reunion trip with my father in South Africa. After that, each time I pulled out a card to charge a hotel room, or a cash advance to pay for food or drugs, was an unconscious "fuck you" to my father.

Today, in our age of DIY and OnlyFans porn, some people think that porn stars once made a decent living from the old "studio system." Some undoubtedly did, but they also worked their asses off in order to do so. They might film dozens of scenes a year and then likely supplement that work with live performances, appearances and personal appointments. My income from Titan was limited because my contract was limited: I could make just four movies a year for them, for each of which I'd get about $1,200. The idea was that, by making me a Titan exclusive, they were giving me not so much a livable income as they were a framework for building that if I wanted to. And my contract with the state of Vermont to assess their Migrant Education Grant had long since come to an end.

Hence, my money was beginning to run out and my credit card debt was growing. I pulled in some money escorting—just enough to keep me afloat. All in all, throughout my time in the porn business, I'd only escorted less than a dozen times. I'd never considered going into porn as anything more than a short-term adventure, so I wasn't necessarily concerned about the lack of funds. I spent time with my mother in Lancaster and then with my sister in Leesburg, Virginia, so I had places to stay temporarily. I eventually asked my sister if I could live with them for an extended period of time and use her house as a homebase for traveling. With Leesburg so close to Dulles, it was the perfect hub, and she had the space and a separate guest quarters. Both she and my brother-in-law agreed.

My older sister and I hadn't spent much time together over the previous two decades, so this opportunity to get reacquainted with her and spend time with my two young nephews was a blessing. She and her husband both knew I was doing porn porn. On one of my first nights with her, over happy hour, she and I had a True Confessions moment—about more than just the porn. She'd never known, for example, about all that had happened in South Africa, including some of my parents' more lively behavior. When she'd been off with friends, I'd been home watching the adults. Suddenly, she said, so much made sense to her about our childhood and teen years. To me, she'd always been the one who could do no wrong in my father's eyes.

Now, she said, finding out the origin point for my parents' spouse-swapping years later was more of a shock to her than learning that I was a porn star—which, in fact, made her laugh. Like my stepsister, she was supportive and said that if anyone could start a porn career at 36, it was me. She also couldn't wait to tell my brother-in-law, who found it downright cool. He even said, after asking to see some photographic stills, that I had a nice cock. Yes, my brother-in-law admired my dick.

I traveled from Vermont to Virginia not just to plant myself for a couple of weeks before heading back to film my next movie, *Cirque Noir*, in June, but also because Johannes, my three-week South African tryst, was flying to D.C. to see his sister—but also me. Johannes, the Afrikaner heartstopper who fucked me from behind against a wall in a bathhouse while I was on that trip to Cape Town after my father left, had been a wonderful rebound distraction from the breakup with Henry seven months earlier—the heaviness of which I hadn't really shared with him.

In fact, when I left Cape Town, I clearly signaled to him that I was leaving the door open for the two of us.

During our time together, Johannes picked up on my enthusiasm at being newly unattached and free, in South Africa after 30 years away, and he'd also found my burgeoning porn career fascinating. But some of my enthusiasm was at times tempered by moments of contemplation which often turned into flashbacks when we'd visit places I'd been as a child. Some of the memories were good, some not so good. But mostly Johannes managed to distract me with good South African weed and his beautiful uncut cock. In addition to sex, we'd spent much of those three weeks together going out to dinner or to classical concerts, or taking road trips—including one to Knysna, where I bungee-jumped from the highest jump in Africa and world's highest commercially operated bungee jump. Once again, jumping off a bridge two-and-a-half football fields high on a reinforced rope became an act of proof that I was brave enough, man enough—even if my father wasn't there to witness it.

I suppose that the energy, enthusiasm and positivity I exuded at that time were attractive to Johannes. I was this American who'd ridden in on a chariot, full of life and affirmation, spear in hand and ready to conquer the world. But while I wanted to explore, to live fast and hard and experience what I felt I had been missing all those years with Henry, Johannes was looking for more. At brunch one Sunday, at a beach restaurant across the bay from the city, I told him I was thinking that Cape Town could be a new home for me at some point in the future. It would mean giving up the porn career I'd just started, but I couldn't imagine doing porn for too long, at least once I seriously started writing.

I realized my mistake as soon as I'd said it. To Johannes, my words meant we had a possible future together. In truth, as hot he was, as good as the sex was, and however much I enjoyed someone taking care of me, which he had essentially been doing, he wasn't someone with whom I could have a relationship. Our personalities and needs were simply too different. Our conversations outside of discussing what our plans were for this day or that weekend, brunch with his friends, a concert, a short trip, didn't have the substance I craved. I wanted to talk about the journey of life, about meaningful books and their lessons for living, about art and the creative process. He wanted to start dating seriously and have a serious relationship; I had been single for seven months, the only seven months of my entire adulthood.

Yet because I had no prior experience in dating at that point, just coming off my long tenure with Henry, I didn't know how to extricate myself from our affair. In fact, I was grateful that I didn't need to know how, because I was going back to America. So I walked back my musings about the future by letting him know that my living in South Africa wasn't really realistic.

But now here he was on his way to the States, wanting to connect with me again. He knew I was staying with my sister and her family just outside D.C., not far from where his own sister lived. While I felt obligated to spend some time with him during his visit, I feared his desire to continue some sort of relationship with me. If I couldn't move to South Africa, he told me, he could move to America. I knew I would eventually have to find a way to say there was nothing to us—or to ghost him like I'd done to Andrew just a few weeks before.

I picked up Johannes at Dulles, where we spent a night in a hotel. He could tell something was different about me; he said I seemed manic. And he was right. Emotionally, I was off, operating as a different Spencer than the one he knew in South Africa.

We made an overnight visit to his sister, where he would eventually go back and spend a few weeks. Then we went to my sister's in Leesburg, where we spent several days together, then overnight to the gay beach resort of Rehoboth, Delaware, before I took him back to his family and escaped to San Francisco.

By the time we said our goodbyes, we both knew that it was over because of my passive-aggressive behavior towards him. I'd been distant, cold and callous—at least that's how I remember it. I wasn't proud of my behavior, just as I wasn't proud about how I'd left Andrew, but I told myself there really wasn't anything to feel badly about. That's what happens in relationships, when you're testing the waters and dating, I told myself. It was all new to me. It would take practice for me to learn to have short-term relationships that wouldn't turn into 17-year commitments, I told myself, because from the moment I'd been sexually abused as a child, I didn't know that I had the right to say no.

Both during and after both Andrew and Johannes, I spent a lot of time alone and in my head during the car drives, on the flights across the country, and in the empty hotel rooms. I had a lot of time to think and began to process what was happening. I realized if I wasn't careful, it'd happen again: at some point, I'd give in to another guy, lead them on and have them fall in love with me when all I wanted was sex and company. I was still like a teenager, incapable of breaking up with someone face-to-face.

But I also realized that I didn't know how to be alone, so my default would continue to be to allow people into my life when I was in no position to do so. I had no idea who I was by myself. Yet, I thought, if I continued to have emotional entanglements with every guy I had sex with, I'd continue to hurt people.

By that logic, I figured, having sex only on-set and or while on meth made sense. Both porn and meth put up a kind of wall between me and the other person, I thought, that would keep me from getting involved with them.

My next film was described to me as a fantasy with a circus theme; I didn't exactly find that appealing. But the title was changed prior to my arrival from something suggesting a carnival to the more provocative and intriguing *Cirque Noir.* It's amazing how a name can change everything, even with porn. How could I not picture aerialists in a Cirque du Soleil setting? That was exactly what Titan was going for in my scene—a threesome including an acrobat who promised to be quite flexible. Titan had booked a room in downtown San Francisco, something that still filled me with excitement. San Francisco!

But that excitement was quickly tempered by my inability, yet again, to say no. It was the next and last lesson in my course on dating.

When I'd left Andrew earlier that spring to drive across the country back to a desperate Henry, he knew that I was set to film again in June and had suggested that he'd drive up from L.A. to see me. At the time, I'd hoped that by ignoring his phone calls or appearing unexcited when I did take them that I'd be able to get out of that. But when he did call, he nearly pleaded to see me—and, unable to draw a line, I agreed that he could drive up and stay with me for the three nights I was booked in the hotel during the filming of *Cirque Noir.* It would be the official end, I told myself, during which I would have the decency to give him a proper and direct goodbye.

By then, though, word that I had been hanging out with Andrew, who was known to be a meth addict, had traveled through the gay network that connected L.A. and San Francisco—all the way to someone at Titan. Keith Webb, one of my contacts with Titan, called me, expressing his concern. I was shocked that Andrew had such a significant reputation as a meth user that I was receiving a call from my porn company. But Titan was serious about their image as a safer-sex and drug-free company.

My being an exclusive, a performer they were actively promoting as a face of the company, brought with it responsibilities on my part, I was told. I'd believed, in fact, that I *was* being responsible—by keeping my drug use off the set. Despite all this, Keith cared enough to reach out and tell me to be careful. It was at this point I realized the folks at Titan, in addition to protecting their no-drugs reputation, actually cared about me. I was touched by the call.

On top of that realization, I was also just beginning to understand how my life was changing in a truly amazing way. I hadn't yet realized that I was becoming somewhat famous. In the porn world, I was *the* current newcomer, so when I showed up with Andrew in L.A. to friends' houses, people took notice.

Despite the warnings from Titan, I still agreed to let Andrew stay with me at my hotel, partly because I knew we wouldn't be using. I never used drugs before or during a performance. It was a line I wouldn't cross—and never did throughout my career. And, as I also made clear to Andrew in advance of his arriving in San Francisco, we wouldn't be having sex because I needed to honor Titan's rule of no sex prior to filming.

The other reason I had to sever the relationship with Andrew was that he had called me a week or so before I arrived on the West Coast to tell me that he'd tested positive for HIV—and that he was convinced I'd infected him. At first I worried that he might be right. But then I tested immediately—and was still negative. I wasn't the one who infected him, and over a phone call, I told him. I don't know whether he believed me or not.

For some men reading this who lived within the HIV/AIDS crisis, my naivety may feel frustrating and anger inducing. But I'd wager there are many men who didn't live in urban centers all those years who might actually relate to my naivety. We've heard about survivor's guilt, and while I know it is not the same, my guilt comes from my ignorance and disregard for the pain and suffering others were going through while I engaged in risky behavior. Because this memoir isn't just about the how and the what, I'm taking the time in this narrative to go back to the why. The whole purpose of this book is for me to examine the why, so I beg your patience.

This many months into my quest, I was only just coming to terms with being a sexually active gay man in a world still defined by HIV/ AIDS. (PrEP, the HIV prevention pill, was still seven years away; the FDA did not approve it until 2012.) Of course, HIV had been lurking around all along. As much as my guilt wants me to embellish the number of guys with whom I had condomless sex since leaving Henry, in reality, it was around a dozen guys at this point. Perhaps that was a lot, but I told myself it couldn't possibly be. With nearly all of them I'd had discussions about status, and, even with meth in my system or in a party scenario, made choices with these men whether to be safe or not.

I was part of that Gen X generation of gay men who came of age aware and fearful of HIV but not hit as hard by it as the generation just a decade or two older than us. Unless you were growing up in an inner city in the 1980s and 1990s, HIV/AIDS often remained a creature you knew existed out there—it came up on TV and in the media—but had never seen up close in your own life. And yet, of course, and especially as we became sexually active, it was out there, waiting patiently for us to make even one bad decision.

Soon after meth took hold in the gay community in the nineties and aughts, however, it quickly became clear that it had the power to make users throw most of their previously adhered-to safe-sex rules out the window. I didn't do that—not at first. My initial experience with meth may have landed me in a San Antonio bathhouse for two full days, but the sex I'd had was still safe. Just two guys had fucked me, both with condoms. But I had sucked cock, which I believed at the time to be lower risk for HIV than getting fucked, but not exactly zero risk either. (The CDC has since declared that there is "little to no risk" of getting HIV from oral sex.) When I came back to Vermont, I told our rural small-town doctor that I wanted the test for the virus. He explained that transmission would have been unlikely, but we tested mostly for my piece of mind.

As a young gay man growing into his sexuality in the eighties, I'd sit rigid when the TV news aired something about AIDS. I'd feel like I was destined to die from it and would wonder if my family knew as much. Granted, there likely wasn't much HIV circulating in rural Pennsylvania Amish country. But despite my fear, I *was* still having sex with older men. Nobody talked about HIV. Yes, there was one gay guy, in his mid-twenties, who'd at one point worked at The Loft, Lancaster's gay restaurant where I worked, and who apparently had HIV. I only knew him on the periphery of the circle of staff currently working at the restaurant. But he was hot, a seventies porn star hot, and I'd jerked off to thoughts of him more than once.

At a high school graduation party for my peers and I, I got drunk and hooked up with this fantasy guy. We ended up sixty-nining in the back of his van. I came in his mouth. I distinctly remember him saying, "It's been a long time since I let someone do that." I tried to get him off by continuing to suck him but at some point he took over with his hand, and while he didn't come in my face, I remember watching the cum pour out of him thinking that perhaps I had more to learn about how best to perform oral sex.

It turned out that he was definitely HIV-positive. I found out because Kathy, the older girl who would get me drunk and coerce me into fucking her throughout high school, found out that he and I had done something. She slapped me in the face and asked how I could do that to her, since she and I had had sex after my encounter with him. In my mind, all I could think was that she deserved some fear, because I'd never wanted to have sex with her in the first place. I was able to confirm later that he was positive. While shrouded in a sense of secrecy, once I made inquiries through other people, I discovered the truth.

The following summer, when Henry and I landed in London and ended up having sex with guys in exchange for a place to stay and for spending money, condoms were always used. But again, nobody really talked about HIV.

I used HIV for my own purposes the first time when Henry and I came home with our tails between our legs after just three months of being away. The trip to Europe was a disaster in the eyes of our parents. We'd been bailed out by them with our plane tickets home from England– we were penniless by then. My parents had also gotten my freshman year grades in the mail while we were away. I had failed four of my five fresh-man classes. The final straw was that I had stolen the deposit for my room/board for Sophomore year to use for the trip. I was a nice guy, a good kid, but I could manipulate.

By the time I graduated high school, I was an expert at it, so in order to deflect attention away from my grades, the 'misappropriation' of their money and the consequences of both, I told my mother I thought I might have HIV. I knew I didn't, or at least I couldn't imagine how. All her anger and disappointment in me immediately turned to utter fear which was what I wanted to happen. While all I wanted was to deflect attention from the damage I'd done, I brought sheer terror to my mother with my sleight of hand. My mother still remembers that moment as one of the scariest of her life. She remembers standing outside of the doctors office jumping with joy with her jogging buddy after hearing that my test was negative.

I was relieved my plan had worked, and if I felt any guilt about what I had put her through, I quickly squashed it by calling forth a decade of resentments against her. I thought back to the previous summer, the summer after high school, and remembered her response to Kathy who openly told her we were having sex. My mother said to her it was too bad I hadn't gotten her pregnant; it was her solution to my being gay. I thought about her forcing me to secretly carry all the weight of things that had happened in South Africa when, the night my parents confronted me senior year in high school about being gay, she gave me a drink and I became her confessor. I thought about her sitting at the kitchen table in middle school and doing nothing while my father humiliated and tore me apart.

The second and last time someone slapped me over HIV was the morning after Halloween in 1995. Henry and I had gone clubbing in Pittsburgh the previous night then landed at the after-hours gay club with a group of friends. I'd been tripping on cold medicine and alcohol for several hours and finally blacked out. My last memory was seeing a guy on the street outside of the club who I only knew through mutual acquaintances. He was dressed in drag, leaning into my car window, and then I came to and awoke from my blackout while fucking him in his apartment. It was one of the few times I'd fucked anyone since Henry and I had been together. I came in him. I tried to find my car but ended up having to walk home where I faced Henry who asked if I'd gone home with the guy and whether we had sex. I told the truth and the slap came fast and hard. "You know he's HIV+," he screamed. It was a few months later when I had the DXM split, a true psychotic break, that landed me in Western Psychiatric Hospital and when I gave up drinking and drugging for the first time.

HIV simply wasn't present in our lives after that. The only person I knew who had AIDS and who eventually passed away was my mother's cousin, Art Maharg, a founder of RazorMaid records in San Francisco. I met him once on a trip back from Hawaii in 10th grade. He could barely look at me; I was newly aware of my own sexuality at 16 and was probably making him uncomfortable with my staring. Even at that age, I was learning how to seduce. That 70's porn star look I will always find incredibly sexy. It was soon after that Art started sending my mother, (in my mind he was secretly sending them to me), various Razor Maid albums. These were cutting edge music mixes, the club mixes used in all the San Francisco gay clubs, which brought a level of coolness to my senior year parties. One of the songs, "Don't be so Fucking Serious" became an anthem for my classmates. When he died from AIDS in the early 90's, I didn't know what to feel. His life was so far removed from mine, from the life Henry and I had started. His death was sad, tragic for his parents, but it wasn't the symbolic or monumental moment in my HIV awareness as it might have been.

When I chose to send my photos to Titan, I chose them because they had safe sex public service blips at the start of their movies. They made wearing condoms cool. The sex I watched was so incredibly hot, fucking bareback wasn't something that even crossed my mind. I didn't even know the terms "bareback" or "raw" yet. If I was going to sow my oats at 36 as a first-time single man, the only sowing would be into a condom. Sure the breeding and seeding of 70's porn was a turn on, but millions of people had died from AIDS at this point. Unsafe sex simply wasn't an option. I was completely unaware of what was going on medically with HIV transmission and prevention at the time. I was clueless, utterly. I experienced nothing of the 90's, knew nothing of that horror, knew nothing of the current drug-treatments and their efficacy, or the longevity of those infected and not treated. Nothing. I believed HIV was still a death sentence even in our first-world country. I didn't know there were drugs making living with HIV possible. HIV still meant death to me.

After coming back from South Africa and meeting Andrew during the GAYVN awards, we did talk about it. He reassured me he was an exclusive top which was supposed to mean something even though I ended up fucking him that night making me question his definition of the term 'exclusive.' We were also negative, or so we both said, and we proceeded to smoke meth and fuck for weeks, both under the assumption we were only fucking each other and therefore would stay negative. I had tested in a free clinic in Palm Springs shortly before seeking solace and temporarily moving in with him in LA after Jessie died. The counselor, with whom I was completely honest about my use and new career, gave me my negative result along with a prediction that I would soon be positive if I didn't change my behavior.

I headed back to San Francisco to film *Cirque Noir* with relief, knowing that even if Andrew was coming, I'd set the rules and we wouldn't be having sex. The day I flew in, Andrew drove up from L.A. with his dog. When he got there, he told me he'd never even considered that the hotel might have a no-pets policy, which it did. He ended up sneaking the dog in and out the back stairs several times a day while I was on set. It irked me that he was risking getting me in trouble in a hotel for which Titan was paying. It was yet another thing, I told myself, that would allow me to finally walk away from him without guilt.

The set of *Cirque Noir* was simple and beautiful. Elegant, even, with a black backdrop and flowing neon-green curtains draped at angles. A trapeze was at the center of it all.

And so was I, about to get double-fucked. I can't remember whether this was Brian Mill's suggestion or mine, but I think it must have been the latter because I continued to want to push the boundaries of what I would do on camera. At any rate, Titan was more than willing to make this happen. Other sex acts would precede it, but the culmination of the scene would be me crouching down onto two dicks while I held onto the trapeze above my head. I knew I could do this, but I also knew I'd have to prepare, so I spent 20 minutes using progressively larger dildos to stretch me out. If there's any one image that symbolizes my comfort and security in my sexuality at that point, it was me casually sitting on dildos on set while the crew adjusted equipment, chatted and ate. La di da.

I remember thinking at the time what a meditative process it was, slowing stretching, getting comfortable, breathing. It wasn't necessarily sexual for me. I was still blogging at this point, and after finishing the scene I wrote a post about it. That sort of says it all in terms of the persona I was desperately trying to create: funny, down-to-earth, thoughtful, cheeky.

The other two performers and I would go on to win a GayVN award for Best Threesome for that scene, perhaps not so much for the double-fuck but because it was as close to cinematic art as porn could get. It was visually stunning because the set design was so simple: an empty stage, the floor lit in dark cobalt blue, two draped curtains in the back lit in a neon lime-yellow, and a solitary trapeze hanging front and center. And, of course, the three bodies twisted, contorted, and melding into one as though we had become a six legged, six armed, and three dicked creature of skin and sweat.

On checkout day from the hotel, Andrew left before me; we barely said anything. At this point, our lack of words expressed a mutual understanding we may not see each other again. I then managed to get myself to the airport. I didn't feel well—exhaustion I thought—and was looking forward to sleeping more on the plane. Fortunately it was only half-full, so I had a row to myself. I was shivering uncontrollably, fatigued like I'd never had been before, and losing my mind a bit. It felt like that K-hole I had slipped into the previous fall, when I woke up with the old guy on top of me. I was confused, on the verge of losing consciousness. Thankfully, in a feverish sleep, I got through the five-hour flight to Dulles. When we landed, I had a scary 20-minute drive to my sister in Leesburg, where I crashed for two days, still sick and in isolation for fear that whatever I had might be catching.

Somehow I again rallied and drove myself the three hours to my mother's house in Lancaster, where I again proceeded to crash for another five days. It wouldn't stop: the fever, the malaise, the inability to stay awake, and the degrading of my mental state. I couldn't tell reality from my dreams—I didn't know who I was for days.

But during those moments of clarity, when I was able to sit up and eat something my mother brought me, not once did I think that I might be seroconverting to HIV. I'd just tested HIV-negative weeks before, after all. This was the flu, I told myself, and, after it finally let go of its hold on me, I joined my extended family for their annual family vacation in the mountains of North Central Pennsylvania. From there, I continued to drive north to stay yet again with Henry for a few days before heading to Provincetown for my visit with Laura—the visit where she and I would finally have a chance to say goodbye to Jessie.

I'd been meth-free for weeks now and felt good despite the fact that I'd just seroconverted and still didn't know it. I'd had enough warning signs of the dangers of being out of control with meth. I'd watched Andrew lose his job. On top of that, another sexual partner from Philadelphia the previous fall had called me recently to tell me about being hospitalized with the belief that bugs were crawling under his skin.

I'd heard about this phenomenon with extreme meth use, how such people have delusions that creatures are burrowing below the surface of the skin that need to be scratched or cut out. (Some users would go so far as to do just that.) I was so floored by this confession of his, and the fact that even after being released from the hospital he still thought he was carrying bugs, that I promised myself I'd stop using. Or at least take a break for as long as I could manage. I thought of the impending trip to Provincetown as a time to be connected with Jessie's spirit, far beyond the world of porn and sex. I needed a spiritual retreat, a time to focus on my health and my writing, and decided that Provincetown would be it.

Chapter Eighteen

⌄

As a child who'd spent years traveling the world, living in places of profound beauty and connecting with the universal truth that exists in the natural world, I found that Provincetown opened within me a sense of belonging and of coming home. At first it wasn't the town itself but the massive open expanses of dunes and scrub pines, which immediately took my senses back to South Africa as a child. The vastness of sky and sand suggested I could get lost here, that I could explore and feel the same feelings of awe and wonder I had as a child in the seventies. Just as Palm Springs' heat and intense mountain views had caught me in a deep sense of nostalgia, the Cape Cod National Seashore did the same, but on a much more intense level. As there had been in Cape Town, there was so much light on the tip of Cape Cod that I felt closer to the sun and sky. It'd be years before I understood there was, literally, more light in Provincetown. It was surrounded on three sides by water, which captured and reflected light back to the town, and to the thousands of artists who'd made it an art colony for more than a hundred years.

There was also the town itself, which gave me yet another sense of belonging. I had been to Provincetown as a child, a side trip during regular stays on the Cape throughout middle school. Three of my father's aunts lived in nearby Orleans, and in fact one had been there since the 1950s, when her husband brought Kodak development to the Cape. His business, Cape Cod Photos, had not only been a fixture in the center of Orleans for decades but also had had a satellite store in Provincetown, Town Camera Shop, next to the Portuguese Bakery. So while I couldn't exactly say I had roots in Provincetown, I had a visible connection to it, a literal sign above a window, and I felt that connection whenever I passed it.

Of course, another sense of belonging was even greater. Provincetown gave me a vision of what gay life could be and offered possibilities of creating a new home there—if not permanently, at least temporarily. I decided it would be a perfect landing spot for me, a newly single porn star who wanted a creative and soulful life. As I wandered the dunes, the beach and the town's main strip, Commercial Street, I realized that Jessie may have left me, but she'd given me Provincetown.

Laura was best friends with a woman named Beth, a true Ptown-townie whose family owned nightclubs, bars and one of the town's most historically distinctive houses. I stayed in Beth's condo, which was in a well-known house in the East End with an old-fashioned ship's figurehead of a woman mounted over its portico. Laura and Beth took me under their wing and introduced me to their friends, which immediately made me feel like I was in the Ptown in-crowd.

After only a week in Ptown, I decided I'd stay, find a place to rent after the season ended on Labor Day, and establish some roots there myself. I found a rental on Cottage Street in Kensington Gardens. This was 2005, when the off-season in Provincetown actually started in September, and when rentals were harder to find because the town hadn't gentrified yet and turned into a profit hub for some second homeowners solely interested in making money. It was back when you had to rely on classifieds in the paper or flyers on the notice board at the post office to find a place. There weren't many options, so I ended up in a three-bedroom, full kitchen, dining room, living room, shared pool, hot tub and sauna unit all for myself. I wasn't worried about my rent which was almost $1000/month—I figured I could turn a few tricks in town when I needed the cash. I'd have income from a couple of movies. I had my credit cards. I didn't really spend a lot of money and wasn't one to go out, so I decided I could make what I had stretch. I would move in the weekend after Labor Day.

Meanwhile, Laura and I still needed to find a way to grieve and to celebrate Jessie. We decided we would get a matching tattoo in her honor; Laura would design it. It would be a bird, to symbolize Jessie's true passion—the passion I'd wanted to encourage her to follow after that visit to New Jersey a year before but had never gotten the chance to. We'd get the tattoos later, Laura and I decided, after I moved to town, because I didn't want to have to avoid getting mine wet in the middle of summer—there was still swimming to do.

Meanwhile, I began to see Jessie everywhere in Provincetown. I'd begun talking to every bird I encountered, especially the ones that landed close to me, who looked at me directly before flying away. Of course there were seagulls, all of them Jonathan Livingston, or descendents of, and terns and the protected piping plovers. I saw Jessie everywhere and found the comfort I needed in knowing she had never actually left me and never would. When I saw the birds, I felt like Jessie was telling me, "Stay, you belong here, live the life you have, there's no need to check out early." That had been her phrase, "check out." And as much as I'd been jealous of her checking out, as much as I'd thought of a thousand ways to die since that phone call, now I was staying alive for her because that's what she'd want. The birds told me so. It's really hard to want to "check out" when your best friend, your soulmate, is whispering to you through every feathered creature to stay alive. Jessie was everywhere.

It was now nearing the middle of July 2005, and I decided that until I came back to Provincetown in September, my best plan would be to go back to my sister's. I had two trips to California in July and, again, my sister's proximity to both Dulles and BWI made staying with her convenient. Meanwhile, Titan was moving forward with plans for my future. The last of my four contracted films for 2005 would be *Spy Quest 2*. (There was even talk of a third in the series pending the reception of the second.) Once again, Titan wanted to keep me happy and to help me push my sexual boundaries. They were going to give me the gangbang I really wanted. This time, instead of the scenes in *Manplay 18* and *Alabama Takedown*, where everyone was fucking everyone else, I was going to get all the dicks. I wanted to be tag-teamed by one guy after another. Titan was already looking for a group of co-stars with big dicks but smaller hands, because I also wanted to get fisted in *SpyQuest 2*.

Meanwhile, Titan continued to promote me as their new exclusive. My rise wasn't simply luck; it was a part of a methodical and well-planned campaign by the company. I was getting interviewed by a number of porn websites, and Titan had got me the cover of *Men* magazine for July. And I was prominently featured on the cover cases of all my movies. It was a heady experience. I'd like to say I was keeping my ego in check, and while that's hard to do when you feel like you're riding a rocket, the underlying issues of loss and self-destruction were there the whole time. Those heavy feelings were dormant when I was clean and sober, but all it would take was a drink and I'd slide to the dark side.

I was also aware while in Ptown that I'd become a bit of a star in the gay male world. Eyes would dart in my direction and friends would whisper to one another as they recognized me walking down Commercial Street. At the local leather bars, The Vault or Macho Bar, I'd be standing alongside the other patrons while they watched me fucking or getting fucked on the video screens hanging above. I enjoyed the attention, the knowing stares, the hard dicks I'd see pushing against jeans as guys turned to show me what they had in the hopes of bagging the guy they saw on the screen. But at the same time, I still didn't know how to interact with the public in places like that and I'd usually last just a few minutes before discomfort made me leave. I wanted the desire and lust, but I still felt like I was faking my confidence and, after that first drink, I'd feel utterly alone, lost in the crowd. My mind would immediately think of how, when I was high, I felt like the life of the party, my appetite voracious and insatiable.

My first of the two trips to California was for a new deal Titan had secured with a chain of hotels. They wanted me to be the face of the campaign. Through a short video spot, I'd lure hotel guests into watching the on-demand porn available on the hotel's TV network. But money was becoming an issue for me, as much as I wanted to pretend it wasn't, so I set up an escorting job for the first night in L.A. the day before filming.

I hadn't used meth in weeks and I had no intention to, which was how I started every porn-related trip to the west coast—with the best of intentions. But when I arrived at the apartment of the guy who hired me, I was immediately offered meth. It wasn't in me to say no, the pull of meth was so strong. So I got fucked while high and then purchased a stash from him to take back to the hotel, where I ordered in several more guys to fuck me that night. No condoms, just drug-fueled bareback sex. At this point, it wasn't just that my inhibitions would fall to the wayside when high, it was that getting fuck without condoms was no different than the nights I spend drunk and burning myself in college. It was another act of self-harm, and I was in a place where my darkness was catching up to me. Self-harm had always been and continued to be a coping mechanism that provided a sense of control and comfort.

By sun-up, I was still tweaking and horny, so I found another couple I could have sex with before heading to the shoot. We ended up in a bathhouse. I eventually headed back to the hotel to clean up and then got to set. I don't know how I managed to get through filming, but my sheer determination and ability to act sober while coming off a high was still remarkable, and I did just that. Except for my profuse sweating, I don't think I gave any clue that I was exhausted, crashing, still horny as fuck and out of my mind. It was literally a 15 second spot. I'd memorized the two lines, I took their direction, and I finished the job. Then I slept through the night and got on the plane back to Virginia the next day.

Two weeks later, I was slated to do an appearance after Dore Alley, an outdoor leather and fetish fair in San Francisco. The event was sponsored in part by Troy Anicete, Mr. San Francisco Leather 2003, who had created the leather gear for *Horse* as well as my custom leather pants for *Spy Quest*. I'll admit, the thought of even going to Dore Alley, Folsom Street Fair's little brother, made me nervous—it's true name, after all, was Up Your Alley. I could have sex on the set, where I felt like I was playing a role, or in a bathhouse, at a rest stop and on meth, obviously, but being leathered up and watching guys having sex in an open public-venue free-for-all made me feel inhibited. Even after 13 months of exploring who I was sexually, and as much as I wanted to be the guy who took any dick put before me, I was jealous of guys who felt free enough to have sex out in the street.

Fortunately, Brian Mills went to the Dore Alley with me. We walked around and chatted with the many guys there who Brian knew, but as much as I wanted to let go, watch or even have public sex like some other guys there, I just could not. Overall, I just felt awkward.

And yet, upon leaving Dore Alley, all I wanted was to have hardcore, base and animalistic sex. For months, often while on meth, I'd been watching the 2004 Treasure Island Media porn video *Dawson's 20-Load Weekend*, featuring a hot young bottom named Dawson (who went public with his HIV-positive status shortly after the film came out) taking load after load with no condoms. The film was a huge hit, as well as controversial, with some gay activists saying that it was glamorizing unprotected sex. (This was still several years before the HIV prevention regimen PrEP widely repopularized bareback sex among gay men.) I saw Dawson as a mythical demi-god, half-man and half-creature, who drew men in and let them pillage him, cum in him and fuck him mercilessly while he begged them for more.

I wanted to be Dawson. And I found that wearing leather was like wearing a magical cloak that melted away any of my remaining inhibitions. That's how I felt after leaving Dore Alley, so after I spent a few hours with escort clients mainly talking, because that's what they wanted, I got on the sex hookup site Manhunt and found a source for meth. I spent the night in the Castro with a guy who gave me what I wanted for eight hours, even if it was only one dick. The next morning, I boarded my plane for the East Coast in nearly the same state of fatigue I'd had weeks before—only this time I was only crashing from meth, not seroconverting.

Believe it or not, I was feeling pretty good at this point in my journey. I felt connected to Jessie and to Provincetown, and before my two trips to California, I'd been clean for three weeks. In meth circles, users would say that it was okay to use only once a month, which I'd conveniently cut back to three weeks.

By now, it was early August, a month away from my moving to the Cape, so I entered what I saw as another necessary three weeks of not using. I managed to do this even though I stopped off in New York City for some escorting jobs. I could've been more successful at escorting had I made an effort to promote myself more on Rentboy and other such sites. But enough men managed to find me via my website.

Overall, I think I was a good escort. I was clearly good at fucking and I knew how to fulfill anyone's desire. But I also think my clients saw something in me that was appealing beyond sex, based on my interviews and blogging. They saw me as authentic and "not just a pornstar." So many of my clients wanted to talk as much as they wanted to fuck. What they got with me was someone who listened, who asked them questions about their lives and who was genuinely interested in their stories. I gave them sympathy and empathy, encouragement and support, a feeling of acceptance. I actually cared, and even if I was expensive, I gave them an emotional outlet they couldn't find elsewhere. One guy just held me. One guy painted a portrait of me. I was therapist, friend and lover, even if only for an hour.

Chapter Nineteen

⌄

L abor Day was fast approaching, so I headed back to Lancaster to gather some of the belongings I'd left with my mother and stepfather in preparation for my move. I'd spent the month of August clean, but now my brain, demanding meth, told me it was time to use again. Besides the short stay in D.C. with Johannes in June, I'd over the past year made a small group of party friends in that city. It had started the previous fall, when I was attending a National Migrant Education conference for my consulting work for Vermont's Department of Education. Initially, I'd simply had a few hook-ups via Manhunt, a couple of blow jobs to professionals on their work break. This was when I'd had my first experience of what it feels like to get cum in your eye; I'd quickly developed symptoms, similar to red-eye, that burned for days. The guy who shot cum in my eye worked in the Capitol—and also introduced me to Patrick, a lawyer with whom I soon had occasional meth sessions. As I initially had with Andrew, I felt comfortable with these job-holding men who gave the impression that they could handle their meth use.

But I was also finding that the usual conversations about HIV I'd have before sex were fading away. Early into my porn career, I'd naively assumed that, while discussing HIV, men who were employed and looked "healthy" and tested regularly would be honest and open about their status, as I tried to be. I didn't feel it was such a big deal to have condomless sex with these guys, as long as we'd had that conversation and they didn't cum in either my mouth or ass. But once meth came into the picture, sex with one man turned into two, then into a small group. The more meth and the more men I had, the more friends of friends of friends who joined the party, the less likely it became that I, or anyone, would initiate the HIV conversation before fucking. And despite my recent serious flu, HIV wasn't in my mind. Despite the amount of condomless sex I'd had since Andrew told me he was positive and I'd subsequently tested negative, I still hadn't been tested again. That meant, I'd later understand, that I'd arrived in D.C. highly infectious, just shortly after transmission, when the virus is raging in the body before it settles down to a baseline.

In preparation for filming *Spy Quest 2* soon, I took a mail-in test before heading to D.C. Back then, results took days, so I didn't expect to get them until after the Labor Day weekend. In D.C., Patrick and I marathon partied with a small group. It was unsafe sex—exchange of fluid, watersports, fisting, the whole meth experience. The morning after, it was just Patrick and I who watched on TV Hurricane Katrina's devastation of New Orleans. Then we smoked and fucked again. This wouldn't be the first time I was high out of my mind during significant moments in history, including the Boston Marathon bombing in 2013, the shooting down of the Malaysia Airlines plane in 2014 and the January 6th insurrection of the Capitol in 2021.

Before going back to Provincetown to start my seasonal rental on Cottage Street—coincidentally named Kensington Gardens, the name of the street where Henry and I had found shelter in London 20 years before—I went to my mother's to pick up my belongings. Almost as an afterthought, I called to find out my HIV result. I was distracted, gathering my toiletries, expecting an all-clear.

But it wasn't. This was a national HIV testing company, not a super-sensitive gay community center, so the gentleman on the other end of the line said, with all the emotion of a robocall, "Your result came back positive." There was an awkward pause in the conversation as I took a beat to say 'ok' and then another awkward pause as I waited for some form of comfort to come through the phone, some words of advice or reassurance. It didn't come. The voice didn't offer anything so I simply said, 'thank you,' and hung up.

I stood there in my old childhood bedroom, my bags packed, key in hand. *It had happened. I'd done it.* Honestly, that's all I could feel at the moment, three minutes of shock after which I went downstairs and said goodbye to my mother as if my life hadn't just done a 180. I faked the smile I'd so expertly mastered all my life and started driving east towards the Cape.

I could feel myself splitting on that drive, but this time purposely so. Ignore, suppress, dismiss, diminish, move on. Protect myself at all costs. This was too much: the loss of Henry, the triggering of old trauma, the self-destructive desires and actions that followed, the growing addiction, Jessie and my desperate need to join her. Now, on top of all that, I knew I had HIV coursing through my body.

But on the other side, I was driving towards light: Provincetown, healing, creative inspiration, a sense of belonging, purpose, home. I was exhausted, so utterly exhausted from the past year, from the years leading up to the last year, from the decades of endless ups and downs. Again, it was the perpetual dichotomy: the dark and light, the depression and the grandiosity and me trying to find mental and emotional balance, to reach the center of the seesaw. I was rising fast in my career (the light) and falling equally fast in my personal life (the dark). At times over the years, I'd managed to find my footing between extremes, gently rocking myself back and forth over the center, where I felt my most authentic. Life felt better in the middle. But then all it would take was a trigger, a brief memory, feeling or thought, and seeds would grow into invasive, choking and potentially deadly weeds, wrapping themselves around me and pulling me toward depression, mania or both.

Driving Interstate 78 between Allentown and Morrisville, New Jersey, I told myself that when I got to Provincetown, I'd get a confirmatory HIV test. Those mail-in things had to have a high percentage of false positives, I convinced myself.

At some point on the road, I called Andrew, thinking that he would know what I was going through and empathize. But when he picked up, he actually asked who was calling, indicating that he'd deleted my number from his phone. And once I told him the news, he gave me a non-reaction. He didn't say anything other than an "ok," and while I wanted to believe he couldn't talk because perhaps he had found another job and was at work, it felt as though I was a random stranger to him and that he was wondering why I was calling to tell him in the first place.

This left me hurt, baffled and, once again, feeling that I cared too much. Even through the dysfunctional haze of meth, I was still drawn to people, offered too much of myself, and then believed when I left them that I'd given them a gift they would carry with them for life. I didn't know that such thinking was rather arrogant and narcissistic, as was my idea that my stamp on people was nothing but positive. It took me time to realize that I might've actually hurt Andrew with my passive-aggressive chilliness the last time we'd seen each other, rather than having lovingly but firmly told him I couldn't see him again in the first place. I was blind to my own selfish and dark side.

On the rest of my ride to the Cape, I came to accept that my positive HIV status was not only likely true but of my own doing. I even wondered if I'd let myself be exposed to HIV because it would be the easiest way to die (even as I knew, on some rational level, that not going on treatment and letting myself advance to AIDS would actually result in a slow and horrible death, far from an easy one.)

But also on the drive, I thought about how I'd jeopardized the porn career I'd established. Despite the new trend in bareback porn, Titan was very much a 100% condom, safe sex company. Even if condoms were used, I imagined, they wouldn't want someone positive on the set. Didn't even oral sex carry a tiny risk? (Not really, we've since learned.)

I wasn't ready yet to tell Titan about my status. I arrived in Provincetown, moved into my rental and looked up a place to get that confirmatory test.

In Provincetown, The Men's Health Project, the testing and outreach office of the AIDS Support Group of Cape Cod, was a tiny place, both an HIV testing site and a needle exchange. Behind a sliding door, in a cupboard cut in half by the sloped ceiling, an intake was done, risky behavior was discussed, and a rapid test was given. Unlike when I got my first result over the phone, I felt at ease enough to cry when the counselor gave me the second positive result from the rapid test. But there was a final test to take, the antigen test, which would be the true confirmation. By this point, though, I was resigned to the idea that the chance of two false positives was highly unlikely.

And so the counselor helped me think through what was to come once my positive status was confirmed. Who, including former sexual partners, did I have to tell? I'd been highly infectious for months, and I hadn't exactly been celibate.

Sure enough, the antigen test came back positive. I went back to the counselor at the support group and we went through my list of sex partners or at least the ones I remembered. My status would be reported to the state of Massachuesetts, he said, but self-reporting through sharing with my previous partners was important, he added. He provided the basis for the decision making process. We broke up the list into several columns: the "Of Course I'll Tell" column, the "Not Sure I Should Tell" column and the "I Don't Need to Tell" column. The last two categories could be divided further based on sexual acts weighed against the science. They were also influenced by whether I'd been paid for sex and whether it was meth sex. The counselor suggested that my escorting hookups had been relatively safe for the tops, not just because tops face less HIV risk than bottoms but because we'd used condoms. The counselor told me I could cross them all off the list if I wanted to, and I happily did.

We then talked about the hookups I'd had while partying. Essentially it was up to me, the counselor said. I shouldn't blame myself for possible transmission, he said, because when people engage in drug-fueled bareback sex, everyone is responsible, no matter who might infect who. But if I actually had contacts, phone numbers, for the guys I'd hooked up with, he said, then I should consider telling them, because if I'd infected someone and didn't alert them to that possibility, to be tested themselves, then HIV would spread.

But I also felt that telling them was the moral thing to do. And so, I called Patrick, with whom I'd spent Labor Day weekend partying. The initial call was cut and dry: I told him I'd just found out I was positive and that he should get tested.

But the second call, when Patrick called me back to tell me that he, too, had tested positive, would haunt me for years. I don't remember the words, but I remember feeling his pain. It was pure anguish, the anguish of someone who felt his life was over. Initially his crying tore a hole in my heart. I had done this to him and I was willing to take the blame he was directing at me. I didn't understand, he said. He was a lawyer from a distinguished D.C. family—one that would never accept his HIV diagnosis. His life was ruined, he told me, and *I'd* ruined it!

After that, there wasn't much more I could say, so I got off the phone with him as soon as possible. As much as I felt he was in denial about his own part in it—after all, we'd barebacked together, at a time when either of us could've already been positive—I knew I needed to let him feel and say what he needed to, because he'd just gotten his results whereas I'd had some time between my own diagnosis and when I'd told him to accept that my diagnosis was my own responsibility.

Yet I could only be apologetic with him for so long before I parroted back to him what the counselor had told me, which was that we'd *both* engaged in drug-fueled unsafe sex. Weren't we both responsible? He countered by saying that I'd lied about how much unsafe sex I'd had over the previous year. And true, yes, I hadn't told him everything. I'd likely misled him into thinking I was more stable than I was. But it's not like we'd been dating. We'd essentially been two strangers making bad choices together.

It wasn't until after the call that I began to question the timeline. We'd partied only two weeks ago. Would an infection from me show up that quickly on a test? Maybe he'd already been positive that weekend and just didn't know it yet.

That may have been the last time we spoke. I'm not sure; I began blocking out a lot. I think I wrote him to further apologize. I think he wrote back saying I was a horrible human being, but perhaps he didn't and I've made that up thinking he deserved the last word. I used that last word, whether imaginary or not, as the impetus to change my behavior. For starters, going forward, I determined I would always tell my partners I was positive before we had sex.

$$\smile$$

That left me with the other phone call which needed to happen. I had to call Titan, or more specifically, Brian who had become a good friend. Strangely, I actually don't remember the call well, but I do have the follow-up email Brian sent, which contained more of what he'd said on the phone: He'd been, as I'd hoped, compassionate, understanding and comforting, and said that it didn't make a difference. They had other HIV-positive porn stars who worked for them, he said, and it didn't matter because everyone used condoms. (This was also about five years before a series of large studies worldwide confirmed that HIV-positive people who were on HIV meds and undetectable were basically 100% incapable of passing HIV to their sexual partners.)

While the conversation with Brian relieved me, especially in learning that I'd not ruined my career, it also left me in a minor state of shock: I'd honestly not thought that I'd been having sex with positive people on the set without having been told first. Sure, we used condoms and there was never any cum in the mouth when filming, but why wouldn't a safer-sex company disclose HIV status to scene partners? In retrospect, I can understand that, admirably, they had a status-neutral policy: as long as everyone was using condoms then it didn't really matter who on set was positive or negative.

But I was still in a zone where I needed to place at least some blame on someone other than myself, because I felt so stupid. (I could even hear my father calling me that, telling me I should've known better.) So I told

Brian I felt duped by Titan for not letting me know about the other actors' status. And once again, he responded with nothing but professionalism and understanding. He offered an apology for not having discussed these things.

Perhaps he knew that his gentle response would quickly melt away my righteous and not very well-founded anger. He was right. After the exchange, I was left with just my own excuses which, once scrubbed of all the external blame, didn't hold up. Rather than assume there were no positive men on the set of my first film, I could've asked about that before I started filling out paperwork. And off-set, I could've not engaged in behavior I knew damn well wasn't safe. Just as my porn career hadn't turned me into a meth addict, it didn't give me HIV either. That was all on me.

So I resumed my commitment to changing, to doing the right thing and becoming more responsible in my own life. And for me, that meant I insisted from then on that all my scene partners be told my status before they showed up on set. It was important for me to know they were given the facts and a choice—a choice that, regardless of my own behaviors, I felt like I hadn't been given. Brian commended this choice, which I needed to hear—to know that there was still good in me.

The next person I called to tell was Henry. "You didn't do this," he told me. "The disease did." Maybe he said that because he was scared of what I'd do if he made me feel guilty and self-hating over the diagnosis, but at any rate, his words gave me great comfort for a long time to come.

With September coming to a close, and despite having adhered to my rule of not using meth for three weeks, I was a total wreck waiting to happen. I'm not talking about a car careening headfirst into a concrete barrier. I'm talking about a bullet train that's jumped the rails and is in a mid-air arch to the bottom of a deep ravine. Three weeks off meth wasn't enough to dull its power; inside, I was a pressure cooker just waiting to blow. I didn't know it, but I was about to embark on a 15-month period that, years later, a therapist would simply stare at me in shock as I recounted it. At the time, I was so dissociated I didn't even know how bad it was. I was alone, without other people to help me keep one foot in reality, and didn't know who I was any more. Of course, walking around Provincetown as fall set in, I pretended that I had it all together.

But really, I wanted to use, be abused, and hurt myself—again and again. My inner darkness tried to convince me that I didn't have the ability to change. Everything I'd felt when I first arrived in Provincetown, all the birds through which I spoke to Jessie, all the hope and optimism and faith in myself, was gone. Even with the kindness of Provincetown, the attention from fans and the press, the support of my ex, friends and Titan in terms of my HIV status, my guilt, shame and profound loss were like a sword I imagined sinking deep into my gut.

One of the people I felt the need to convince I was doing okay was my mother, so I invited her to visit so I could show her my resilience in the face of the loss of both Henry and Jessie. But once she arrived, the woman who, in younger years, had done "blow job" shots and held South African lobsters over her naked breasts for a photo now seemed visibly uncomfortable by the gay sexual energy in the streets of Provincetown.

She arrived during Mates Leather Weekend, when the town was full of randy guys in harnesses and chaps. As we walked around town, she didn't understand why I was shirtless, didn't understand the looks I was getting, and didn't understand why so many people seemed to know me despite my having moved to town just a few weeks before. The last night of her stay, she told me she was embarrassed by my display of overt sexuality. Even though I'd spent most of our time showing her the natural beauty of the beaches and the dunes, going so far as to take her plein-air painting along with Laura, the only thing she could focus on was her embarrassment of being seen with me on Commercial Street without my shirt on.

To hear this from her was shocking—she'd spent the previous decade proud of my accomplishments, my sobriety and my relationship with Henry. In retrospect, I can understand that visiting Provincetown where I had chosen to live was hard enough for her to fathom. She was my mother, and mother's spend a lifetime worrying about their children, something I couldn't understand. I was 37 years-old. When she was 37 years-old she had a 15 and a 17 year-old. Here I was in my mid-30's flaunting my sexuality as though I was in my 20's, something she had done as well at that age. What she couldn't understand, however, was that in some ways, I was in my 20's. Emotionally and sexually I was a young adult trying to find his way in a strange and wonderful world.

We proceeded to have the biggest fight of our lives. She seemed disgusted with me, and I, in turn, became disgusted with her. The woman who had initially protected me from my father's disgust as a child, who was once my hero saving me from his wrath, had somehow become him. And so my natural reaction, after minutes of devastating hurt, was to make her feel ashamed and guilty for the pain she just inflicted, to strike as significant a blow as possible. I confessed I had just found out I was HIV positive. But instead of retreating into remorse, she looked at me with fire in her eyes and said, calmly, "I wondered when that would happen."

She drove back to Pennsylvania the next day after asking, "How could you tell me that last night and then make me drive eight hours with no sleep?" Of course she was justified in asking me the question because my throwing my status at her was selfish, a bit cruel, and childish in the way I wanted to hurt her back for her hurting me. But given she'd yet to respond with what I felt would be an appropriate amount of out-wardly concern or compassion since I told her my HIV news, we seemed to have stepped back into an old pattern of behavior.

I knew she had it in her, but I hadn't seen this part of her since my breakdown in 1996. The first time she deployed this sort of counterattack had been when I was in fifth grade. We'd just moved back to Lancaster, her hometown, after spending a horrible winter in Buffalo—our reality check after South Africa. My parents' relationship was crumbling, having yet found relief with the neighborhood couple. I was yet again the new kid, feeling alone and disregarded, but she insisted that having a birthday party would solve my growing depression. I pleaded with her that I didn't want to have a party, finally saying to her, "I have no friends and you don't even know that—you don't even care." I then left for school. When I got home, she immediately asked me how I could say that to her, how hurt she was, and that I made her cry all morning.

I eventually learned that when I was in crisis, her guilt over what she had or hadn't done as a mother led her from compassion for me and instead to judgment of how I was making her feel. She knew her part in all of my issues, but having to face it directly was too much for her. Then again, this sort of reaction usually only showed up when I was struggling. If I appeared stable and happy to her, all was well, so I learned through high school and into adulthood to create a protective facade that would then become a real thing, a real person, and I'd eventually split. It might take me years for it to happen, but at some point the mask would fall off and I'd be in crisis.

When it came to the essential nature of our relationship, I was resentful at her for my dysfunction. In those moments of crisis, the ones that had root causes in what I experienced as a child, I never felt like my mother could get beyond her own guilt. While processing my deeper traumas eventually took over a decade of therapeutic work, I'd been able to as early as high school, but on a more superficial level, move from what had happened in my past and turn these things into fodder for a good story. When life became too much, however, and I went into a significant crisis, I just wanted unconditional support from my mother. But there was alway a roadblock in the way. Her initial reaction would always be: "I'm such a bad mother." In that simple sentence she'd shift the focus off of me, and I'd spend more time trying to tell her she wasn't a bad mother instead of having my needs met while in crisis.

When she left Provincetown, I tried to justify my reaction and my anger, but I was distraught by what had happened and my part in it. Nothing about her visit had been healthy. My intention of showing her how stable and happy I was had been destroyed by the person I'd become over the previous year. It's quite possible her trip was doomed from the beginning, because I was looking to explode at someone or something. I was an angry and hurt child. It turned out she was just the first person I'd attack over the next several months.

Chapter Twenty

⌄

After my mother's visit, which hit me hard, not only was I craving meth, not having used in three weeks, I also wanted to hurt myself, to be used and abused. I had to find the drug. All I had to do was go on Manhunt and look for guys looking to "party and play," or simply "PnP." Just seeing those letters sent a shock wave through my fingers to my dick, taking my cravings to another dimension. Anticipating that first inhalation off the glass pipe, that touch of someone's dick, the feel of it entering me, the shudder I'd feel in every cell that wouldn't stop for hours—it would all drive me crazy until I heard the knock on the door. Once my guest brought out the drug, I'd be immediately on my knees.

It wasn't hard to find someone who'd offer their stash to a porn star, and I used that. The off-season Provincetown PnP community was a relatively tight-knit group. All it took was connecting to one guy and I had access to a dozen. On some occasions, it felt like they were all in the master bedroom of my Kensington Gardens condo, taking their turns with me. The appeal of being used, of letting the rougher guys hurt me, was as addicting as the drug itself.

No one cared about my HIV status. Half of them were positive themselves and the other half felt completely comfortable having sex without a condom. Typically, we'd be surrounded by a sling, a glass pipe, leather gear, dildos, lube, Crisco—and a Treasure Island porn flick on the TV screen.

Once, while glancing at the screen while fooling around with a couple of guys, I noticed an actor who looked familiar. Then it hit me: This was the guy Titan had planned to pair me with in *110° in Tucson*. He was supposed to have been the construction foreman, the top, but Titan ended up replacing him with me because he'd gone AWOL. It occurred to me that maybe Titan couldn't reach or find him because he'd been in the thick of a drug addiction. I was connecting Treasure Island videos with my own drug use, so it made sense to me that Treasure Island videos were drug fueled productions, an unfair assumption but not illogical during my using. I was starting to recognize some 'what-ifs' that could happen to me if I spun too far out of control with my own addiction and disappearing might be one of them. I figured that was what had happened to this model.

What struck me was that I'd seen his name and face recently with the promotion of a new Titan movie. But there he was in a bareback movie, the line Titan had drawn in the sand. No actor who performed bareback with another company would ever be hired by Titan, they'd told me. But once again, perhaps I made an assumption in this regard in terms of the word "told." Perhaps it wasn't written in some formal company contract, but it was, at the very least, suggested.

Throughout an increasingly chilly October in Provincetown, I continued to use regularly. I'd party for 24 hours, crash for another 24 hours, then attempt to stay clean for the rest of the week by working on my website, blogging, knitting and trying to paint. This on-again, off-again life, with crystal distorting my mind even when I wasn't using, gave time a weirdly fluid quality, as if it were slipping by faster than usual.

Meanwhile, as the filming of *Spy Quest 2* approached, I started to get anxious about how I looked. I was still buff and ripped; meth helped with that, with its long periods of not eating. But I started to become obsessed with my face. Did I look worn? Would Titan be able to tell? My summer tan was fading and the circles under my eyes felt darker. As late October arrived, I tried to stop partying, promising myself to hit the gym religiously and use a tanning bed. I was successful and started to see more of my old self in the mirror, someone whose body and eyes appeared more healthy. But even so, even as I looked in the mirror, I knew the truth: I was an addict and a faker. I hurt people, was to blame for too much pain, and didn't deserve happiness. I tried to distract myself from the dark call of meth, roamed room to room in the sprawling condo. I started muttering to myself words of self-hatred: pathetic, loser, fat, stupid. I wasn't aware enough at the time to realize those were the words my father had used all those years ago.

The only writing I'd been doing was for my blog, and while some of it was good and was reaching people, the full-on book I wanted to write was elusive. I'd confused having a story to tell with being able to actually write it. My mind was all over the place, my addiction thriving, my yet-to-be-diagnosed bipolar disorder having a field day with my brain while I struggled to live alone for the first time.

I was painting, though, which brought some peace for the few hours I could concentrate. I'd continued to paint after leaving Pittsburgh, doing commissions here and there, but now I was making an attempt to capture scenes in Provincetown. As a watercolorist, oils and canvas were new to me, creating a learning curve which, rather than accept, I let feed my feelings of worthlessness. I covered an entire wall of the condo with canvases and large sheets of watercolor paper. They hung there the entire ensuing winter, splashes of color here and there but no completed work.

I was also knitting. After years of not having cable TV and simply spending nights by the woodstove in Vermont, I'd become a voracious knitter. Some fans called me "the knitting porn star," because I posted on my blog photos of me sitting shirtless, in the middle of winter, knitting away. I'd even knit and send fisherman caps off to some very dedicated fans.

As the November film shoot approached, I managed to get some clean time. Brian emailed prior to the shoot to assure me he'd spoken with my scene partners and they were fine with my HIV status. He again emphasized how admirable it was that I had insisted on telling them before filming.

But by this point in the year, I was too exhausted to take much pride in that. Mainly I felt lonely, angry, hurt, tired, frustrated. The novelty of being a porn star was fading. Sure, I was getting attention, emails and accolades, but I was still just a loner trying desperately not to be a loser. I was desperate for something to latch onto, to validate a deeper, more confident and soulful self.

The more I thought about Titan using that bareback pornstar I'd seen in the Treasure Island video, the angrier I became. The anger wasn't necessarily rational; it was certainly self-righteous. I didn't know what was happening in terms of Titan's professional relationship with this man. I sent what I thought was a clear and concise email to Keith Webb at Titan expressing my confusion over what they were doing, conveniently disregarding my own hypocrisy over the fact that I was barebacking left and right while still working with Titan (even if it was with condoms).

But Titan actually responded to me graciously, apologizing and admitting the discrepancy. They also went on to explain how this actor had been torn apart by his meth addiction—a familiar story in the gay porn world—but that he was now clean and attending 12-step meetings and trying to build a new life. They also said they believed in second chances. Lastly, they said they were starting a new campaign with the San Francisco Department of Public Health warning of the dangers of meth, and this performer would be the face of the campaign.

Second chances. I'd spent my life preaching it—to others. Call me a hopeless life coach or say that I had a messiah complex, but I'd always felt that if I could help someone believe in themselves enough to make positive change, then my own life would have purpose. I incorporated that message in all my blog posts and in conversations with friends, fans, and family. Even while partying, I asked people about their lives and they shared openly, meth being a truth serum of sorts. So I'd suggest, even with a glass pipe in my hand or a dick in my ass, that they start painting again, exercise, write, go back to school

So then how could I not appreciate what Titan was doing for this actor? Faced with Titan's response, with Keith's honesty and compassion, my righteousness again quickly morphed into shame and guilt.

As the filming of *Spy Quest 2* got closer, I realized I was going to run out of money soon. Escorting in Provincetown during the tourist-free winter wasn't an option, and *Spy Quest 2* was to be the last film in my yearly contract with Titan, meaning that I wasn't getting any more work until 2006. I attempted to negotiate with Titan an increased fee for this coming film, citing my growing popularity. Considering I'd pulled in less than $6,000 for the three films that year (*Spy Quest, Alabama Takedown and Cirque Noir*), I couldn't help but think I deserved more for this one.

Titan actually agreed to adjust my rate slightly, but barely enough to lighten my financial burden. The heat alone for my huge and drafty condo was approaching the actual rent, something I hadn't figured on when taking the lease. I'd always known that four films a year at $2,000 a pop wasn't going to make ends meet, but I'd loved the freedom of not worrying about finances after decades of such close attention to them. I'd been able to use credit cards for food and travel—but rent and heat was something else.

So Titan and I had the conversation: I needed to end the exclusive contract and start to reach out to other companies, I told them—and, perhaps because of my growing pushiness, as well as their growing sense that I wasn't as stable as they'd originally thought, they easily agreed. Brian even offered to connect me with other companies, some of which had already spoken to him about my availability. (This led to an initial conversation with the pornmaker-slash-drag-queen Chi Chi LaRue.)

I suppose in my gut I'd hoped Titan would ask me to remain as their exclusive and simply give me more money, but that wasn't the case. Even though I'd instigated the conversation, I couldn't help but feel a sense of abandonment. After the conversation, my goal was simply to stay clean, start looking better, nail the next movie—and hope I hadn't just destroyed my relationship with Titan.

Of all the films I made, I remember the least about *Spy Quest 2*. Between the haze of what I'd consider long-term meth use, even though it wasn't constant, and the mental deterioration from my losses and struggles over the past year, my memories of this movie don't have the same clarity as do the memories of all my other films. I do remember that it was in a new studio, and that Brian had to shave my back because I hadn't bothered to do it myself before arriving on set. This was a time before we had all these advanced man-grooming devices to buy from Amazon. There were no such things as shavers with handles long enough for a person to be able to shave his own back. But I had been able to jury-rig just that—a long back scratcher taped to a regular razor. Between almost being double jointed (yes, that's how I managed to get into all sorts of positions on the set), I could shave my own back.

I remember that I had a scene with Jake Decker in a sleek black Mustang–I think it was a Mustang. I remember sitting in the driver's seat with Jake standing over me but facing front. I remember opening the access zipper in the back of his leather pants so that I could rim him, and I remember it being incredibly hot. As for the other scene I shot, I actually don't remember a single thing about it. I think I may have fisted someone, since Titan and I had decided that, were I to get fisted, I might lose a part of my fan base for whom fisting was too extreme. I didn't get gangbanged. Overall, I think I remember so little of this film because, at the time I made it, I was so lost. It's not that I wasn't enjoying what I was doing. It had more to do with knowing, in my heart, I wasn't my best self and that I was letting everyone down including myself. I could feel myself squandering my draining potential.

I left San Francisco relieved that I'd made it through the filming without anyone mentioning that I seemed to have changed since the filming of the first *Spy Quest* back in March. But I can see it on the cover of the DVD when I look at it now. My eyes have no light or shine—they look guilty and ashamed. My smile, while still a smirk, was less true sexual confidence and more an attempt to look confident and sexy. To me I look lost. My dark side was winning, pulling me away from faith and confidence in myself.

I also don't remember much of that Provincetown winter of 2005-6. I know I spent some time with my family and that I went to Belize for two weeks. But I also struggled to pay the electric bill which was, in the coldest months, nearly $800. I partied with the core group of locals.

But I certainly remember something that happened that winter that would change my life for the next decade. I injected meth for the first time, which is called slamming. I can't and won't describe the intensity of the high because by doing so I'd be glorifying it, which is the last thing I want to do. At first I thought it was just a one-and-done that I'd forget about. But the memory of it was so powerful that it haunted me, and it wasn't to be the last time I did it—by far.

Chapter Twenty-One

⌄

The year 2006 felt like me at my worst, but ironically it also ended up being a whirlwind of exposure, publicity, and awards. Titan put me on the cover of their 2006 calendar and also gave me the month of June. There were numerous spreads, interviews and articles in different magazines. I was voted the fourth top porn star in the business by the readers of *Men* magazine, which wasn't bad considering how few movies I'd actually made. I was the poster boy for the GayVNs in magazine ads and even for the AVN (straight porn) expo.

Then, when the GayVN award nominations came out in February, I was nominated for Best Newcomer, Best Sex Scene and Best Threesome. I ended up winning Best Threesome for the trapeze double-fuck in *Cirque Noir* and soon after won Best Non-European Actor at the David Awards, sort of the European version of the GayVNs, and Porn Star of the Year for the Hard Choice Awards, yet another porn competition. While these accolades may seem obscure and perhaps somewhat funny to the general public, studio films were all there were at the time when it came to porn—a massive system employing hundreds of people—so to win an award was a big deal. There was no OnlyFans, or even iPhones, that could let virtually anyone try their hand at being a pornstar. The awards made me feel that the work I was doing was not only good but important, no matter how low I felt on the inside.

Then, sometime in late winter or early spring, I got a phone call that would again change my life. Michael Lucas, the Russia-born king of gay porn, whose films pushed the boundaries of what a porn film could be, asked me to be in a film—and I hadn't even reached out to him first! It felt like an offering from the heavens. Following his successful gay-porn remake of Roger Vadim's 1959 classic Les Liaisons Dangereuses, Michael Lucas was now set to film the a gay-porn remake of Fellini's 1960 La Dolce Vita—and not only did he want me to star in it with him, he was offering me residuals for the film. I'd make a percentage of each DVD sold. That was virtually unheard-of among porn actors. In other words, just as I was about to fall completely to the dark side, Michael was offering me a career-changing opportunity and a chance to continue making a living in New York City. Like Henry said, perhaps I was charmed. I decided that the opportunity could be yet another beginning, a chance to do right and get back on track.

I would have a meeting with Michael in New York in early spring, but in the meantime, I had to get through the long, dark Provincetown winter. I went this way and then that, dark, light, up, down. I sought out locals with drugs, became attached to a few, using meth with them on a regular basis. I'd gone from trying not to use it for three weeks between sessions to struggling to get a week or 10 days between sessions. But I tried; I never stopped trying to curb the use. I'd rarely party for more than one night and into two nights when, having started at night the first evening, I'd use through the next day into the next night until crashing 36 hours later.

On the lighter side, I'd also hang out with Laura and her gang who provided me with what felt like honest friendship partly because they didn't want anything from me sexually. They gave me support for my creative endeavors. I began to feel like I belonged in Provincetown outside of its drug world. One thing I did that winter to maintain some sanity was start listening to music again, which I'd stopped doing. I began to sing again. I brought my keyboard with me on my last trip back from Vermont and started to play again, posting videos on my website and getting attention for being not just the knitting porn star but the singing porn star. I rekindled my high school obsession with Linda Rondstadt and Nelson Riddle's 1980s albums of standards, wandering through my castle of a condo and belting out every single word in perfect lip synch. I knew these three albums by heart and had piano music for all three of them. And while I would cry through a mournful song and dance through another, the ear worm that dug in those weeks was "Straighten Up and Fly Right," the story of the buzzard and the monkey. I would straighten up and fly right from now on, I told myself. And I did—maybe not completely straight or right, but more in control than before.

In early spring I went to New York City to meet with Michael. I found the door to his office tucked into a sidewalk of construction scaffolding and made my way up. I met a few staff, tried to be nice and charming, then Michael ushered me into his office. We shook hands, embraced, kissed, then had a deeper kiss followed by my touching his hard dick through his pants and finally dropping to my knees with his cock in my mouth. It wasn't coercive at all. Michael was gorgeous, sexy, powerful—and had a beautiful dick. Of course I wanted to service it. I made him cum, then we talked business. Michael had a reputation for being a bit of an egomaniac—perhaps not surprisingly, being the king of Gay Porn—but the two of us instantly hit it off. He took me under his wing, and I couldn't help being a bit awed and infatuated with him. He made me feel special, not just sexually, but as a person.

As for New York City, I knew my way around as a tourist but that was it. Michael happened to live right across the street from where I was staying on 23rd St. in Chelsea, so over the following months I was there regularly. He'd invite me to gatherings, easing my discomfort and introducing me to the people I should know. He wanted me by his side; I believe he genuinely liked me. And I liked him, regardless of how dissimilar we were. Essentially, I was his country mouse to his city mouse. He was about flash and custom tailored clothing and I shopped at T.J. Maxx. I spent much of my time trying to please people, and he seemed to walk through life not feeling compelled to do so. He demanded and expected of others and I asked without expectations. Our dissimilarities seemed to fit like yin and yang. I also liked NYC. Unlike San Francisco, where I felt like a child exploring a fabled city, in New York City I felt quickly at home. I wondered if I might be able to build a life in both places: the city and Provincetown, two Ithakas where I'd finally find a true home within myself.

During that short visit, we had a shoot to get some stills for the company. Michael had said they were just going to take a couple of pictures, but it actually was a full photoshoot to promote me as a new Lucas model. I was grateful I'd stayed clean and looked pretty good. The photo series was very fifties, with me in a light-blue tailored crooner jacket and thin black tie, sitting on a sleek, low mid-century leather couch. I could have been Frank Sinatra. They shot me clothed, then partially clothed, then showing off a hard-on and my ass. Fortunately, the young guy in charge of wardrobe stepped up to be a fluffer, which I appreciated because, unlike with Titan, no Viagra had been offered.

While I didn't especially like my overdone makeup, the photos turned out to be among the favorites of my career. I loved the environment of the shoot, the large open studio, the sound of car horns and New York City traffic coming through the open windows, the smell of the streets, the fluffer's mouth encouraging my erection, the sound of Michael's distinct and sexy voice from behind the camera. But what I loved most was the relationship I felt I had with Michael, even a few weeks before we started actual filming.

⌄

After the still shoot, I headed back to Provincetown and focused on my body in preparation for filming *La Dolce Vita*. My character was Preston Connors, a wealthy intellectual, impeccable in dress and with an affinity for barely legal young men. Appealingly to me, I'd be actually acting as much as having sex. I'd have poignant dialogue, moments of thoughtful reflection, an admission of guilt for an imprisonable crime, regret, acceptance—and then a final scene of being arrested for having sex with a minor. It was a thrilling concept for me. It was taking porn into the realm of cinema. I loved the idea of playing a role where the character had motivation, goals and a tragic flaw.

While waiting for my trip to NYC to film, I was again contacted out of the blue. David Guertin, a theater producer, had discovered that I could sing and asked if I wanted to join the cast of the iconic New York City show *Naked Boys Singing* to headline a short run off-Broadway. Along with doing several ensemble numbers, each member of the cast had a featured song. Mine would be "Perky Little Porn Star." I couldn't have been happier. I was still blogging at this point, attempting to build up more fans while creating the persona of an artist, someone trying to distinguish himself as being on a spiritual journey of self-exploration. I'd hated myself just weeks before, had pictured myself with a liquor bottle in my hand and a bungee cord around my neck, but now another second chance was at my door and I was rebounding.

I also started to believe once again that I had a superpower of helping and healing others. I thought that by blogging I'd connect with people and perhaps give them a glimmer of hope that they could change their lives if they wanted or needed to. That meant offering all of myself up to the public—the knitting pornstar, the painting pornstar, and the singing pornstar. Being in a show off-Broadway was a part of a lesson I could share with others, an example of taking chances and embracing opportunity. I quickly said yes to his offer of joining the cast for a short run.

Once again, I could hear Henry's voice saying that my life was "charmed." How was all this happening? Was it a gift from the universe, a sign saying, "You got this…you are someone….you are a nice guy"? Was it a test of recovery, a gauge of my desire to step away from the drug life? Was it an opportunity to convince myself that I was balancing successfully on the seesaw I called my life? I settled on it being yet another chance to test my strength, to straighten up and fly right, but mostly to walk into fear and through my insecurities. It was a yet-explored road in my current quest, so of course I took it.

Even having been to New York City several times, I'd never heard of *Naked Boys Singing*. But I heard "naked," "boys" and "singing" and figured I could do it. It was a dream come true: twenty years after first stepping on the stage in middle school and dreaming of going to New York to join the theater, I was about to be headlining an off-Broadway musical at the New World Stages.

I had to audition first, which initially didn't faze me. I could sing. I may have missed seeing a decade and a half of Broadway shows outside of *Les Miserables*, but I could still belt out a classic—perhaps something from Ronstadt and Riddle, I told myself. But the idea of dancing was like waiting to walk into a blazing fire of humiliation, because I couldn't dance. I was a klutz, *doplic* as we said in Pennsylvania Dutch. But, I told myself, I still had to try.

We timed the audition to take place during the filming of *La Dolce Vita*. New York City took on an even greater appeal and magic in those weeks. I felt like I belonged, like I was bushwhacking away much of the weeds that had begun to strangle me the previous fall and winter. I was easily slipping back into a persona of outward confidence. I decided to once again lock away my feelings, my memories and everything bad that had happened over the previous year and a half. I tossed the key down a storm drain.

The New Worlds Stages theater on 50th St. and Eighth Avenue was a newly renovated three-stage venue for off-Broadway shows, a former movie theater, and a place where many productions moved once their run on Broadway ended. *Avenue Q* and *Jersey Boys* eventually landed there. *Naked Boys Singing*, a fixture in the Village for years, had relocated there a year before. I was taken aback when I saw the theater for the first time. It wasn't some tucked-away old building that had seen better days. It was modern, sitting between tall office buildings with an outdoor plaza adjacent to its doors. While there was no marquee as such, there was still a large *Naked Boys Singing* Poster surrounded by globes of lights. If I landed the role, I'd be performing next to several other shows, including one with Eartha Kitt. Mandy Patinkin had recently given a solo concert at the venue. Yes, *Naked Boys Singing* had a reputation for being a gay show, light and silly and written for Village audiences, but still, here it was, up with all the other theaters.

David and I met the musical director on stage at his piano. I hadn't bothered preparing anything from the show to sing—another sign of my naivete, ignorance, arrogance, or a combination of all three—so I sang Linda's Nelson Riddle arrangement of "Bewitched, Bothered and Bewildered." When they asked if I knew anything upbeat and current, I had to admit that I wasn't really up on contemporary musical theater. So they took me through a few pages of music from the show, which I quickly got under my belt. (I could read music, which helped.) They told me—unenthusiastically, I thought—that I had a "nice" voice.

Then we moved to the dancing part. Right up front, I confessed my utter lack of ability. The director walked me through a few movements. I listened, watched, and took directions.

And, much to my surprise, it was enough. They cast me and said that my run would start in October and go for three months. My rehearsal time would be the two weeks prior. That felt scant to me, but the company wasn't going to give me special treatment. Two weeks was the norm to learn a role for an already running show, and that's what I would get.

Meanwhile, I focused on *La Dolce Vita*. I was in several non-sex scenes, which we filmed first. One was a fully produced fashion-show scene where Michael and I sat next to each other in the front row, talking and pointing to either the clothes or the men strutting on the catwalk. The casual vibe between us wasn't hard to pull off because we were becoming friends. I remember being backstage beforehand, though, in the flurry of models, clothes and dressers, and feeling unbelievably out of place. I was grateful again for Michael's continued personal attention.

Then there was another non-sex scene, a party at my character's home (filmed in Michael's real home) where I saw for the first time the character played by Jamie Donovan, the young man with whom I would be filming a scene. In a later scene, towards the end of the movie, I'm with Michael, discussing mistakes I'd made, waiting for the police to come arrest me for having sex with a minor. This was the scene for which I won Best Supporting Actor. In it, Michael enters my home and asks what happened and I explain, nearly in tears, that I had a problem (younger men), that I didn't know Jamie was underage, and that I needed help.

I also had some lines about Daedalus flying too close to the sun, which was an all-too-appropriate reference to that hero's journey I felt I was on. Throughout the scene, I channeled my current rise, fall and further rise in the porn business, my own feelings of indestructibility and subsequent self-destruction from addictive behaviors. Describing it now, I imagine that if you've never seen the film you might be scoffing to hear of quality acting in a porn flick, but twenty years later, I'm still struck by the depth of my emotion in that scene. I was truly in angst, both as my character and as myself.

The last non-sex scene was me being led out of the building in handcuffs and put into a police car, with paparazzi snapping away. Looking back, I feel that even this one-minute clip holds a level of emotional intensity. The shame and guilt on my face is real. I was in the public eye, both in real life and in the movie, being captured on film and video, and all I felt deep inside was guilt and shame. I was broken and about to be locked away—and I distinctly remember feeling a moment of premonition, as though this were Circe's warning, an alert to the danger to come.

I had one sex scene in the film that was a part of the actual story line—my scene with Jamie Donovan. Filming took place in Michael's walk-in closet in the lower level of his home. My character had, in the party scene, asked Jamie to join him downstairs for a tour. I proceed to seduce him surrounded by Michael's impressive wardrobe. I'd had my scenes with younger men before, including the incomparable Blu Kennedy, but this scene with this beautiful boy was all about intimacy and affection. I was beside myself with pleasure and sexual excitement.

There had been so many things I'd been able to explore over the past two years, from group sex to double-fucking, but having sex with someone this young and beautiful made me realize that, even at 38, I could be a daddy. Jamie the actor was well above legal age, of course, and the use of the word "boy" did not mean that he was a minor. In this context, it simply meant someone young and beautiful whom I wanted to take care of—or put on a pedestal to gaze upon, like a statue of David. I wanted to write him a love note, slide it into his school locker and wait around the corner to watch him read it. I wanted to let him know he would be okay, that he'd find a world where he belonged, where he could not only be who he wanted but could genuinely be loved. I wanted to give him everything I had hoped for as a young boy.

While rimming him was one of the most sensual moments of my career and clearly driven by sexual desire, I also wanted to be a gentle, loving father figure, to let him know he was adored. In reality, he was me—my younger self, or at least the part of my younger self that had been haunting me since South Africa.

It was on this shoot that I was also offered something I'd long heard about but couldn't imagine ever doing: Caverject, which is a drug you shoot into your penis to make it as hard and huge as possible. Up to this point, Viagra had always been sufficient for me—along with hormones, lust and the thrill of being on camera, of course. I'd always thought of Caverject as taboo—something that guys who used meth often relied on, because when it came to maintaining an erection on meth, Viagra just didn't cut it. Michael recommended it, so I decided to try it. It worked.

It was also only the second time in my life where I'd stuck a needle in myself, and while this certainly wasn't like shooting up meth the previous winter, it was similar in that the results were almost instantaneous. Getting that hard that fast fired all those same neurotransmitters in my brain equating needles to sex. At this point in my journey, I was addicted to speed, adrenalin, and the rush of a stimulant And, to me, drawing blood meant affection and comfort, the comfort my father gave me in my childhood when I'd fall, hurt myself and need stitches.

Then, at the end of regular filming, Michael brought up *our* scene together. It wasn't in the script, Michael explained, but it would be a bonus feature on the DVD. I don't know if this was an afterthought on his part or the plan all along, but Michael and I had created some serious chemistry over the previous weeks together. We both wanted to fuck the other, so it felt necessary and natural to do it on camera. Which we did, without dialogue and in his actual bed. It felt intimate and romantic, as though we were alone and simply enjoying ourselves. And we did. I also achieved yet another sexual milestone of my on-screen career: while on my back with my ass in the air, Michael pissed onto and into my ass.

Interestingly, a decade later, I had a fan who happened upon me in my gallery in Provincetown; he left and then returned with flowers for me, explaining, with tears in his eyes, how watching my scene with Michael had changed his life by showing him what intimacy with another man could be.

As my off-season rental in Provincetown was ending in May, I had to find other accommodations if I was to continue living there part time. So, as much as I felt I was doing well controlling my meth habit, I moved in with someone who was known to be, or at least had been, a drug dealer. I'd find myself doing this often in the future, attaching myself to drug dealers and giving up my body and pieces of my soul for free access to all the meth I wanted. It wasn't a far jump from taking money for sex. The summer sped by, my debt creeping ever higher, my partying sporadic. *Naked Boys Singing* was on the horizon. I swore to myself I would not fuck it up.

The summer of 2006 was also my first real experience with being the "lite" version of a celebrity. I would never be as famous as fellow porn star Johnny Hazzard, who also called Provincetown home during the summer, but I was certainly getting enough press to be recognized on the streets. I was on the cover of *Men* magazine that July and my videos were both being carried in the town sex shops and video stores *and* shown at The Vault and The Macho Bar. There's nothing quite like going into a bar, this time with friends, and seeing yourself fucking on the screen behind the bartender. Both Titan and Lucas were putting out the press, and when the two biggest porn companies promote you, you get noticed.

I decided I was famous enough to advertise and hold a benefit at the sex shop Toys of Eros for the AIDS Support Group of Cape Cod. The concept was that my fans would bring an item from racks in the shop to have me try on for them in the private dressing room. Two fans from Australia were vacationing in town. I offered to pick them up from the ferry in a motorboat and drive them across the harbor to the Provincetown Inn. They ended up being two of the few who came to the event. Another man fell so quickly to his knees after dressing me in a kilt that he got me all the way down his throat before I knew it. Hey, it was for charity, so I let him go at it for a few minutes.

I was also surprised that Johnny Hazzard stopped by; I still didn't believe someone like him would even know who I was. In all, about a dozen guys shelled out money—not a great take but not a bad one either. The experience helped keep my ego in check. It also got some attention from a magazine, whose name escapes me, that named me Porn Star of the Year in part because of the charity work I had done.

Playbill announced my upcoming role in *Naked Boys Singing*, so now I was getting attention for a new reason and via a different audience. There was a low-frequency buzz, part of which came from my continuing to build a fan base via my website. I had plenty of time that summer, so

I tried to write. I also set up my easel in the tiny attic bedroom in which I was staying. Regardless of where I'd drifted since leaving Henry, even in the thick of filming or drug-induced sex, my intention to live a creative life never went away.

Now I was about to do theater again after all these years, and while a part of me didn't want to give up thinking of Provincetown as my new home, it also felt like New York was where I was meant to be, in part because Michael had another film after *La Dolce Vita* on deck.

Chapter Twenty-Two

⌄

M eanwhile, my mother and step-father were wondering what I was doing for a living since my consulting work had ended over a year before. I truly don't remember whether she asked me, and if she did, what I said. It's possible I simply defaulted to saying I was waiting tables, it being a logical answer since I spent so much of my teen years working in restaurants. Our relationship had mended over the previous year after she visited Provincetown when I threw my HIV status at her. She had had time to process, to ask questions, and I provided answers that reassured her I was physically fine and would continue to be fine with medication. While a mother's worry never ends, I did my best to show her the stable and happy son I had been since Michael Lucas had pulled me from despair back in the previous winter. She may not have known everything that was happening, but she had the sense I was actually happy.

My father hadn't been a huge part of my life since we'd come back from South Africa in early 2005. He was present but not a part of my life outside of regular phone calls. He wasn't really occupying time in my head, at least consciously. He'd since retired to a private golf island in

South Carolina, so my contact with him was only by phone and email. He'd offered me support when Jessie died, and in the following months I did my best to be the son I thought I should be with my regular phone calls and my somewhat feigned interest in his golf life. The symbolism of our return to South Africa, father and son on a healing journey, slowly began to fade and was replaced by an inner turmoil I felt bubbling inside but couldn't name at this point.

⌄

I had done a masterful job of weaving my father's life story together in the previous decades in an attempt to find empathy for him, to see his perspective, and to find forgiveness. He was the cause of my suffering, yes, but there was a cause to his suffering as a child as well. Now as I write this, it makes sense. He makes sense. His priorities, his goals, his obsessions, his political beliefs, his treatment of me as a child all make sense. That perspective allowed me to eventually accept his behavior although I'm still working on forgiveness.

With both a younger and older sibling with cerebral palsy, my father grew up in a world of disability. Normal was a word to describe other families, not his. He was forced to step into a role of responsibility as a young child, forced to suppress any natural childhood need for attention. My aunt's and uncle's disability demanded extra help and attention (sight, hearing, walking were issues.) While a parent's affection is endless, there is only so much attention that can be given to each child. My father may simply have chosen to withhold attention from me, but his parents had a limited amount to give him in light of his sibling's needs.

The degree of their challenge wasn't great enough to be sent to special schools or institutions. Plenty of parents would have done that in the 50's but not my grandparents. I can only imagine their childhood. I can only imagine my father's lack of one. His was a hard-working blue-collar family from York, PA, where post-war modest living was enough, where factory work was enough, and where people like my grandparents had the guts to not just support their two children with disabilities, they changed the entire community. They were saints. They founded the Handicap Club of York and created a support system for others.

His parents were selfless, and by default, my father had to become selfless. Throughout his life his needs were put to the side even though my grandparents surely did their best. They had their struggles though; their life was hard and while my father refuses to believe addiction was an issue, there was a story when my grandparents got so drunk on Christmas Eve, they came home, passed out having never played Santa. Their three kids, aged two-six, awoke to no presents under the Christmas tree.

It's not hard to imagine the cruelty of children in the 1950's towards school mates who were different, and while my father has never shared just what it was like, he was literally in the middle. His sister was just two years older, his brother two years younger. I like to think he was by their side in every grade, standing up to bullies and cruel children. But perhaps he was simply embarrassed by them, doing his best never to be seen in their company. By the time he hit high school, he was football-player cool, and again, I like to think, a protector of his siblings, if only by default. You don't mess with a football player's siblings unless you want to come up against the entire team.

My father must have worked really hard to suppress resentments towards his entire family for what was a lost childhood. Once he left for Penn State, he spent the rest of his life trying to escape his family, first by getting my mother pregnant with my sister their freshman year to eventually moving his family 8000 miles away to the otherside of the world. He managed to permanently escape his family when he and I returned from our recent trip to South Africa and he fled to his new golf island home, six states away from where his parents lived during their ailing final years and where his siblings still live, his sister now in a home for cerebral palsy.

His desire to succeed, to fit into a society, one not filled by handicaps, dysfunction, scraping by, and selfless charity turned him into someone who demanded attention and acknowledgment in adulthood. To him, no one got a free ride. There were no charity cases. No one had a right to complain. There was no sympathy for anyone with issues, whether physical, mental or emotional, a direct path to landing in a political party that felt social services should be eliminated. All his resentment of the attention, funds, and sympathy attributed to humane social services was driven by the fact he hadn't gotten what a child deserves to get. He never had the normal he always wanted.

While I've already touched on my fear of my father as a child, it's the why behind his treatment that I'll continue to try to understand on my journey toward forgiveness. Of course the why is just a story I'm writing and offering to you, but it does make sense. By the time I was two-years-old, it was clear to him I wasn't his kind of normal, that I didn't fit the mold of what he wanted as a son. He was already living deeply in a pit of resentment towards his upbringing, towards my mother's parents, and eventually towards my mother herself. He was moody but not in a gentle Eeyore way. Now he had a son who also pulled attention, who was already an entertainer, but who was also too sensitive, who felt too much and therefore pulled even more attention.

His resentment towards life itself bubbled over into our home, and most of it landed on me. He transferred all of his anger and hurt towards me, his weird, awkward, girlish, crybaby, bed-wetting, goofy, Donald Duck-talking son. He intentionally tried to destroy any sense of self-worth or identity I was forming as a child. His ruthless mocking, bullying, and humiliation was the first impetus that caused me to split. I learned to dissociate early because he was so utterly cruel at times. He made me feel like I was the one with special needs, with a disability, with a handicap. He made me feel like I *was* a disability to him. I was the problem in his life, his embarrassment, and he was determined to fix me.

When my parents discovered I was gay my senior year of high school, my father walking half a block from where he lived two door down to confront me upon my return from St. Thomas where I spent Christmas with former employees of the Loft (my parents being either so naive or trusting they let their kid go to St. Thomas on his own), it was clear I was now even more disappointing, even less normal, and certainly more of an embarrassment to him. I didn't learn until later that he likely equated my being gay to his sister's short marriage in the 70's when a man decided a wife with cerebral palsy would make the perfect coat hanger upon which to hang his secrets in his closet of shame. My aunt and her new husband honeymooned on Cape Cod with the rest of the family, and it was my father who had to drag her new husband out of a motel room he booked so he could have sex with his boyfriend. I was going to be that kind of gay, the only gay he knew. I would bring him further shame.

He also resented kindness and people who were inherently full of life, those people who pulled attention because of their joy, people to whom other people were naturally drawn. He resented my mother because of this very thing. She may have been a princess as a teenager, but she had a light, a spark and a shine that seemed natural for people who grew up in her family and in her hometown. Her parents owned an ice cream factory; that sort of says it all.

As I got older and started to develop an identity despite him, his resentments continued to grow. He'd gifted us South Africa, given me perspective starting at the age of six, and as I discovered an understanding of how I fit into and who I was within a world of pain and beauty, he resented the soulfulness he saw in my eyes. I inherited kindness, compassion, empathy, love and joy for other people from his family and from my mother's family. It was too much for him. I was, to him, all of his family's dysfunction and resilience and all of their vulnerability and courage. I was their goodness and it felt like he loathed me for it.

My father's story, his experiences with growing up in a family of disability and the subsequent treatment of me as a child, both the cause of his trauma and much of my trauma, soon became an integral part of the next few months after filming La Dolce Vita and while preparing for Naked Boys Singing. It started when a famous NYC drag personality used the word 'retarded' in her act in public. She was a close friend of Michael Lucas who then, too, used the word publicly in describing the drag performer's act while lauding her for her show. I don't remember where I read Michael's words, whether it was a review of the drag performer's show online or some other article in a magazine, but when I read it, everything exploded in me. That turmoil triggered by my trip to South Africa, the turmoil of feeling less than normal in the eyes of my father as a child and teen, finally bubbled to the surface.

Since a child I had always taken the word personally, and that's exactly what I did again when Michael used the word. It was a tiny incident. It was one word. But that's all it takes sometimes for trauma to take over: eight letters, perhaps even less. I've learned since then that while there may be a difference between being hurtful, being mean and being a bully, a person scarred in childhood will often conflate all three. I was so angry I called Michael out on my blog. It was a gut-reaction, an emotional impulsive reaction to pain I couldn't define at the moment.

Even a decade ago, if a comedian, drag performer or any celebrity used 'retarded' in public, they might have been pulled aside after the show and told they crossed a line. Today they'd simply be canceled. Or they'd be elected president. In 2006, society wasn't there yet. As a culture we weren't yet protecting people from harmful words. I was beside myself with anger and righteous indignation at this incident because it hurt. With an aunt and uncle with cerebral palsy, I spent decades calling people out for the use of the term, and sadly, I still do because it's still necessary. The word deeply hurt. It felt like the same hurt I felt when my father had bullied me. It hurt even more because it came from a friend. It also offended me because my father's family had worked so hard to dispel the stigma of living with disabilities since the 1950's.

I suppose all my years of anger at people who used the word landed on Michael. It might not make sense, but a lot didn't make sense by this point in time. I couldn't bear when others called me names as a child, including my father, and I couldn't bear other people being bullied and hurt. I believe a piece of my inner child wanted to come out swinging and screaming, "don't hurt anyone with your words, please just don't hurt anyone!" I didn't realize I was actually begging mercy for myself.

With this incident several things happened. My past started to slowly choke me, the twisted weeds, the monsters, the voices, everything that ever hurt me came rushing at me. I also pissed off Michael. While I never intended to be cruel by calling him out, his revenge felt intentional. He went to Michael Musto and the Village Voice a few weeks later and decided to describe a sexual encounter Michael and I had off-set in our personal lives that had, essentially, a rather messy ending, 'messy' being the operative term. I had had sex earlier that day that included watersports. Suffice it to say I think I ruined his suit. He was graphic in describing the incident to Musto, all of which made it into the paper.

Michael decided to offer a story that was so humiliating to me, so much like the malicious attacks of my father, it became a part of my nose dive over the next few months. But I had played with the big boys, poked a hornets' nest and got stung, so I had no choice but to push my embarrassment aside and pretend it never happened. Michael and I never spoke of it; neither of us ever broached the subject.

The incident also made clear to me that my blog had become a powerful platform upon which to share my own feelings and vulnerabilities. I started writing about loss, about losing Jessie, about leaving my relationship with my partner and the devastation of both. I wrote about bullies, hurtful people, and I wrote about the joy in the world around me. I wrote about childhood and about my father, about being molested as a child and about becoming both HIV-positive and an addict. I sought to create a writing voice that I hoped combined humor, honesty, sexiness and soulfulness. Blogging became my attempt to salvage parts of myself, good parts, that I felt I'd been leaving behind.

For some time, I had been getting emails from fans telling me how some of my scenes, especially the erotic seduction of *110° in Tucson*, had changed their lives and helped them come to terms with their own desires. But as my blog posts got more thoughtful and vulnerable, so did the incoming emails. People weren't just pointing out how hot they felt I was or how accessible I seemed on screen or in my magazine interviews. Now, dozens of people were reaching out to me because they saw in my words something that touched them deeply.

Susan, a straight married woman from Iowa, wrote to tell me when her husband had died recently, she somehow found solace in my porn. Also, my writing about Jessie helped her get through her own loss. She ended up commissioning from me an oil painting of her deceased husband's favorite vacation location, the cliffs and rocks of a beach in Mexico. That painting now hangs above the mantle of her fireplace in the home she shares with her new husband. When I went to rehab, Susan emailed me every day for the 90 days I was there because she wanted me to know how important I was to her.

Jack, a teacher in Connecticut, reached out to me. His son had recently died in Iraq and he was going through a level of loss that I simply couldn't imagine. He also had another son with Down Syndrome, so my posts brought him comfort and support on two different fronts. Jack would come to stay with me several years later while I was working at a guest house in Provincetown; we're still in touch on Facebook, as I am with many people I met during my porn career almost two decades ago. (Sadly, a day after we last messaged on Facebook this past November when I asked how he was doing having recently had a foot amputated, he died. No obituary was released until just this May when I felt a similar shock of when I found Jessie had died weeks before my knowing.)

Chris, a licensed social worker from Buffalo, became like a brother to me. He was drawn to my creative journey and his encouragement through the years has been invaluable, so much so that he's a big part of why I wrote this memoir. When he comes to Provincetown each summer, he cat-sits for me while I go to New York City to see some of the shows he has recommended.

Arthur, a sober leather daddy from Minnesota, was drawn to me through my movies, but with the keen knowing eye of a fellow addict, he was able to see through my words the deeper hurt I was feeling. He expressed concern for me from the very start. He told me he could see how the look in my eyes was changing from movie to movie as I dug myself ever deeper into darkness. Even though his concern annoyed me at times, at other times I felt like he was the only person who actually knew what I was going through. He sends me cookies at Christmas and recently reminded me how important I was to him by sending an image of the wall in his house where photos of generations of his family hang. I'm tucked in there along with relatives and loved ones.

James, another gentleman who picks me up from the airport in Ft. Lauderdale when I visit, has a beautiful watercolor of me he purchased from an artist who had painted it while the artist was living in Provincetown. Through our connections to the AIDS Support Group, we connected and I modeled for him. James jokes that he thinks of me every day because the painting is above his toilet. He insisted that I include this section of this book where I talk about all the people I've touched over the years. I helped him come to terms with his sexuality, he told me, and he just recently trusted me enough to tell me that he wanted to explore anal play with a dildo for the first time in his life. I'm coaching him through the process.

All these people comforted me then and have supported me for nearly two decades. They've helped me come to terms with the disconnect between who they see me to be and what I think of myself. During some of my darkest days of addiction through the 2010s, they were the green lights across the water reminding me of the someone I wanted to be again.

As recently as this past summer, a gentleman and his wife in their late seventies came into my gallery, assisted by canes. The husband was quiet, the wife gregarious—but after they left, the husband snuck back in and told me he knew who I was from my past porn life and that he wanted me to know how much I'd helped him all those years ago because he'd been struggling with his sexuality. In his fifties, he told me, he'd desperately wanted a family, which to him meant marrying a woman. And he did—the woman, in fact, he'd slipped away from to come back to the gallery to talk to me. He revealed that my blogging had made it clear that I'd been having a rough journey back then, and he wanted me to know that I was the reason he'd gotten through his own tough time.

Unfortunately, while I desperately wanted to believe all these admiring fans who saw such good in me, my returning and growing moments of darkness were becoming more frequent and more intense to take their words as the gift they were. I saw the kindness and love they were pouring out to me as proof that I was as far from real and authentic as I could be at that point. Only I knew the truth: I was a selfish, cruel, self-absorbed and self-righteous meth addict. I wanted to blow myself up.

I moved to New York City in September, just before the two-week rehearsal period for *Naked Boys Singing*. I was at the height of my career; I had success, publicity, accolades and connections not only within the porn industry but now within the theater community, too. There was potential for so much more as well. Who knew what might happen if the three-month run went well?

I had to nail the show, though. It's fair to say that I work best under pressure. Throughout my education, I often waited until the last minute to attack major deadlines. (I wrote my master's thesis in three days.) I took the NBS rehearsals seriously, listened to the director, took his direction and practiced in front of the wall of mirrors in the place I was living. I had to learn how to dance, which reminded me of first learning to swim—a lot of flailing, embarrassment, gasping for breath, fear and doubt. I was clumsy, but sheer will and determination got me through. During one rehearsal, the director singled me out, saying, "Thank you, Spencer, for being the only one to take the note I gave yesterday and fixing the issue."

I enjoyed the compliment, but I also distinctly sensed that the rest of the cast didn't appreciate being shown up by a pornstar. I couldn't help but feel like they were saying to one another, "Who the hell does he think he is?" Whether they were or not didn't matter, and it's likely they didn't. What it felt like was that many in the cast had been in the show long enough that their investment in it had slipped; it was a job to them, a secure job providing much needed stability and income between their daytime gigs. To me it was so much more. I had something to prove to myself and everyone else, so I made sure I took every note.

Meanwhile, even as New York City was putting career opportunities in front of me, it was also opening me up to more men and more drugs, which I couldn't help but sample. 10 days before opening night, I overdosed on GHB, a drug that must be carefully measured, waking up covered in vomit with one of my sex partners, phone in hand, about to call an ambulance. But that didn't stop me from using more. Days later, I was up for two sleepless nights of partying, the Monday and Tuesday night prior to my first night on stage. I smoked meth, got fucked by at least a half dozen guys and got no sleep, yet still somehow managed to nail my first performance three days later. It was far from perfect, but no one expected it to be. Everyone was relieved that I'd pulled it off—especially me. I felt a relief so powerful I again couldn't help but think that the gods were on my side—and that I'd pulled off a miracle.

Several people I knew came to see me in my first performance in the middle of October 2006 including my youngest step-sister from Colorado, Laura, who came to opening night with her fiancé. Two best friends from high school, Jane and Carrie, drove in from Lancaster County. It was Carrie whose house was a favorite hang out in high school in part because of her father's massive collection of porn. Hers was a household where sex, at least the porn, wasn't hidden; entering her home felt safe especially during a time when I was coming out. It was Jane who'd introduced me to New York City in 9th grade and to shows including *The Fantasticks, A Chorus Line,* and *Sunday in the Park with George.* Michael Lucas was there, along with Randy Jones, the cowboy from The

Village People. There were fans and press. Looking today at photos from a post-show party we had, I think it's remarkable how healthy and happy I look, with a genuine smile on my face. That might've been due in part to the fact that, again, I'd gotten away with it, so I was exhibiting a sense of relief. But there was genuine happiness, happiness I felt I deserved on one hand and on the other didn't.

With five shows a week to crank out for three months, I now fell into the routine of a working actor in New York City. Having pulled off opening night, I convinced myself that I wasn't an imposter after all. Most importantly, I felt like I was back on the upward path that had appeared before me two years earlier, with that first email from Titan. After each show, the cast would hang out at the entrance of the theater to meet members of the audience who might want a photo. I was blessed to have existing fans of my porn come see me, some with whom I had already established an online friendship. Quite a few of these people are still in my life 18 years later. These moments were a blessing; seeing their faces, their excitement and then feeling their relief that while I may have been a pornstar, I was essentially just a nice guy who had sex on camera.

Then each night leaving the theater, I'd either take the subway or, when I was feeling more contemplative, I'd walk the 20 blocks home through the theater district down into Chelsea and acknowledge the opportunities and those blessings I'd been given and would feel a deep sense of gratitude. Life had given me something tremendous. I felt like I was in control, that I had a handle on my usage of meth, and that the show had the potential to lead to more opportunities. I was determined to stay on track, to excel, and to continue to forge a life in the city. But at least once or twice a week, I'd still get high and get fucked as much as possible.

Eventually I sought out a drug dealer to whom I could attach myself in a drugs-for-sex deal. My memory of this time in early December 2006 is vague. I was still managing fairly well through the shows even with using once or twice during the days the show was dark. If I felt guilty going into a night of partying, with a day or two of sleep before a show I arrived at the theater feeling stable and competent if not a little tired. I hadn't been showing up high, per se, since my run opened even if there might have been lingering drugs in my system. Only an addict would see it that way. One night, I accidentally kicked a stage light during my solo song, "Perky Little Porn Star." I stopped the song to start over. There were a few other embarrassing incidents like that which I casually brushed off, so while I may have been trying to convince myself I had it all together, I wasn't exactly at the top of my game.

The truth was that by December I wanted to stop using and was beginning to understand I couldn't. When the thought of meth came into my head, I'd end up using within hours. I stopped enjoying being in the show and began to wonder when I'd really fuck up. The time between my using and doing a show began to shorten until my habit became such that I'd use the night before and arrive at the theater the following night tweaking or crashing. Tweaking and paranoia go hand-in-hand. There is nothing quite like performing in front of an audience, dancing, no less, high on meth. There's also nothing like performing naked in front of an audience with a red, chaffed and swollen dick from hours of sex you had the night before.

Eventually, my ability to manage the show and my addiction began to falter. With the paranoia came even more depression and self-hatred. My imposter syndrome came roaring back. I wondered if the cast saw the changes in me I felt were so glaring. I wondered if the audience was disappointed in seeing this version of me, not the buff, powerful, and sexual being in my movies but instead someone withering, fading, and falling apart. I'd spend hours in the mirror looking for signs that I was turning into someone else, that gaunt, hollow-eyed person everyone would look at and know they were an addict. My desire and need to self-destruct, a desire that had been mostly subconscious up to this point, began to find the light of day. With my insecurities taking hold, my default need to take myself further into the comfort of my darkness began to grow. I knew I was about to blow my life up with intent and purpose. I was back on a precipice and I wanted to jump.

Just before Christmas, with the show dark for a few days, I decided I needed to get away and spend the holiday with Henry in Vermont. I needed the safety of Henry, our cat and our past. Before leaving for Vermont, I bought an eight-ball of meth from my dealer. From there, I headed north, knowing I'd not be coming back. That jump from the precipice wasn't going to be a leap of faith like diving into a gorge on a bungee. I'd be making a jump but without a cord and into the peace I assumed Jessie had found in her own final act.

Chapter Twenty-Three

⌄

I n the hours it took me to drive from New York City to the top of Vermont, I gave over to the darkness. I spent the time sobbing and snorting meth, flying up I-91. At one point, a park ranger pulled me over because I had flown by him at 80mph. I threw something over the baggie of meth sitting out in the open on the passenger's seat and proceeded to cry to him, explaining I was just having a bad day. He let me go.

The crying was authentic, though. I was thinking that I had destroyed my life and hurt those I loved, that all I did was create pain and chaos, and that I would never be able to stop using. I was no longer the self I'd always wanted to be, my best self. If I could simply slip away, finally ending this life, I'd be okay. Everything would be okay. I'd had a full life, I told myself, even at just 39 years old. My dying would be tragic to those left behind, of course, but I needed to somehow make sure they felt no guilt or responsibility for my death. I certainly didn't want anyone to feel like I'd felt after Jessie's death. If I could show those I'd hurt that it wasn't about them but about me and my demons, then perhaps they'd forgive me for hurting them.

Henry met me with a smile and a hug. I hadn't seen him since my first months in Provincetown, when he'd come to visit. We'd both missed each other, that was clear. I was tweaking on meth upon arrival, yes, but it didn't faze him because he'd lived with my on-and-off mania for so many years.

Nothing had changed in the house. The furniture was still arranged the same way and Henry hadn't thrown my handmade stick chairs, TV stand and bench into the wood burning fireplace—something I'd imagined he might have done at some point since we broke up. Outside the house, Vermont was covered in snow. While I felt a tinge of joy seeing our log cabin surrounded by snowy whiteness, it was fleeting.

Henry and I had happy hour together and a typical quiet evening, me once again with the knitting I'd left behind, him with a new manuscript splayed across the floor. Then we set up the cot in the room I had once called my own and said goodnight. I then pulled out my bag of meth, ready to kill myself.

I needed to make it look like a drug overdose because, I thought, it would be easier for those I was leaving behind if my death looked accidental. I had only meth to work with, so I figured that if I could simply do enough, I would blow out my heart. My tolerance was high at this point, though, so I decided I'd have a better chance of killing myself if I injected multiple large amounts.

The only trouble was, I hadn't thought to bring syringes with me when I left the city. Then I remembered that the cabin held a supply of subcutaneous syringes, used a while back for the cat. I decided I'd somehow be able to find a vein, even though they weren't the right gauge or meant for intravenous use. I spent six hours that night, snorting, shaking and trying to stick the pencil-tip-wide needle into the few veins I had available. I only managed to hit a vein twice—not enough to do heart damage. Still, it was a lot of meth to inject, and as my body temperature skyrocketed, my mind felt like it was beginning to melt. I was hallucinating, hearing things, voices and noises. My heart was beating so violently I thought Henry would be able to hear it from the other room. I tried to shoot up more but all I managed to do was bloody and bruise myself, creating pockets of liquid under my skin that left my arms and feet looking like I had leprosy. By the time morning came, I was out of my mind, zombie-like, covered in blood.

And still alive. Which is how I was found that morning by Henry, to whom I managed to coherently say that I needed help.

Within a week, I decided on the Clear Haven Center, a rehab program in Quebec, just north of Montreal. The first person I called was Susan, my straight fan from Iowa who'd lost her husband and had written to me that I had helped her. I knew she would provide the emotional support I needed. I called my mother, telling her that Henry, not I, was struggling, so I wouldn't be coming home for Christmas. I called *Naked Boys Singing!* producer David Gersten and said I'd had a breakdown and couldn't return to finish the run of the show.

I decided that 30 days rehab wouldn't be enough, so I paid $24,000 to Clear Haven up front on three credit cards so that I could go for three months. I'd start examining my life with the assistance of professional help. I'd end up retiring from porn while in rehab. These would both be the first steps in my journey of recovery—steps that continue to this day.

But within weeks of leaving Clear Haven, I used meth again—and I fell even further.

Epilogue

⌣

This is where my porn quest ends. After 120 days in rehab, I came home to my Ithaka, with its log cabin and forest of cedars. But I had yet to fully understand that Vermont and Henry were no longer actually home. Even the cat Henry had given me in 1987 had died while I was at Clear Haven—the ultimate symbolic end to our relationship.

I suppose, having entrenched myself in metaphor for a year while writing this, it would be important to try to separate for you the figurative from the literal images I used in this book to describe my quest. But the truth is, I believe they are one and the same. I could not have lived the life I lived if it weren't for taking a class on myth and storytelling my freshman year of college, in which Joseph Campbell's *The Hero with a Thousand Faces* was the primary text. Campbell taught me that we can and should interpret our experience through myth, as a way to find a deeper understanding of the human condition. Myth has been present with humankind since the first mask or animal or weapon was drawn on a cave wall. Campbell's research and storytelling prove, to me, that we are all on a mythic quest. In looking back on my own life and labeling it as such in these pages, I hoped to provide context, understanding and connection to and for others.

But an equally powerful gift of Joseph Cambell was that, once I discovered his work, not only could I look back at all the adventures I had experienced in the first 20 years of my life and honor them as necessary and meaningful, not only could I see them as the stepping stones on the path to follow my bliss, I was also able to purposely seek out adventure and meaning in future decisions I would make over the next three decades of my life.

People say that what we're all seeking is a meaning for life. I don't think that's what we're really seeking. I think what we're seeking is an experience of being alive. Again, I chose my porn name for a reason. I was, have always been, and will always be on a quest to be alive. My choice to describe this adventure the way I did was not due to delusions of grandeur, although mental health and addiction issues took me to those places on my porn quest. It's because writing this book was an adventure itself. Walking on broken glass in order to get these words down on paper was a trial no less significant than any other hero's tests. Relapsing while writing it was no different than succumbing to the lotus eaters. Having a breakdown and physically hurting myself after I completed my first draft was momentarily being in the mouth of a monster. But I escaped my demons once again, and am now writing the epilogue. I plan to continue to live my next decades as the hero of my own journey.

Friends have told me that I can't end the story with a quick note about leaving rehab only to relapse again, that readers will feel cheated. Where's the redemption? Where's the happy ending? Where's the hope? Where's the recovery?

But here's the thing with my recovery: It's neither a straight path, nor a level one. It doesn't stick to a coherent plot line. It's also not circular or any other two-dimensional shape. It's three-dimensional at the very minimum—even more dimensions if you're a fan of quantum theory. For me, recovery isn't a thing I get or learn or earn or buy. It's not the default minimum reward, the prize, or badge I can wear for staying clean and sober. My recovery hasn't been achieved. Instead, I'm living it every day. It will never end.

Recovery is done through a day-to-day, one-step-at-a-time philosophy, whether we're talking about recovery from substances or from trauma. From the moment we leave the womb, we begin a lifetime of healing. Each moment of living is then an act of recovery, whether you are searching for your past, your youth, your inner child, or your authentic, best self. Living is an act of recovery when you decide you've had enough of the crippling self-hatred, the bullying voices, and the debilitating guilt and shame. When you decide to seek out help in order to pull yourself from the morass of self-destruction. When you realize that the pretty chokeweed flowers will continue to grow and will strangle and eventually kill you. Even in the midst of the chaos and hell, when we're digging the pit even deeper, recovery is happening on some level because every act of self-destruction and self-hatred becomes another lens through which we can see how far we've fallen, see what we've become, and—even over a growing distance from the light above us—who we could yet be. As long as there is an ounce of awareness, there is recovery.

Recovery also necessitates growth. And because growth is limitless, I'll always consider myself in the process of recovery.

My intentional recovery—"intentional" meaning I finally accepted I had issues with which only professionals could help—began with a therapist in 2007, along with my first psychiatric medication when I returned to Provincetown. Neither lasted for more than a couple of months. In 2010, I started seeing a psychiatric nurse who again put me on medication for depression and who started to provide therapy sessions as well.

By 2012, my addiction had become so bad that she let me go, saying she couldn't help me any more. She said I needed to get clean all over again. So I went for 30 days to The Pride Institute, the LGBTQ-specializing 12-Step rehabilitation facility in Minnesota. Upon my return, with no personnel commitment but rather a commitment to those around me—that is, I wasn't doing it for myself—I entered the Provincetown recovery community. I managed to get ten months under my belt before I secretly started using while continuing to go to daily meetings and counting days. I lied for the following two months until I received a one-year chip. Then, distraught by my lies, I confessed to my home group and spiraled again into using.

Then, in 2013, I began seeing a psychiatrist who diagnosed me with bipolar and then started me on the difficult journey of finding the right combination of medications. I also began to see another therapist, a gay man who helped me delve into issues regarding my sexuality, porn career and other lifelong patterns of destructive behaviors. In 2016, after my psychiatrist suggested that we gradually take me off one of my medications because it was pushing me towards mania, I went ahead and did so cold turkey. Two weeks later, I cut my wrists in the bathtub. I was taken to the hospital, where I managed to then drain two liters of blood from my wounds with a plastic straw I pushed into them. A psychiatric hospital came next, then seven months of sobriety. I continued to struggle with my addictions, getting a little time and then relapsing again, until, during COVID, I got nearly three years of sobriety under my belt: no drugs, alcohol or purging.

Nearly this entire time, from 2012 on, I went to daily AA meetings. I became entrenched in the program, did service, chaired meetings and

I thought I'd succeeded in portraying someone who "got it." I fooled some, but those closest to me saw right through the facade, especially when I'd again count days even while I was using. I was a chronic relapser for nine years until finally, during COVID, I got a true full year of sobriety…and then two years…then 30 months…and then I started writing this book.

Over all these years, a few people in the rooms even told me to my face they thought I was a lost cause.

In trying to align my journey with the heroes of myth and purpose, I suppose this tale is more akin to Dante being led into the Inferno rather than Odysseus finding his way home. I think most addicts can relate more to Dante; I certainly worked my way through several circles of hell, including lust, wrath and fraud, before getting to the center of my own personal underworld.

But that was my internal journey, one most people didn't see except in the rooms of AA. Besides writing this memoir for my own catharsis, I've also hoped to tell a story of someone who appears to have it all but who is no different than anyone else in his suffering. My body, my talents and my outward shine all came with a cost. What we see on people's outsides isn't always the truth. Today, what I show externally is as authentic as I can be—for now.

After I moved to Provincetown permanently in 2007, I'm sure that I appeared to many of the town folks to have it all together. In fact, I don't think I had more than a year of uninterrupted sobriety until 2020. But in the meantime, starting in 2008, for four years I was the manager of the Men's Health Project for the AIDS Support Group of Cape Cod (ASGCC) where I had gotten my second positive HIV result 3 years before. I was in charge of street outreach, doing HIV testing and counseling, working in the needle exchange and co-facilitating a health enhancement course for those living with HIV/AIDS. I was hired in part because I was a porn star and in part because of my experience in education and as a manager of a learning center. But I was eventually let go from that job because of my severe IV drug use. Unbeknownst to anyone prior to my firing, I'd steal used, meth-encrusted needles from the hazard container in hopes of salvaging a high. Eventually I nearly died because I was on the verge of going septic. When I returned from the Pride Institute rehab, the ASGCC asked me to not return because they couldn't risk having me still employed there.

But prior to that, while I was working at the AIDS Support Group, I was a poster child for HIV prevention. I earned the title of King of Carnival in Provincetown, the same year the drag performer Coco Peru was the Grand Marshall. While riding in a convertible through town with my crown, I also had "HIV+" written in large letters across my back. That same summer, I starred in a production of *Two Boys in a Bed on a Cold Winter Night*, directed by David Drake, the writer and star of the one-man show *The Night Larry Kramer Kissed Me*. We took *Two Boys* to the Gay and Lesbian Theater Festival in Dublin in 2009, where *The Irish Times* gave me a significant shout out for my acting—proving to me, for a moment at least, that I wasn't a washed-up porn star. That was a moniker I struggled with for years.

Over the following years in Provincetown, I also played the lead roles in Marlowe's *Edward II* and in David Ives' *Venus in Fur* and managed a gut-wrenching performance as Felix in Larry Kramer's *The Normal Heart* at the Provincetown Theater. I started painting again, had two successful shows, and was a part of a fledgling musical we took to New York City in order to find backers. I wrote a play that had multiple readings and was slated for a short summer run before the theater went through a major upheaval and the opportunity was lost in the shuffle.

Provincetown, Jessie's gift to me, gave me everything I ever wanted. It gave me all the chances to be creative I could ever dream of. But sadly, while the town, for the most part, saw me as a success, I kept picking up meth again.

Then, also at the start of COVID, the right therapist came into my life—one who not only had decades of recovery but was also a specialist in trauma work. She made all the difference in changing the trajectory of my path of recovery; she is in large part why I was able to get 30 months clean and sober before I started to write this book. I cherish my 12-Step recovery program, but I have learned that everything has its roadblocks. For me, childhood trauma could not be healed simply by getting sober. Finding someone who could blend the steps, through her own experiences, into the science of trauma was essential and a gift I'll forever carry with me even through future dark times. I'd likely still be floundering had I not been given full rights to claim ownership of my childhood experiences.

Ironically, I was doing so well before deciding to tackle this project, we both agreed I didn't need to see her any more. When I started writing and began to struggle again, I decided it wouldn't be a good idea to go back to her even while I sunk further into reliving my trauma. In fact, I thought it would be a bad idea because a part of me didn't want to be in a good place while writing this—part of me wanted to feel every ounce of pain my story would bring up for me. I wanted to stomp on that broken glass. Regardless, she is still why I did make it through this process and why I'm still alive. I am actually seeing her once again as I make the attempt to get this book published.

While acting, painting, writing, using, drinking and hurting myself, I've spent the same 12 years I've spent in the program establishing myself as a figure in the arts community. With a friend and mentor, I have become a gallerist, auctioneer, and educator specializing in historic Provincetown art. Provincetown has been one of the largest and most significant art communities in the U.S. for well over a century—and, much to my surprise, people now look to me for expertise and advice on that. They tune into our online auctions, where I entertain, educate and auction Provincetown art.

⌄

My sense of being a "washed-up pornstar" slowly faded until finally, several years ago, I began to embrace my journey and story. Whereas once it was just the gay men in town who knew my past, now everyone knows. Many of my gallery and auction clients know. The local paper did a full-page feature on me and my career, even printing an image of the cover of *100° in Tucson*, and my road to Provincetown and the art world. On social media I've started to embrace my sexuality, creativity, and humanity, which brings me joy and a sense of authenticity I've never had before. I'm now doing exactly what I always wanted: trying to help people see all their parts, from their desire to their compassion to their struggles. I am helping people feel not so alone.

I couldn't be more proud of my porn career. Not only was it the adventure of a lifetime, the work was important as evidenced by messages I get from new followers on social media all the time. They tell me my porn was significant for them in so many ways. They tell me how my scenes saved them during a difficult time. Porn saved *me*, too; it was that beacon keeping me on course during the turbulent time of my breakup. It gave me something to cling to while I struggled to stay afloat during a time of great loss. I've finally embraced the fact, and am quite public about it, that I'm an exhibitionist, that I love sex, but that I have quite a few talents beyond what people saw in my movies. I embrace it all. I'm becoming whole.

About the same time I retired from porn, the iPhone became a common device, shortly after which porn began to go mainstream. Sites like OnlyFans became outlets for anyone with a phone to offer up skin and sex. While these people collecting $10 a month for subscriptions may not consider themselves such, they're actually part of a whole new generation of sex workers. Condom usage started to dwindle as science confirmed that those like me living with HIV were unable to transmit the virus if we were on HIV medications—and then, of course, science gave us the first medical HIV prevention regimen, known as PrEP. Hence, bareback sex lost its shock value and became the route many porn companies took. Eventually, the term "sex positive" entered the lexicon of our younger generations. Shame and guilt over having sex on camera seemed to fade away, and the social stigma associated with it mellowed too, even if it hasn't necessarily gone away completely.

Witnessing all this, on one hand, yes, I'm jealous of younger guys who don't have to grow up in a world where sex is so taboo and stigmatized. On the other hand, I'm genuinely grateful my career took place when it did. It was a special time, at least that's how I see it. It was the beginning of the end of an era. With the proliferation of porn on the internet happening soon after my career ended, it's fun to look back and remember the days of video stores. I feel sorry for the younger generation who never experienced going into one to not just look at the covers, pick them up, and choose their evening entertainment, but to perhaps also catch the eye of the guy next to you doing his own browsing. It was a kick for me to go into a store in Chelsea and see my face on posters and to see not just one, but multiple copies of 3 different videos with me on the cover. There was something tangible on the shelf, something that would be taken home, touched, and then carried back—perhaps incurring a late fee.

Essentially, I took my favorite pornstars home with me and many men took me home. In doing so, a relationship was created, call it a "porn-date." That felt a lot different than it does now when I simply google what I want and am finished and cleaned up in 90 seconds. There is little planning beyond the initial urge and a few strokes—on the keyboard and elsewhere. The industry is obviously bigger than ever, and perhaps that's why 20 years ago, it felt more special, more intimate. I don't know, perhaps there are films or scenes being made now that will be, in 20 years, called classics. Certainly there are no more DVDs to slide out of view when guests arrive.

⌄

The most important piece of my recovery has been the evolution of my relationship with those closest to me, including my family and my husband. Within several years of my retiring from porn in 2009, my father and I entered into another eight-year estrangement. I was still a mess: using, trying to find the right psychiatric meds and seeing therapists who hadn't yet helped me deal with the trauma in my life. Returning to South Africa with my father triggered such anger in me toward him that I decided I couldn't have him in my life. I spent those eight years trying to heal; I don't know what my father was doing during that time, but I question whether there was much self-reflection.

In 2017, I ended our silence with a phone call that changed the trajectory of our relationship. I suppose it was in part my most recent suicide attempt and in part getting older, my 50th was approaching. My recovery program and therapy helped me realize I didn't want to end up by his deathbed without having reconciled. But before we could reconcile, I had a lot to get off my chest. I told him everything: all of the episodes of self-harm throughout my life, the suicide attempts, the molestation, the HIV diagnosis, the porn career. He told me how hurt he'd been when I didn't show up to his mother's funeral. I told him I'd been in a psychiatric ward after trying to kill myself at the time. He asked me how I could be so selfish, how I could do that to him. He then asked if it was because of him, and I, not protecting him for the first time, gave him an honest answer. Yes, I told him.

He cried and apologized, and then told me he never wanted to talk about it again. He soon after asked me if I'd resolved my "issues" because he was updating his will and wasn't going to include me if I hadn't straightened myself out. All I could do was roll my eyes in the realization the man would never truly change, that he would never understand or accept he was the root of many of my "issues," and that saying anything other than, "yes, Dad," would be pointless.

Since then, however, for the past seven years, we talk on the phone every two weeks. After asking about my husband and sending him his regards, he says he loves me at the end of each call. We both say "Cheers"— something we still carry with us from South Africa. He tells me what an amazing human being I am, how proud he is of me, and that I am a far better person than he. One of the pieces of sheet music I asked my mother to send to my first rehab was her copy of the *Theme from Brian's Song*, the one she had from the seventies. It was the song I learned in the hopes of capturing my father's attention in middle school during the years I truly thought he wished I just wasn't around, when I thought he was both ashamed and disgusted by me. For some reason, I still pull it out and play it around Father's Day each year with the thought that I'll record it on video and share it with him. Each year I play it, but I've yet to send him a video. I'm just not there yet, and perhaps I never will be.

I've always adored my mother. She was a goddess to me as a child, and then she wasn't for a while. Now I simply see her as human with her own past, her own upbringing, unrealistic expectations, and traumas.

We've talked about them recently as I try to let her know it's okay to be vulnerable and it's okay to share things she might never have thought she could share. I'm her confidant.

From her I got every ounce of creativity in my body, her kindness and compassion, her love of simplicity and nature—and while I continue to tell her this as often as possible, she still questions her role as a mother. She knows about the porn and everything else that I've gone through, and now, when I share my struggles on social media or a video of me singing or playing the piano, or even a thirst trap photo of me in a jockstrap, she comments: "And I am his mother and am so proud of him." In yet another way, I have returned home to find the best of my parents waiting for me.

The question begs to be asked of how I could write this book without mentioning my husband. I said in the beginning that I would not be weaving him into this narrative because, even though he was with me for part of my time while in the porn business, we were on our own very different paths. We are also very different people from each other; I was obviously publicly 'out there' and he was and is a very private person. We met in 2005, 15 months into my porn career, a month before I tested positive for HIV and moved to Provincetown. Essentially we've been together ever since. The term "together" evolved over the years from casually dating initially, to qualifying ourselves as boyfriends albeit long-distance, to him leaving a job in New York City and getting a job in Boston to be closer to me, to living together part-time, to renting a place in Provincetown together, to buying our house and to eventually getting married 17 years after we first met. I started to fall for him while we were walking to the Eagle in New York City the night we met; he stopped on the sidewalk, went over to a homeless person on the stairs of a church and spoke with her for 15 minutes. He then explained to me he knew the woman from the soup kitchen and wanted to make sure she was okay. This person was who I had been looking for—a soulful, kind and compassionate man who saw not just my sexuality but my own soul and gifts beyond my skin.

He was there during my downfall that landed me in rehab 16 months later, and he was there after. Over the next decade and a half, while we were together as a couple the whole time, if not necessarily living together full-time, our journey through life couldn't have been further apart. Everyone's journey starts with childhood. He could never relate to my trauma, having had a very different childhood with supportive parents and no emotional abuse or trauma, sexual or otherwise. To me, his childhood has always seemed idyllic, although I'm very aware there were issues. He could have left me many, many times during my worst years as I put him through the hell of my addictions and endless relapses, but he didn't. He was stability, I was chaos. That's the kind of person he was and still is. Like his parents, he is a man of faith, and somehow he never lost it. We have a blessed life and daily let each other know how grateful we are for that life and for each other.

After 12 years of trying to stay in touch, Henry and I stopped calling each other on our birthdays. He had come to Provincetown several times to visit before then, one time bringing a boyfriend, one time hooking up with a friend of mine in the guest room. He found a partner a few years after we split and opened a bookstore, his lifelong dream. I hope he is living a life of joy despite his continued frustrations with still not having a book published (we are still friends on Facebook, so I do occasionally see his posts.) I have a copy of all of his manuscripts written through 2010; at the time he gave them to me he asked that if he died, I would try to publish them.

Of course there is also my relationship with myself. I am both different and the same as I was in childhood, young adulthood and in the adult industry. Hopefully you gathered that while reading. I have an awareness of both the light and dark in me now, and I accept them both. I suppose most importantly I have learned and come to believe I am a nice guy after all. I'm also a little bent.

Finally, it took years for me to reestablish my love affair with Provincetown that began when Jessie first brought me to its shore. My struggles through the years opened up spaces in my initial appreciation for its endless beauty and creative opportunities. I often took it for granted, which, I believe, is easy to do unless one sets out and works for intentional gratitude. I use forms of the word "intention" a lot these days because setting my intention in the morning allows me to see the gift of Provincetown anew every single day. So, with intention, I think of the hours to come and thus feel poised for the wonder at all that life is offering me for the day. Then I swim, bike, walk, paint, write, sing, play, recover, sit, laugh, cry, pray, and let go of my own "barbaric yawp," because I am free and at peace.

Life is beautiful but hard. Life cares not, I believe, who I am, where I've been or how I've lived. But I believe life, or the universe, or the energy or whatever I know I'm connected to, watches over me and cares whether I stay on my journey. I've felt the embrace of something larger in every sign I've been able to see. Serendipity or synchronicity are constant companions suggesting I'm always right where I should be, even if I'm in the wrong place. I'm open to what's out there. I've flung open the doors and windows, and my future has come rushing in on a breeze. So while I don't believe something is out there either answering my prayers or judging my life, whatever is out there certainly isn't on a balcony throwing bottles three stories down to smash at my feet anymore. Life may not care, but I now care for life.

A journey is only a quest if the self-proclaimed hero understands their larger purpose. I've always believed that my purpose was to guide, teach, inspire and help. To offer up my pain in the hope of relieving someone else's. I've never forgotten that, and it has saved me.

Today, I can still be hit by dark, triggering memories, but they no longer derail me from my purpose: to be kind. I stand in front of the mirror now, not just for vanity's sake or to pick apart everything I see, but to assure myself on a daily basis that regardless of what I am feeling in that moment, it makes perfect sense. And then I move forward, towards the light and my best self.

I started this quest twenty years ago with the intention of writing a book. Well, this is it.

"Live all you can — it's a mistake not to. It doesn't so much matter what you do in particular, so long as you have your life. If you haven't had that, what have you had?"

—Henry James

Acknowledgements

⌄

How does one go about acknowledging a lifetime of people who have made me who I am? I hope, in one way, this book does just that. There isn't a single person with whom I've come in contact in my life who hasn't taught me or given me something. To all of you, my deepest thanks and gratitude. Whether you intended to or not, you changed me.

About the Author

〜

Spencer Keasey received his Master's of Arts in Teaching at the University of Pittsburgh in 1992. Since then he's worked several jobs including as a high school English teacher, mediator, fitness instructor, athletic director, educational grant coordinator, Vermont Department of Education consultant, and HIV outreach and testing counselor. He currently serves as the director of an art gallery and auction house specializing in historic Provincetown art. He has called Provincetown home for nearly 2 decades and continues to explore his creative side as a musician, artist, actor, and now, writer. This is his first book. He lives a charmed life with his husband and cats.